BROWNING THE REVISIONARY

Browning the Revisionary

John Woolford

Lecturer in English
King's College, London

MACMILLAN
PRESS

First published 1988

Published by
THE MACMILLAN PRESS LTD
Houndmills, Basingstoke, Hampshire RG21 2XS
and London
Companies and representatives
throughout the world

Typeset by
Vine & Gorfin Ltd,
Exmouth, Devon

Printed in Hong Kong

British Library Cataloguing in Publication Data
Woolford, John
Browning the revisionary
1. Browning, Robert, 1812–1889—
Criticism and interpretation
I. Title
821'.8   PR4238
ISBN 0-333-38872-0

For Sylvia

Contents

Preface

In calling this book *Browning the Revisionary*, I have in mind two of the many senses of the word 'revision': first, an author's revision of his work; secondly, his revision of a system of values, the process or attitude sometimes called 'revisionism'. In Browning's case there is an unusually intimate connection between the two.

In 1852 Browning produced his only acknowledged prose statement on aesthetics, in the form of an introductory essay to a collection of supposed letters by Shelley (actually forgeries). Shelley had always represented for him the apotheosis of Romantic poetry; Browning's comments in this essay, therefore, amount to an articulation of what he saw as the essential character of Romanticism, which he defines as a preoccupation with 'subjective' vision – what we would now term an idealist or a transcendentalist outlook. The subjective poet 'is impelled to embody the thing he perceives, not so much with reference to the many below as to the one above him, the supreme Intelligence which apprehends all things in their absolute truth' (*Penguin* i 1002). Browning goes on, 'Not with the combination of humanity in action, but with the primal elements of humanity he has to do; and he digs where he stands, – preferring to seek them in his own soul as the nearest reflex of that absolute Mind' (ibid.). What emerges from this account is what Browning identifies as the essential solipsism of Romanticism. As a visionary, the Romantic feels no allegiance to his fellow men ('the many below'), but seeks through introspection to reach some kind of vision of the absolute, which he then renders as best he can in his work. That work, Browning makes clear, will normally 'fail in art' because of the essentially incommunicable character of its material, but will be redeemed by its approximation to its governing vision, and by the felt presence within it of the poet's sovereign subjectivity.

In describing and paying tribute to this poetry of introspective transcendence, however, Browning is also engaged in and justifying his own deviation from it, his revision of Romanticism. He does this by defining what he regards as a contrary, co-existent poetic personality, that of the 'objective poet', the representative of a realist or pragmatic outlook. The worship the subjective poet devotes to his vision the objective poet transfers to the world around him. His 'endeavour has been to reproduce things external', the 'doings of men'. Such subject-matter forces itself on him as a consequence of 'a sense of duty or of love', 'an irresistible sympathy with men' (*Penguin* 1001, 1002). And such love

viii

influences not only his choice of subject-matter, but also his relation with his audience. The subjective poet has, in a sense, no audience; at least, his work is produced without reference to an imagined reader, and gains currency only, so to speak, by accident. The objective poet, conversely, finds his 'sympathy with men' directing him to write 'with an immediate reference, in every case, to the common eye and apprehension of his fellow men', making an 'appeal to the aggregate human mind' (*Penguin* 1001, 1003). He is conscious of an audience, and this consciousness parallels and extends the devotion to 'men and women' which is the mainspring of his poetry's content. Nor does this concern make him inferior to the subjective poet. Both are necessary, being inspired by the same 'fuller perception of nature and man' (1002); and 'If the subjective might seem to be the ultimate requirement of every age, the objective, in the strictest state, must still retain its original value' (1003). By this argument, Browning manages at once to do homage to what he sees as the Romantic achievement, and to construct a centre for his own poetic activity. For while his characterisation of the objective poet does not altogether coincide with his sense of his own poetic character, it comprises and explains one leading feature of his career, the feature with which my book is concerned, his preoccupation with the reception of his work by a contemporary audience.

In a letter to his future wife, Elizabeth Barrett, Browning wrote, 'you must read books in order to get words and forms for "the public" if you *write*, and *that* you needs must do, if you fear God' (11 March 1845; *LK* 39). This statement makes it clear that Browning saw nothing disreputable in courting a contemporary audience; its slightly defensive tone arises from his consciousness that Elizabeth Barrett (hereafter E.B.B.) held a different view, the view, in fact, appropriate to a Romantic transcendentalist, that the poet should 'await the coming age' for recognition, and pay no attention to his or her contemporary reception. Browning expressed, in another letter, his concern that this position might cause E.B.B. to misunderstand his having taken 'another course', that of taking his produce to the market with the intention of selling it like any other trader.

It was this intention, consistently maintained, as I shall argue, throughout the first thirty-six years of his career, which produced *self-revision*, as the practical application of his revision of Romantic aesthetics. Giving as he did a high priority to pleasing a contemporary audience, Browning found himself compelled into a continuous modification of his work, a long-sustained quest for 'words and forms' with which to achieve popularity.

For he was not the kind of poet who naturally or easily pleases. On the contrary, his work was, from its inception, difficult in style and recondite in meaning; he is one of the few genuine intellectuals in the history of English poetry. Critics invariably complained about the resulting interpretative difficulties, and the public responded by refusing to buy or read his work. It was not until *The Ring and the Book* in 1869 that he achieved something like a popular success, and that success, I argue, resulted from a long revisionary process, during which he adjusted – always painfully, frequently with reluctance – his manner and matter to fit contemporary taste.

This revisionary process did not, I should emphasise, involve *re-writing* his work in accordance with critical objections. Such a course is the one he believed Tennyson had taken. Tennyson's *Poems* of 1842 contains substantially re-written versions of the poems published in 1830 and 1833, and Browning quite explicitly condemned the alterations in a letter to E.B.B.: – 'Tennyson reads the "Quarterly" and does as they bid him, with the most solemn face in the world – out goes this, in goes that, all is changed and ranged. . Oh me!' (*LK* 19). Browning's own procedure was different. If a work failed, as so many did, to attract critical approval, his response was not to alter it, but to set about producing another which would more nearly satisfy what he conceived as his audience's requirements. That process is the subject of this book.

This study falls into two parts, the first of which, Chapters 1–4, is concerned with Browning's interactions with his audience, while the second, Chapters 5–7, contains a more purely critical study of the works which I regard as the culmination of the major phase of his career, the revised *Men and Women* (1863), *Dramatis Personae* (1864), and *The Ring and the Book* (1869). In the first chapter, *The Problem of Power*, I set out the grounds on which I regard Browning as motivated by 'sympathy with mankind'. I argue that the earliest influences conducing to such a concern were Romantic, but that he came to regard Romantic humanism as radically defective both in what he took to be its elevation of the poet above mankind and in its anti-religious tendency (especially in the case of Shelley). This critique led him to formulate a religious humanism based on the equality of all mankind in the eye of God; the poet, *sub specie aeternitatis*, is no better, no more privileged, than the least of his fellow-men, and his duty is to use his powers on their behalf, equalising them with himself. Such a priority necessarily demands that he should involve them in the poetic process, both as its chosen recipients and as constitutors of its full meaning. In my second chapter, *The Problem of Audience*, I argue that Browning confronted an immediate difficulty arising out of this need at once to please his readers, and to draw them into the poetic act. For the two aims, if not mutually exclusive, were at any rate extremely difficult to combine. If the reader is to contribute to the poetic meaning, the poem cannot be internally complete; it must position an area of difficulty within its boundaries to prompt the reader to complete it. But difficulty was not what Browning's readers wanted, and they inclined to regard the difficulty of his works as the product of a lofty disregard for them, rather than of the love of which it was actually, in his eyes, the product. The problem, then, was to find a form capable of harmonising Browning's double aim of pleasing and involving his reader; and my third chapter, *The Problem of Form*, studies his early formal experiments, up to and including his development of the dramatic monologue in the early 1840s, as possible vehicles for his populist aesthetic. The 1830s were dominated by drama (*Paracelsus, Strafford*) and epic (*Sordello*): both forms, I argue, adopted in response to what Browning imagined to be his public's preferences, but made problematic by that area of difficulty which he felt obliged to retain. Dramatic monologue proved to be the way forward. For the display of character with which dramatic monologue is centrally concerned was calculated to appeal to an audience increasingly addicted to novels, while the element of enigma, formally accommodated as the mystery about the response of the monologue's fictitious auditor, could restrict itself to the kind of speculation about the moral placing of character – the speaker's character – which novel-readers naturally enjoy.

I do not, however, believe that dramatic monologue in itself solved Browning's problem with his audience. This is made evident by the derisive reception accorded Browning's first major collection of dramatic monologues, *Men and Women*, published in 1855. In chapter four, *The Structured Collection*, I tell the story of that reception, and trace the reviewers' hostility to their consensus that Browning, in dedicating himself to what were essentially short poems, was failing in the duty to produce large-scale works. The 'structured collection' was Browning's response. While indeed setting about the production of a long poem – *The Ring and the Book*, eventually published in 1869 – he experimented in introducing a structural principle into two collections of shorter poems – the revised *Men and Women* of 1863, and *Dramatis Personae* (1864) – by which they might be read either as collections of single poems, or as thematic sequences. Chapter four concludes with an examination of the provenance and character of the structured collection form; chapters five and six are devoted to, respectively, the revised *Men and Women* and *Dramatis Personae*, in their character as structured collections. I argue that in each case, a detailed study of the individual poems not only reveals their place within a larger design, but also characterises that design as including, in the case of the revised *Men and Women*, a direct concern with the very questions which had led to its adoption: the relation between popularity and vision, the subjective and objective modes. In *Dramatis Personae* Browning modifies this design by turning his attention more directly on the metaphysical implications of the structured collection form itself, as a dialectic between unity and disorder which reflects the orders and disorders evident in human experience. Chapter seven, *The Unity of The Ring and the Book*, argues that the unity of that poem was the outcome of those two previous experiments, and that with it the structured collection evolved into an explicit long poem. *The Ring and the Book* marks the culmination of Browning's career, with the achievement of both a formal and a popular success.

Many valuable studies of Browning's work have been published, but most have concerned themselves with individual poems, with short stretches of his career, or with his contribution to the development of the dramatic monologue. What I have tried to do here is to link together the poems produced during his major creative phase as a developing series, and to put forward the idea that his mature collections have an internal coherence beyond the conveniences of publication. My primary concern has been to demonstrate that Browning's work *does* develop, and that its development arises out of his creative interaction with contemporary readers. It was the element of interaction which represented, in his own eyes, his revision of Romantic poetics, and stimulated his progressive revision of poetic form.

My thanks are due to John Murray for permission to use material relating to Browning, and to Macmillan for the patience and helpfulness of their editorial staff, in particular Julia Steward and Frances Arnold. Two institutions, King's College, Cambridge and King's College, London, have promoted, respectively, the earlier and later stages of this project – King's, Cambridge by awarding me a Research Fellowship which enabled me to begin it, and King's, London for giving me a year's leave of absence to complete it. Many members of both institutions have offered helpful advice at every stage.

The scholars to whom I wish to express more particular indebtedness include Jeremy Prynne, John Rathmell and Tony Tanner, who first stimulated my interest in Browning, and Theodore Redpath and the late Hugh Sykes Davies, who guided the early stages of my research. My debt to Robert Langbaum's seminal work on Browning will be obvious throughout, and both he and John Beer have been most generous in putting their time and scholarship at my disposal. My father, Jack

Woolford, has read the manuscript in its entirety and made many valuable comments. My principal debts are to Danny Karlin, who has laboured to make my style less Browningesque, and, most of all, to my wife, Sylvia Adamson, who has helped me to organise the layout of my material, and bring my arguments into focus.

List of Abbreviations

I have tried to keep abbreviations to a minimum. Where I refer frequently to one of Browning's poems, I abbreviate as transparently as possible: for example, *The Ring and the Book* becomes *Ring*, the revised *Men and Women* 2*M&W*. Other works are referred to by abbreviated titles; biographies are usually *Life*, for example. Less transparent abbreviations are listed below:

Allott: Matthew Arnold, *Poems*, ed. K. Allott (1965).
Brimley: Fraser's liii (Jan. 1856) 105–16 (G. Brimley).
CH: Browning: the Critical Heritage, eds Boyd Litzinger and Donald Smalley (1970).
Correspondence: The Brownings' Correspondence, ed. P. Kelley and R. Hudson (Winfield, Kansas, 1984).
DeVane: W. C. DeVane, *A Browning Handbook* (2nd edn, New York, 1955).
DI: Dearest Isa, ed. N. MacAleer (Texas, 1951).
Hayden: Wordsworth, *Poems*, ed. J. O. Hayden (Harmondsworth, Middx, 1977).
Kenyon: The Letters of Elizabeth Barrett Browning, ed. F. G. Kenyon (1898).
Langbaum: R. Langbaum, *The Poetry of Experience* (repr. 1972).
LJW: Robert Browning and Julia Wedgwood, ed. R. Curle (New York, 1936).
LK: The Letters of Robert Browning and Elizabeth Barrett Barrett ed. E. Kintner (Harvard, 1969).
LH: Letters, ed T. L. Hood (1933).
NL: New Letters, eds W. C. DeVane and K. L. Knickerbocker (Yale, 1950).
Oxford: The Poetical Works of Robert Browning, eds I. R. J. Jack *et al.* (Oxford 1983).
Penguin: Poems, eds J. Pettigrew and T. J. Collins (Harmondsworth, Middx, 1981).
PMLA: Publications of the Modern Language Association of America.
RB & AD: Robert Browning and Alfred Domett, ed. F. G. Kenyon (1907).
VP: Victorian Poetry.

For notes on the works used in this book please see the Bibliography.

1
The Problem of Power

I

'The predominating sentiment of Shelley throughout his whole life', according to Browning, was 'his sympathy with the oppressed.'[1] It was a sentiment Browning shared. 'Do you know,' he wrote to his future wife, Elizabeth Barrett,

> that I hever *used* to dream unless indisposed, and rarely then . . . and *those* nightmare dreams have invariably been of *one* sort – I stand by (powerless to interpose by a word even) and see the infliction of tyranny on the unresisting – man or beast (generally the last) – and I wake just in time not to die[.]
>
> 18 Jan. 1846 (*The Letters of Robert Browning and Elizabeth Barrett Barrett*, ed. E. Kintner (Harvard, 1969) [hereafter *LK*] 399)

His early work (1835–45) accordingly centres, almost invariably, on the resistance to despotism, whether that of the eighteenth-century *ancien régime* (*King Victor and King Charles*), or of the feuding aristocratic dynasties of fourteenth-century Italy (*Sordello*). *Instans Tyrannus*, a poem of 1855, is spoken by a despot who, like the nameless one of Browning's dreams, takes a sadistic delight in heaping torment and ignominy upon the meanest of his subjects. The fact that Browning's account of those dreams was provoked by E.B.B's revelation of her father's practice of keeping his children in bondage at home, forbidding them to marry on pain of being disowned and financially ruined,[2] indicates that domestic tyranny was equally repugnant to him; his response, to advocate and finally bring about an elopement which has become legendary, reappears time and again in his work, and is the central motif of his longest poem, *The Ring and the Book*. Such treatments represent, not simply their intrinsic Romance interest, but a political manifesto ubiquitous at every level of life.

These preoccupations mark the typical Romantic humanist. From Shelley, his first Mentor in social and poetic theory, Browning inherited the central principle – that tyranny is always evil and resistance to tyranny

1

always justified – which runs like a *leitmotif* through Romantic thought, from Rousseau to Byron. The direct influence of the Romantic humanists, in particular Goethe, Wordsworth, Byron, Shelley and Carlyle, is traceable everywhere in his work, not only in the negative gesture of denouncing despotism, but in the positive underlying belief that Man is great and glorious, having an inherent dignity, a semi-divine endowment, and a future potential for perfection. *Paracelsus* (1835), the first poem he published under his own name, is dominated by this theme, and concludes with a visionary rhapsody on the evolution of man from the primitive to his eventual perfection at the millenium. Browning's own comment, in a letter to his friend W. J. Fox, indicates the political nature of this theme:

> I shall affix my name & stick my arms akimbo; there are precious bold bits here & there, & the drift & scope are awfully radical, – I am "off" for ever with the other side, but must by all means be "on" with yours – a position once gained, worthier works shall follow.
>
> *Correspondence* iii 134–5

This letter suggests that despite its refusal of overt political discourse (I shall return to this point later), the poem has a political sub-text, and the concidence of Paracelsus's main career with the early stages of the Reformation provided Browning with considerable opportunities for reference to the social and religious ferment of that period. Such references are most strongly concentrated in Pt. iii, which is placed in Basle, one of the intellectual centres of the Reformation, many of whose leaders are directly named; mention is also made of the Peasant Wars which were historically a partial outcome of the ideas of Luther, Zwingli, Oecomalapadius, Karlstadt and Münzer (all mentioned). Of particular significance is Paracelsus's reference to the revolt of the peasantry led by Münzer. By the time of Paracelsus's appointment in Basle (1527); this revolt was actually over, and Münzer had been executed; Browning's Paracelsus, however, refers to it (iii 1006–9) as an insurrection in progress, an anachronism smoothed over by Browning's unhistorical date of 1526 for the events of Pt. iii. Münzer was a radical; he championed the peasantry, advancing the theory that 'all men were equal in the sight of God, and that, therefore, they ought to have all things in common, and should on no account exhibit any marks of subordination or pre-eminence';[3] according to the *Biographie Universelle*,[4] which Browning consulted extensively for *Paracelsus*, 'il déclara la guerre aux nobles, aux souverains, à l'ordre social tout entier' [he declared war on the nobles, sovereigns, and the entire social order]. Karlstadt ('Carolostadius' in the poem) was associated with these principles, and with the insurrectionary drive. Münzer's anarchistic communism bears a distinct resemblance to the extreme Puritan position of John Lilburne, leader of the Levellers in the English Civil War period, whom as we shall see Browning at this period ardently admired, and in Pt. v Paracelsus articulates a similar vision of the future as involving an irresistible tendency towards human equality.

This egalitarian rhapsody, and the pattern out of which it emerges, provides both a succinct definition of this stage of Browning's political thought, and a distinction of its Romantic tenets and tendencies from the versions of humanism which the historical Paracelsus would have encountered. Browning makes Paracelsus a nexus between the (in effect) élitist humanism of thinkers like Erasmus (also present in Basle in the 1520s, and also mentioned in Pt. iii), and the democratic humanism which spread from the French Revolution into nineteenth century political thought. Browning's Paracelsus, like the Paracelsus of history, rejects the classical learning so dear to Renaissance humanists (the historical Paracelsus caused a scandal by venturing to deliver his lectures in the vernacular), and espouses instead a millenarian communism having affinities with extreme Puritan theory, and with the anarchism of Shelley and Godwin. Like Sordello, the hero of Browning's next major poem, Paracelsus is an intellectual democrat born too early to see his ideas' fruition, but crucial as the avatar of a process which the 'child of aftertime' (Browning himself, or more generally the Romantic democrat) will see realised, or at least brought perceptibly closer as a historical possibility. Paracelsus's evolutionary view of history includes himself as an intellectual proponent of the political principles which will eventually release mankind from social, religious and intellectual bondage; his aloofness from political controversy (and by extension, Browning's occultation of the political argument of the poem) can therefore be interpreted as strategic rather than absolute.

The importance of Shelley's influence on *Paracelsus* has frequently been noted;[5] as significant, however, is the influence of Goethe. *Paracelsus* has been called 'the English *Faust*',[6] and the parallels in form, protagonist and theme are indeed evident; Paracelsus's climactic vision, in particular, is clearly indebted to a central Goethean idea:

> Thus [God] dwells in all,
> From Life's minute beginnings, up at last
> To Man – the consummation of this Scheme

Of Being – the completion of this Sphere
Of Life: whose attributes had here & there
Been scattered o'er the visible world before,
Asking to be combined . . . dim fragments meant
To be united in some wondrous Whole, –
Imperfect qualities throughout Creation
Suggesting some one Creature yet to make . . .
. . . some point
Whereto those wandering rays should all converge[.]

Paracelsus v 681–92 (ms. text)

Goethe likewise held that man comprises the quintessence of creation:

To create man, Nature made a lengthened *praeludium* of beings and
shapes, which fall very short of man. Every one of them has a tendency
which connects it with something above it. The animals wear what
afterward enters into the human composition in neat and beautiful
order as ornaments packed together in the disproportionate organs,
such as horns, long tails, manes, etc. None of these things are to be
found in man, who, unornamented and beautiful, through and in
himself represents the idea of perfection[.]
Goethe's Opinions, ed. O. Wenckstern (1853) [hereafter *Wenckstern*]
61[7]

An equally strong influence, especially during the composition of
Browning's next long poem, *Sordello*, was Thomas Carlyle. In a famous
series of essays in *Fraser's Magazine* during the 1830s,[8] Carlyle had
systematically attacked the assumption that history consists of stories of
kings and nobles rather than the doings of the whole people; and the
historiography of *Sordello*, particularly in passages highlighting the
suffering of the common people under feuding aristocratic dynasties
(Book iv, for instance), clearly echoes this polemic. It would be no
exaggeration to say that Browning's thought, from *Paracelsus* to *Sordello*
and beyond, was dominated by the influence of Goethe and Carlyle.
Certainly they were associated in his mind. In a letter of 1842, Browning
mentioned that Carlyle, during their last meeting, 'talked nobly – seemed
to love Goethe more than ever'.[9] Another letter of 1845, however, while
also illustrating this association, shows it turning sour, and Browning
beginning to wonder if Romantic humanism might not have let him
down:

I hate being *master*, and alone, and absolute disposer in points where real love will save me the trouble . . . because there are infinitely more and greater points where the solitary action and will, with their responsibility, cannot be avoided. I suppose *that* is Goethe's meaning when he says every man has liberty enough – political liberty & social: so that when they let him write "Faust" after his own fashion, he does not mind how they dispose of his money, or even limit his own footsteps. Ah, – but there are the good thousands all round who don't want to write Fausts, and only have money to spend and walks to take, and how do *they* like such an arrangement? Moreover, I should be perhaps more refractory than anybody, if what I cheerfully agree to, as happening to take my fancy, were forced on me, as the only reasonable course. All men ought to be independent, whatever Carlyle may say.

to E.B.B. 21 Aug. 1846: *LK* 982

The passage in Goethe to which Browning seems to be referring here comes from the *Conversations with Eckermann*:

Freedom is an odd thing, and every man has enough of it, if he can only satisfy himself. . . . If a man has freedom enough to live healthy, and work at his craft, he has enough; and so much all can easily obtain.
Conversations with Eckermann, trans. J. Oxenford (1850) i 336

Browning may also have in mind the special privileges which, in Goethe's view, the poet has a right to demand from his fellow-man. In *Torquato Tasso*, Tasso tells his patron, Prince Alphonso:

> 'Twas thou alone, who from a bounded life
> To liberty's fair height exalted me!
> Who from my brow each wasting sorrow took,
> And gave me freedom, that my flame-wing'd soul
> Might be unfolded in ennobling song[.]

trans. Des Voeux (1827) 25

Browning's distrust of such élitism may have been reinforced by his awareness of a neo-feudal, oligarchic strain in Goethe's thought, as in such statements as this:

The most reasonable course for every one is to remain in that station of life in which he has been born, and to follow the profession to which he was trained. Let the shoemaker stick to his last, the peasant to his plough, and the prince to his government.

Wenckstern 2[10]

This tolerance of inequality had led Goethe irresistibly towards the linked concepts of *social collectivity* and the *Hero*:

> The case of individuals is also the case of corporations. The bees, a series of individuals, combine, and their combination produces a something which makes a termination, and which may be considered as the head of the whole, namely, the bee-*king* (queen). In a similar manner does a nation produce its heroes, who, like unto demi-gods, stand forth at its head for protection and salvation. Thus, too, did the poetical powers of the French culminate in Voltaire.

Wenckstern 64–5

Carlyle too claimed that ordinary men stand in need of guidance from their natural leaders:

> Liberty? The true liberty of a man, you would say, consisted in his finding out or being forced to find out, the right path, and to walk thereon. . . . Democracy . . . means despair of finding any Heroes to govern you[.] The liberty especially which has to purchase itself by social isolation, and each man standing separate from the other, having 'no business with him' but a cash-account: this is such a liberty as the Earth seldom saw; – as the Earth will not long put up with, recommend it how you may.

Past and Present (*Works* x 212, 215, 219) ch. xii

And Browning himself, in *Paracelsus*, his most Goethean poem, written during the course of Carlyle's famous series of essays for *Fraser's Magazine*, had put forward a similar idea. Paracelsus regards himself as destined to serve mankind, but from a position eternally and infinitely above them, and explicitly espouses the Hero-theory in several places, as e.g.:

> 'Tis in the advance of individual minds
> That the slow crowd should ground their expectation
> Eventually to follow[.]

Pt. iii 871–3

Shortly after this, however, in a panegyric on Luther, Paracelsus qualifies his argument, elucidating the penalties of that 'eventually':

> The so-heavy chain which galled mankind
> Is shattered, and the noblest of us all
> Must bow to the deliverer – nay, the worker
> Of our own project – we who long before
> Had burst our trammels, but forgot the crowd
> We should have taught, still groaned beneath their load[.]
>
> Pt. iii 982-7

This almost casual comment separates Paracelsus from Goethe, and the element of rebuke obtains a sharper focus from the degree to which Browning's conception of Paracelsus's medical aspirations derives from Goethe's scientific interests; Paracelsus's eventual vision of human equality repeats and reinforces the distinction. In a sense, the poem identifies Goethe as a Renaissance rather than a Romantic humanist, at least in his political thought.

By 1843, Browning had altogether rejected the idea that the 'Hero' really differs from the populace. In Book v of *Sordello*, Sordello argues that the historical prominence of the Hero is chimerical, and that we must therefore abandon the belief that, say, Charlemagne and Pope Gregory really controlled and personified their respective epochs:

> Full three hundred years
> Have men to wear away in smiles and tears
> Between the two that nearly seemed to touch,
> Observe you! quit one workman and you clutch
> Another, letting both their trains go by[.] Alack,
> For one thrust forward, fifty such fall back!
> Do the popes coupled there help Gregory
> Alone? Hark – from the hermit Peter's cry
> At Claremont, down to the first serf that says
> Friedrich's no liege of his while he delays
> Getting the Pope's curse off him!
>
> *Sordello* (1840) v 177-81, 189-95

The running-title of the 1863 text puts it that 'we just see Charlemagne, Hildebrand, / in composite work they *end* and *name*' (cp. Goethe's 'something which makes a *termination*' [m.i.]). The Hero is in real terms a shorthand name for larger forces, his apparently individual initiative a result, rather than the cause, of historical change. On the moral level, it is made clear that the principal opportunity accorded the Hero by his social prominence is for wrong-doing: Sordello, therefore, on being offered the leadership of the Ghibillins,[11] repudiates it as a threat to his humanistic principles. It would appear that by 1840 Browning had become sceptical of some of the central premises of Goethe's and Carlyle's thought, though it was not until 1845 that his attitude hardened into open hostility.

Browning's own conception of 'the collective', as developed in *Sordello*, places it within a theory of absolute *individuality*, or 'independence'.[12] The word recurs in another letter:

> I always loved all those wild creatures God "*sets up for themselves*" so independently of us, so successfully, with their strange happy minute inch of a candle, as it were, to light them; while we run about and against each other with our great cressets and fire-pots.
>
> 4 Jan. 1846; *LK* 356-7

Unlike earlier Romantic writers, who almost invariably found themselves, whatever their starting-point, advocating some kind of autocracy as the only practicable social mechanism,[13] Browning drew upon a tradition of religious thought in which liberty was defined not as a social right, but as the result of a contract between the human individual and *God* – a God who has set up all his 'creatures' to pursue 'success' *in isolation*. This concept dominates the sonnet *Why I am a Liberal*,[14] in which Browning, in 1877, put forward his later political principles:

> 'Why?' Because all I haply can and do,
> All that I am now, all I hope to be, –
> Whence comes it save from fortune setting free
> Body and soul the purpose to pursue
> God traced for both? It fetters not a few
> Of prejudice, convention fall from me
> These shall I bid men – each in his degree
> Also God-guided – bear, and gladly too?
> But little can or do the best of us:
> That little is achieved through Liberty.
> Who dares then hold – emancipated thus –
> His brother shall continue bound? Not I
> Who live, love, labour freely, nor discuss
> A brother's right to freedom. That is 'Why'.

The theory advanced here (not quite 'liberal' in the usual nineteenth-century sense) is based upon the premise that since every man is 'God-guided', and because God's purpose differs for every individual case, each man must remain free to realise that purpose in his own way. No man can know better than I what pleases me or what improves me. My life, therefore, must be inwardly shaped by my will and my conscience, without external interference. The point to emphasise is that Browning now deduces the principles of liberty and equality, not from a political but a *religious* premise, as likewise in the passage, whose opening I have already quoted (p. 1), in which he denounced Edward Moulton-Barrett's tyranny over his children:

> [. . . but I] do hold it the most stringent of all who can [sic], to stop a condition, a relation of one human being to another which God never allowed to exist between Him and ourselves – *Trees* live and die, if you please, and accept will for a law – but with us, all commands surely refer to a previously-implanted conviction in ourselves of their rationality and justice – Or why declare that "the Lord *is* holy, just and good" unless there is recognised and independent conception of holiness and goodness, to which the subsequent assertion is referable? "You know what *holiness* is, what it is to be good? Then, He *is* that" – not "*that* is so, because *he* is that" . . . . All God's urgency, so to speak, is on the *justice* of his judgments, *rightness* of his rule: yet why? one might ask – if one does believe that the rule *is* his; why ask further? – Because, his is a "reasonable service", once for all.
>
> R.B. to E.B.B., 18 Jan. 1846, *LK* 400

Liberty here is a theological rather than a social privilege; God's grant of free-will to man emancipates man from the *obligation* to obey God, making obedience a free moral decision: by extension, men ought to accord an equivalent freedom to each other, and E.B.B. must learn to identify the micro-society of her father's home as totalitarian and blasphemous.

Browning's concept of the 'collective' is unusual in being atomistic rather than supra-personal, and his incorporation of God into political theory marks a wider deviation from Romantic humanism. In Shelley's eyes, God, the Christian God, represented the absolute type of political tyranny. J. S. Mill held that humanism, for which 'the end of man . . . is the highest and most harmonious development of his powers to a complete and consistent whole', is in absolute opposition to religion, in which, 'human nature being radically corrupt, there is no redemption for any one until human nature is killed within him'.[15] Though Browning never publically repudiated Shelley (as he did Rousseau and Byron for example[16]), Shelley's atheism clearly bothered him, as witness his rather rash suggestion that 'had Shelley lived he would have finally ranged himself with the Christians';[17] and after 1840 he characteristically used theology – specifically, seventeenth-century Puritan theology – as his primary source of political ideas.

II

Twice in early letters Browning affectionately recalls the leader of the Puritan Levellers, John Lilburne.[18] Politically, Lilburne stood for something very close to the social equality advocated by some Romantic humanists, with the difference that for him equality was primarily a *religious* principle:

> The omnipotent, glorious and wise God, creating man for his own praise; made him more glorious then all the rest of his Creatures that he placed upon earth: creating him in his own Image, (which principally consisted in his reason and understanding) and made him Lord over the earth, and all the things therein contained. . . . But made him not Lord, or gave him dominion over the individuals of Mankind, no further then by free consent, or agreement, by giving up their power, each to other, for their better being; so that originally, he gave no Lordship, nor Soveraignty, to any of Adam's Posterity, . . . to rule over his Brethren-men, but ingraved by nature in the soule of Man, this goulden and everlasting principle, to doe to another, as he would have another to do to him[.]
>
> *The Levellers in the English Revolution*, ed. G. E. Aylmer (1975) 71

This egalitarianism complements and completes the more widespread Puritan belief in the 'inner light' as man's principal route to the divine will:

> [He] that is a true worshipper, must know who God is, and how he is to be worshipped, from the power of light shining in him, if ever he have true peace.
>
> *The Works of Gerrard Winstanley*, ed. G. H. Sabine (Cornell 1941)
> 107

In *Paracelsus*, Browning cites this doctrine, from which, indeed, his concept of the dignity of man derives:[19]

> Truth is within ourselves . . . it takes no rise
> From outward things, whate'er you may believe;
> There is an inmost centre in us all
> Where truth abides in fulness; . . . &, "to *know*"
> Rather consists in opening out a way
> Whence the imprisoned splendour may dart forth,
> Than in effecting entry for the light
> Supposed to be without[.]

Paracelsus i 726–9, 733–7 (ms. text)

Paracelsus' insistence that there is 'an inmost centre *in us all*' follows the lead of Lilburne and others (Gerrard Winstanley, leader of the Diggers, is a good example) in by-passing the Gnostic/Puritan doctrine of the 'elect' to regard all men as '*equally* God-guided'. The ethical and political consequences of this idea receive their fullest exploration in the poem Browning wrote just after *Sordello*, *Pippa Passes* (1841).

Pippa Passes consists of four separate one-act plays, framed by an exordium and a conclusion. All take place on the same day in the town of Asolo in the Trevisan district of the North Italian Veneto; each involves two characters; in each, one of those characters is reformed or converted by hearing a song sung by Pippa, a 'silk-winding girl' who, as the prologue and epilogue indicate, spends this, her one day's holiday of the year, in 'passing' those whom she takes to be 'the Happiest Four in Asolo'. Despite their superficial disparities, all four plays share the same theme. Each involves an attempt on the part of one character to take control of another, expressed in the offer of a 'part', in the form of words or gestures, for him to act. In the first scene, Ottima, young wife of rich old Luca, who has incite her 'paramour' Sebald to murder Luca, commands him to forget his remorse: 'Crown me your queen, your spirit's arbitress, / Magnificent in sin. *Say that!* (i 217–18: m. i.). In the second scene, Phene, a prostitute whom the sculptor Jules has been tricked into marrying, repeats to Jules a long speech which she has been taught by Lutwyche, who, as the speech explains, contrived the marriage to humiliate Jules: it is particularly striking that in the process Lutwyche's identity obliterates hers by appropriating her 'I'. The cruder third scene contains a simpler form of this motif: Luigi wants to leave Asolo in order to assassinate the Austrian Emperor in Vienna; his mother seeks to detain him, in order to prevent what she regards as his own inevitable death if he dares to execute his design. She asks him to state the grounds of his proposed action: his reply stammers into silence and he proves unable to play the part – an experienced, calculating plotter – that she has (disingenuously) required him to assume. She next hints at the part, of the devoted lover of his fiancé (and herself, evidently) which she really wants him to play; he acquiesces. The same device occurs in its most complex form in the fourth scene. There, each character bids for control of the other, as the Bishop ('Monsignor'), arrived to take over his dead brother's estate, endeavours to get his brother's steward (the Intendent) to confess his crimes, only to meet the counter-attacking revelation that his own inheritance is threatened by the existence of an heir – Pippa herself – whom the Intendent has kept hidden until now. In the climactic speech, the Intendent first parodies the conventional repentence that Monsignor is forcing on him, and then starts coercing in turn:

And how my absurd riches encumbered me! I dared not lay claim to above half my possessions. Let me but once unbosom myself, glorify Heaven, and die!
     Sir, you are no brutal, dastardly idiot like your brother I frightened to death . . . let us understand one another. Sir, I will make away with her for you – the girl – here close at hand; not the stupid obvious kind of killing; do not speak – know nothing of her or me. I see her every day – saw her this morning – of course there is no killing; but at Rome the courtesans perish off every three years, and I can entice her thither – have, indeed, begun operations already – there's a certain lusty, blue-eyed, florid-complexioned, English knave I employ occasionally. – You assent, I perceive – no, that's not it – assent I do not say – but you will let me convert my present havings and holdings into cash, and give time to cross the Alps? 'Tis but a little black-eyed, pretty singing Felippa, gay silk-winding girl.

                              Pippa iv 155–71 (1st edn text; *Penguin* line nos)

What stigmatises all these attempts at domination is their mutual opposition to the will of God. Pippa's first song, the 'New Year's Hymn' she sings in the Induction to the play, proposes that

                              each but as God wills
          Can work – God's puppets, best and worst,
          Are we; there is no last nor first.

                                        Intr. 193–5

The phrase 'God's puppets' might seem to imply a complete negation of human free-will; paradoxically, it *affirms* it. Men's equality in subservience to God's will defends them from human attempts to submit them to hierarchies of 'last' to 'first'. Any human attempt to control the lives and words of others is therefore blasphemous by definition. It is no coincidence that the play's tyrants are conscious blasphemers. Ottima mistakenly believes that she and Sebald could evade the attempts of 'God's messenger' to find them making love in a dark wood. Phene tells Jules,

> your friends, speaking of you, used that smile,
> That hateful smirk of boundless self-conceit
> Which seems to take possession of the world
> And make of God a tame confederate,

> ii 157–60 (1888 text; not in 1st edn)

Jules by contrast longs

> to hear
> God's voice plain as I heard it first, before
> They broke in with their laughter! I heard them
> Henceforth, not God.

> ii 303–6

And Luigi, the protagonist of the poem's third part, expresses the same desire:

> "I am the bright and morning-star", saith God –
> And, "to such an one I give the morning-star!"
> The gift of the morning-star – have I God's gift
> Of the morning-star?

> iii 148–51 (1st edn text)

Again, the last scene is the subtlest, in that here it is Monsignor, the worldly priest, who takes upon himself the role of God by presuming to use the divine language. The factor which links together the profusion of Biblical echoes in his speeches is their implicit claim of moral superiority; Monsignor effectively arrogates a divine status, as the Intendent satirically recognises:

> *Monsignor.* How should I dare to say . . .
> *Intendent.* "Forgive us our trespasses."
>
>   iv 109–11

Forgiveness is not in Monsignor's mind, but the quote like most of his
own, comes from the Sermon on the Mount. And when, furious at
learning of the new heir, Monsignor makes as if to strike the Intendent,
the latter provocatively murmurs, 'Ah, so might a father chastise' (146),
echoing 1 *Kings* xii 11, where the unjust ruler Rheaboam tells the
Israelites, 'my father hath chastised you with whips, but I will chastise
you with scorpions'. Monsignor has no right to a divine language, as
Pippa herself unwittingly confirms:

> ah, but, all the same
> No mere mortal has a right
> To carry that exalted air;
> Best people are not angels quite.
>
>   iv 35–8

The revolutionary 'plot' of *Pippa Passes* reflects this metaphysic by
showing God's will at work to frustrate human tyranny. In each scene, a
character reaches a point at which he is about to submit to human
domination. And at that very moment Pippa passes, singing a song which
when applied to his own case provides him with the guidance he requires.
Pippa remains unconscious of her role, thus remaining a pure example of
'God's puppet', and as in much Victorian fiction, *coincidence* is proposed
as the mechanism by which God's will operates within historical time.
The theoretical framework of such operations is the concept of
Providence, famously described by Pope:

> All Nature is but Art, unknown to thee;
> All Chance, Direction which thou canst not see;
> All Discord, Harmony not understood;
> All partial Evil, universal Good.
>
>   *Essay on Man* i 289–92

Dr Johnson complained, in his review of Soame Jenyns' *Free Inquiry*
(1757), that since such a scheme is inaccessible to human intellect, the
mode and scope of its actual operations is likewise inscrutable: the

interest of *Pippa Passes* lies in Browning's illustration – albeit on a consciously fictive, even playful level – of its possible operation. Each scene is left entirely self-contained, having no connection with any of the others: though all characters live in Asolo, and have such knowledge of each other as would be natural in a small community, they do not interact. It is Pippa's passing in song, and the effect of her songs, that provides the sole dramatic continuity.

This dramaturgy both generalises the play's metaphysic by illustrating its applicability to a number of cases, and confirms its central principle by denying to any protagonist a 'heroic' stature which would compromise the absoluteness of God's will. The continuity of standard dramatic narrative necessarily cedes some power, however marginal, to a protagonist, if only in the neutral sense of permitting him to remain 'central'; the profusion of protagonists in *Pippa Passes* denies this status to any character except Pippa, who however has no 'character' beyond that of a naive child, and whose unconsciousness of the effect of her actions, or indeed of the fact that her songs *are* actions, shelters her from heroic possibility. At the same time, the dramaturgy affirms the essential *freedom* of the characters. Each scene lives its own separate life, uninfluenced by the others: even the apparent coerciveness of Pippa's songs is minimised by the suggestion that because they can only act on souls which are ready for them they are not objectively remedies to the situations into which they intrude: of the two characters in each scene, only one reacts to Pippa's song as to a divine message. Where for Sebald, Pippa's morning song admonishes his own commitment to darkness, Ottima is conscious only of a 'little ragged girl!' (i 230) and is absolutely bewildered by Sebald's reaction to her song. Phene, Luigi's mother and the Intendent are left wordless at the conclusions of the following scenes, but in no case is there any hint that they share the reactions of their partners, emphasis falling rather on the act of interpretation by which the central figure has appropriated and internalised the song. Pippa's second song, which involves the soliloquy of a page who admires but dares not aspire to, Catherine Cornaro of Cyprus ('Kate the Queen') mirrors this process by providing two interpretations of itself internally:

> Give her but a least excuse to love me!
> When – where –
> How – can this arm establish her above me,
> If fortune fixed her as my lady there,
> There already, to eternally reprove me?
> ('Hist!' – said Kate the Queen;

> But 'Oh!' – cried the maiden, binding her tresses,
> "Tis only a page that carols unseen,
> Crumbling your hounds their messes!')

ii 253–61

The two reactions of the hearers of the 'page's' song model those of the play's characters to Pippa. To 'Kate the Queen' the song appears an intended defiance of social rank and thus a virtual serenade to herself; her 'maiden', dismissing it, consigns it to random 'Chance'. The delicacy is that *both* interpretations seem to be true. Mere juxtaposition of the two viewpoints does not openly choose between them, giving the reader the option, already exercised by the characters, of adopting either. This is what the play's dramaturgy also allows. The separateness of the individual scenes, and the ambiguity concerning the relation between them and Pippa's songs, leaves the entire metaphysic open to interpretation as either random or controlled, and thus frees the characters from the overall scheme in the same moment at which it subordinates them to it.

This indeterminacy counters the danger that the play might be supposed to affirm a Calvinist predestination, exemplifying the *tyranny of God*. For though God guarantees, as I have argued, human free-will, free-will must for Browning include freedom from divine control. This is the point affirmed in the letter I have quoted (p. 9), in which God's 'reasonable service' is said to be based upon man's willing rather than forced participation. God, then, becomes a kind of anarchist despot, *forcing* men to be free by interposing to protect them from human – and divine – control. Clearly Browning felt that only a power as great as God's could provide such a guarantee: human social codes, by comparison, are too weak, and, in their collectivisation of mankind, too despotic even when benevolent, to do so. It was this near-anarchism which led Browning not only to reject the collectivist and autocratic elements of Romantic humanism, but simultaneously to repudiate the Romantic belief in revolution, and, virtually, any belief that politics as such might assist human improvement.

III

Why I am a Liberal is hardly a revolutionary poem. The 'fetters' from which men are to be emancipated are intellectual rather than political ('prejudice', 'convention'); the removal even of these is compromised by the admission that '[b]ut little can or do the best of us'. In *Instans Tyrannus*, the self-assertion of the common man takes the form, not of rebellion, but of an appeal to God, and its result is not the fall of the despot, but his experience of a metaphysical *frisson*. And in *Pippa Passes* there is no hint that the injustice of a society which condemns girls like Pippa to slave in the silk-mills could or should be resolved by political action. That what is involved is effectively political quietism is confirmed in the *Essay on Shelley* (1852), where Browning reprimands as 'low practical dexterity' Shelley's efforts to bring about a political accomplishment of his vision, 'at a period when the general intellectual powers [he] was impatient to put in motion, were immature and deficient', and locates in his poetry a more satisfying means 'of looking higher than any manifestation yet made of both beauty and good' (*Penguin* i 1009, 1005). Even *Paracelsus*, Browning's most radical poem, evinces this distaste for direct action. Despite the affinities between Münzer's creed and his own, Paracelsus expresses no approval of Münzer, and joins in Festus's praise of Luther, who took the side of the *status quo* during the Peasant Wars; this fact accords both with Paracelsus's historical identity as a 'Luther alter' (cited by Browning in *Monclar*[20]), with his refusal to engage in political controversy, and with Browning's expressed admiration for Luther (see e.g. *The Twins*). Browning appears to perceive an analogy between Luther and Paracelsus as intellectual innovators disengaged from direct political conflict, whose ideas are destined to a future triumph (Festus's role in Pt. iii as a mediator between Luther and the more extreme Oecompaladius, Karlstadt and Zwingli represents a parallel progress towards reconciliation that historically took place, on the theological level, in Marburg in 1529). But though undertaken in the name of historical gradualism, this repudiation of political action has to be seen against the background of Browning's lifelong mistrust of leaders, and of the political machinations by which they rise to power.

Browning's leaders, from Djabal (*The Return of the Druses*, 1843) to Disraeli (*Parleying with George Bubb Dodington*, 1887), are without exception shady characters. Even when their impulse to lead appears in itself noble and disinterested, they find themselves, once in or near power, compelled to degrade their own integrity and deceive their followers in order to maintain their position. This distrust of power arises directly from what Arnold denounced as the inveterate 'opposition mentality' of the Puritan middle-class tradition:

[H]aving never known a beneficent and just State-power, they
enlarged their hatred of a cruel and partial State-power, the only one
they had ever known, into a maxim that no State-power was to be
trusted, that the least action, in certain provinces, was rigorously to be
denied to the State, whenever this denial was possible.

Complete Prose Works ed. R. H. Super ii (1962) 20

Browning grew up in the tradition Arnold describes, and its influence was
reinforced by parallel elements in Romantic thought. Godwin, following
Rousseau, argued that 'the grand moral evils that exist in the world . . .
are to be traced to political institutions as their source', and Shelley
followed with the claim that 'if man were today sinless, tomorrow he
would have a right to demand that government and all its evils would
cease'.[21] Such propositions raise the general 'problem of power' which lay
at the centre of Romantic thought and was to preoccupy Browning
throughout his career.

Revolution, for an anarchist, presents a moral impasse, since the power
he usurps has obviously failed to 'wither away', as desired, by a natural
process. So having taken power – which he shouldn't – what is he to do
next? Reject power as a threat to his integrity (thereby implicitly
restoring it to the despot)? or temporise with his principles by exercising
it himself? This dilemma, which I call *embarrassment at power*, is the
central problem for a humanist of Browning's type. Its most overt
representation in his work is the hero's death in *Sordello*, which enables
Sordello to reject the temptation of a political power which, we learn from
his soliloquy in Book vi, probably *would* have corrupted him.[22] A cluster
of related motifs in the form and the content of the early works explores
the problem further. These motifs are *apostacy* – specifically, apostacy
from liberal causes; *abdication* from political power; and the *resumption* or
arrogation of political power after its abdication.

In his early work, Browning's presentation of radical thought is
complicated by a near-obsession with apostates from its principles. *The
Lost Leader* (1845), with its assault upon Wordsworth for his desertion of
the liberal cause, is a famous example; Chiappino, supposed assassin of
the despotic Provost in *A Soul's Tragedy* (1845), is in the space of about
ten minutes talked into becoming the next Provost; the speaker of *The
Italian in England* (1845) constantly recalls a former friend, 'Charles',
who betrayed the cause of freedom. Such figures appear to attract a
committed Radical fury, and this is indeed the sentiment of the Puritans
in *Strafford* (1837) towards Wentworth's (Strafford's) apostacy:
'Wentworth? Apostate! Judas! Double-dyed / A traitor!' (1 i 190). That it

is the liberal–humanistic cause that Wentworth has betrayed becomes clear when Pym describes how, before Wentworth's defection, he

> Was used to stroll with him, locked arm in arm,
> Along the streets to see the people pass,
> And read in every island-countenance
> Fresh argument for God against the King[.]

1 i 193–6

In taking the King's side in the revolutionary conflict, Wentworth would seem, for these speakers, to have committed himself, openly and criminally, to despotism. Yet Browning's reading reverses theirs. Far from having cynically chosen the stronger side, Wentworth is shown in *Strafford* defending the weaker against what the play represents as the irresistible course of the Puritan insurrection. Far from cynical self-interest he appears motivated by a devotion to the King's actual person which takes on the character of an admirable, if misbestowed, amorous passion. His antagonist Pym, by contrast, rebuffing Wentworth's appeal to him to spare the King's life, and by extension his own earlier love for Wentworth, voluntarily dissolves his individuality into a menacing collective strength.

This opposition between individual sentiment and political power is even more startlingly represented in the final scene of *Colombe's Birthday* (1844), when Valence and Colombe, at last confessing their mutual love, carelessly ignore the generous speech of Berthold, to whom Colombe has just surrendered power over the Duchy of Juliers:

> *The Duchess [with a light joyous laugh as she turns from them]*. Come, Valence, to our friends, God's earth . . .
> *Valence [as she falls into his arms]*.   – And thee!

Colombe's Birthday v 388–9

The elegance of this *pas de deux* can hardly disguise its moral cost. Colombe throughout has been, in intention at least, a liberal and humane ruler, having agreed, for instance, to satisfy Valence's demand of redress for the wrongs of Cleves, a town, part of her duchy, which she has never visited (II 151). Berthold, the pretender to her throne, is by contrast a typical *ancien régime* despot – not ungenerous, quite capable of subtlety of feeling, but acknowledging no principle beyond the imperative to expand his own power whenever this can be accomplished at no expense to his obligation to act becomingly to his equals. That obligation becomes the means by which Valence manoeuvres him in turn into agreeing to 'redress the wrongs of Cleves' (v 390), but the general character of his régime, as intimated in his farewell address to the courtiers, is hardly encouraging:

> You happy handful that remain with me
> . . . That is, with Dietrich the black Barnabite
> I shall leave o'er you – will earn your wages,
> Or Dietrich has forgot to ply his trade!
>
>   v 379–82

The acquisition of Colombe's duchy is for him a minor episode in the larger scheme of dynastic aggrandisment. By abdicating in his favour, Colombe renounces the defiance of tyranny she had earlier expressed in resolving to continue 'Cleves' Duchess' (ii 278); by accepting her on those terms, Valence renounces his own explicit partnership in that defiance, delivered to Berthold personally:

> The People will not have you; nor shall have!
> . . . never, in this gentle spot of earth,
> Can you become our Colombe, our play-queen[.] . . .
> – Our conqueror? Yes! – Our despot? Yes! – Our Duke?
> Know yourself, know us!
>
>   iii 250, 264–5, 268–9

Browning attempts to solve the problem by making Valence acknowledge that Berthold's claim to Colombe's duchy is documentarily 'just' (iv 97–9); this is however inconsistent with his earlier belief that the only source of 'true dominion' is popular support. Colombe's abdication and Valence's apostasy represent defections from an explicitly popular cause; the revolution and rebirth implicit in the 'birthday' of the title are the reverse of any revolution from despotic to democratic government; yet we seem to be invited to approve both abdicator and apostate.

A similar problem is raised, rather more subtly, in *King Victor and King Charles* (1842). Here, abdication becomes both a thematic and a

structural pivot when King Victor, having abdicated in favour of his son
Charles, actually resumes the throne by forcing Charles to abdicate in his
turn. Browning uses this pattern to create the same moral dilemma as in
Colombe's Birthday. For all the liberalism of his brief reign, a liberalism
which symmetrically reverses his father's tyranny, Charles restores
power to the despot voluntarily – almost without being asked. The fact
that this second abdication is unhistorical (the 'real' Charles imprisoned
his father for wanting his crown back) emphasizes Browning's interest in
the motif; the fact that it involves a restoration of power to the corrupt
ancien régime illustrates the moral cost of what again seems like a
sentimental infatuation. Charles's abdication appears to be the result of
an overweening and deeply neurotic devotion to his father which takes
precedence over every other feeling, even his love for his wife. She it is
who points out to Charles the moral cost of abdication: 'Your duty is to
live and rule – / . . . What matters happiness? / Duty!' (ii 258, 279–80).
And however stuffily 'Victorian' in phrasing, this argument has real force
for a monarch. A king cannot let Love conquer Duty. His role commits
him to a love of his people which must transcend individual affection.
Moreover, the person urging this is his wife, the legitimate representative
of individual affection in his case. Yet having urged it, Polyxena
unhesitatingly supports Charles when he proceeds to do precisely the
reverse. Again, the play's moral sentinel is apparently seduced into self-
confounding applause for a cowardly, or at best equivocal act.[23]

The conflict between love and power forms one aspect of the larger
conflict between individuality, answerable only to God, and the
collectivity which society imposes on its individuals. Political power,
whoever wields it, necessarily entails an instrumentalist strategy and a
social/collectivist view of men; Browning sees this as inherently
tyrannical, whatever the political colour of the régime. The pattern of
abdication/apostasy enacts the resulting belief that political power
corrupts even – and in a sense, especially – the liberal. When power is in
the hands of the despot there is a natural wish to transfer it to the liberal.
Embarrassment at power dictates however that this should come about,
not through revolutionary resistance, but through the despot's voluntary
abdication. In *King Victor and King Charles*, such an abdication then sets
in motion a further reversal which by removing the liberal in turn from
power rescues him from its poison. But the pattern does not stop there,
the resumption of power once more follows the abdication of power, and
when Victor dies at the end of the play, Charles resumes the throne in his
turn. The difference is that he resumes it by default rather than positive
will; but will is an essential component of power, as Polyxena finally
accepts in characterising Charles's reign to Victor Redux:

                                          Charles
Has never ceased to be your subject, sire –
He reigned at first through setting up yourself
As pattern: if he e'er seemed harsh to you,
'Twas from a too intense appreciation
Of your own character: he acted you[.]

                                              ii 335–40

Superficially a puzzling comment (Charles's reign could hardly have
been more different from Victor's), this can only mean that the very act of
holding power is innate to Victor, and to the despotic ideology he
represents, in a way it cannot be for the liberal Charles. By exercising
power, even liberally, Charles is an apostate to his ideology, and by his
abdication recognises his apostacy; simultaneously, power *must* be held,
and by resuming power on his father's death he recognises that fact in
turn. Browning is embarrassed at power, which he identifies with tyranny
(it is significant that Colombe like Charles holds her power on loan, as it
were, from the *ancien régime*). At the same time, he recognises that it is
irresponsible to retreat from it into private life. The pattern of abdication
and resumption or arrogation of power in his work acts out this
ambivalence.

                                        IV

For Goethe, as for most Romantic theorists, the most exalted power of all
belonged to the artist: 'The artist stands higher than art, and higher than
the object. He uses art for his purposes, and deals with the object after his
own fashion' (Wenckstern 77). Such a view is the natural outcome of the
position, most famously advanced by Coleridge, that creative power is
essentially godlike.[24] Its most notable opponent among the Romantics
was Wordsworth, who in the *Preface to the Lyrical Ballads* (1800–02)
attacked 'poetic diction' on the grounds that no poet for whom poetry is,
as it should be, a celebration of man's 'ordinary life' 'will break in upon
the sanctity and truth of his pictures by transitory and accidental
ornaments, and endeavour to excite admiration of himself by arts, the
necessity of which must manifestly depend upon the assumed meanness
of his subject (*Poems*, ed. J. O. Hayden [1977] i 882). The position taken
up by Norbert in Browning's *In a Balcony* (1855) comes very close to

Wordsworth's, with the innovation of making the artist's power directly analogous to the political:

> We live, and they experiment on life –
> Those poets, painters, all who stand aloof
> To overlook the farther. Let us be
> The thing they look at! I might take your face
> And write of it and paint it – to what end?
> For whom? what pale dictatress in the air
> Feeds, smiling sadly, her fine ghost-like form
> With earth's real flesh and blood, the beauteous life
> She makes despised for ever? You are mine,
> Made for me, not for others in the world,
> Nor yet for that which I should call my art,
> The cold calm power to see how fair you look.

664–75

Through the figure of the 'dictatress' Nobert implicitly compares the injustices of social hierarchy with the artist's control over his subject, extending embarrassment at power to the domain of creativity. Similarly, the eponymous speaker of *Prince Hohenstiel-Schwangau, Saviour of Society* (1871), launches an attack on a certain 'Bard' whose work constantly belittles mankind by scornfully comparing them to the sublimes forces of Nature – mountains, the sea – to which his own allegiance is supposedly given. The Prince's objection is that such a manoeuvre is both hypocritical, in that by it the 'Bard' is courting applause from the very mankind he affects to despise, and tyrannical, in that mankind's response to his ridicule is one of awestruck prostration ('down they go / On the humbled knees of them'). A major point of interest is that the 'Bard's, arrogant tirade closely paraphrases a passage from Byron's *Childe Harold*,[25] showing that for Browning it was the Romantic poets, his own poetic and intellectual forbears, who most overtly illustrated the tyrannical model of poetic discourse. In *La Saisiaz* (1877), Rousseau supplements Byron as an illustration of Romantic tyranny; by 1887, in *Parleyings with Certain People of Importance in their Day*, only Keats, of the Romantics, is found worthy of mention as a great poet: because alone of the Romantics, Keats, at least the Keats of the letters, stood for the doctrine of 'Love' with which Browning sought to replace the preoccupation with 'Power' which he detected in all the others.

Browning felt – on the evidence of these and parallel passages – an acute, polemical guilt at the artist's manipulation of his creatures. Of course, the problem is hardly solved by the easy paradox of having a Norbert defy the power of his creator; in Browning's first poem, *Pauline* (published anonymously in 1833), we find a much more complex and troubled treatment, in which the abdication/arrogation figure is brought to bear on the poetic form itself, affording a structural model of the problem which in various forms was to beset his entire subsequent career.

Pauline, a 'Fragment of a Confession', is spoken, as Browning made clear in a subsequent note, by a 'poet',[26] who confesses that as a result of various adolescent turpitudes – harmless enough, it should be added, from an external view – he has lost the ability to write. Throughout the poem, this speaker identifies creativity with a 'self-supremacy' which is 'Most potent to create, and rule, and call / Upon all things to minister to it' (275–6). (Note the juxtaposition of 'create' and 'rule'.) Since youth he has felt 'a vague sense of powers folded up' (341), believing that ultimately 'I should rule' (343) with a spirit able to 'make / All bow to it' (343–4). Simultaneously he rejects this spirit:

> The soul would never rule –
> It would be first in all things – it would have
> Its utmost pleasure filled – but that complete
> Commanding for commanding sickens it.
> The last point I can trace is, rest beneath
> Some better essence than itself – in weakness[.]
>
>   814–19

This 'better essence' is represented in the poem by three figures, God, Shelley, and Pauline herself, all of whom are identified with a 'love' which is the obverse of the speaker's 'power'. God, as Christ, loves man through his Incarnation; Shelley loves men through his humanist ambitions on their behalf; Pauline loves the speaker; and the speaker battles against his fear that 'I can love nothing' (310) by seeking remorsefully to recognise and emulate these loves. Yet he must also repudiate them. Under the influence of Shelley's love of humanity, he had gone out 'to look upon / Men, and their cares, and hopes, and fears, and joys' (443–4), only to experience a dark reversal:

> First went my hopes of perfecting mankind,
> And faith in them – then freedom in itself,
> And virtue in itself . . . and human love went last.
>
>   458–60, 461

As a result,

> My powers were greater – as some temple seemed
> My soul, where nought is changed, and incense rolls
> Around the altar – only God is gone,
> And some dark spirit sitteth in his seat!

469–72

Love, Shelley's or God's, is deposed. Power resumes its throne:

> So I passed through the temple; and to me
> Knelt troops of shadows; and they cried "Hail, king!
> "We serve thee now, and thou shalt serve no more!
> "Call on us, prove us, let us worship thee!"

473–6

These 'shadows' represent poetic creativity as tyrannical rule. Yet even at this threshold of resumed power comes the longing for a further abdication, or at least a desire to be a subject as well as a ruler:

> And I said "Ye will worship
> "Me; but my heart must worship too." They shouted,
> "Thyself – thou art our king!"So I stood there
> Smiling * * * * * *

485–8

The line ends here (in 1833), as though the poem were literally disintegrating under the strain of its own self-interrogation. Is creativity the result of arbitrarily-wielded power or of love of its subject, is it a tyrannical or a liberal-humanistic poetic régime?

A similar conflict is in evidence in *Paracelsus*, where the polarities of Power and Love are thematised in the contrast between Paracelsus, whose pursuit of 'Knowledge' seeks to acquire and use 'Power', and the poet Aprile, who 'would love infinitely, and be loved'. In the recently-published series of notes he wrote on the poem for his friend Amédée de Ripert-Monclar (see n.20), Browning emphasised that the encounter between Paracelsus, who 'has long since abjured love' for '*knowing only*', and Aprile, '*the nature that only loves*' formed the crux of the poem. Both have 'perished' from the bifurcation of their aims; only in 'the Union of the two' will 'success' be achieved; and that success is the province of 'the perfect nature for whom the accomplishment of the feat is reserved'. In the meantime, Paracelsus's pursuit of Knowledge degenerates into the ignominy of his historical reputation as a trickster and charalatan, while Aprile's ambition to realise his Love in tender portraiture of the human and natural scene is realised only as wistful longing. The 'weakness' which in *Pauline* is projected as the logical condition of Love reappears (Paracelsus recalls, in Pt. iii, how Aprile 'moaned his weakness' to him), and what is involved is not merely physical feebleness (though Aprile, symbolically, *is* physically weak', but inability to create, as Sordello similarly finds the textual declaration of his genius an insurmountable difficulty.

In one sense, *Paracelsus* represents an advance on *Pauline*, in that by thematising his creative problem Browning allows his work to stand as the accomplishment of the proleptic ambition of his protagonists. Lacking Power, Aprile perishes without articulating the poem he conceives; Paracelsus is unable to communicate his ultimate vision in his published works (in his *Note* to the poem, Browning draws attention to the historical Paracelsus's reluctance to publish[27]). Both require Browning, or more precisely, Browning's poem, to turn their informal articulation of their respective visions into poetry. The opening of *Sordello* plays a variation on this device by representing Sordello as a voiceless avatar of Dante, the 'perfect nature' who brings his vague schemes to fruition. Again there is an advance, since now the poem contains, in Dante, a concrete example of poetic performance, which Browning can then treat in turn as a prolepsis of his own yet more perfect achievement. The point is made explicit: stating his poetic ambition, Sordello adumbrates a programme of works, passing from epic (Dante's *Divina Commedia*) through drama (Shakespeare) to some consummating work which he cannot describe. As his conception falters and he stammers into silence (cp. the row of stars in *Pauline*), Browning takes over his discourse, completing his sentence with, 'Why, he writes *Sordello*!', and making the poem in which Sordello appears the historical outcome of Sordello's poetic ambition. But since it is Browning who writes *Sordello*, the poem like *Paracelsus* prophesying itself and thus subsuming previous poetic effort, offers its own substance as 'the accomplishment of the feat'. Simultaneously, the will-to-power apparent in Browning's historical triumph over his protagonists is claimed, implicitly, to be the means by which they historically survive (as Sordello survives in Dante's *Purgatorio*), and thus evidence of his redeeming love for them.

But in another note to *Paracelsus*, Browning remarked that he envisaged 'an eternal *succession* of consummations, rather than [. . .] a tendency to any *one* consummation'.[28] He thereby challenges the status of his own work as 'perfect', and the reason for this, given his premises, is clear enough. He is in danger of claiming that his poems, *Paracelsus* and *Sordello*, form some kind of absolute consummation, 'precluding further advance'; might, in short, erect themselves into the *tyrants* of the literary–historical process. It is significant here that 'Why, he writes *Sordello*' was a line added in 1863; the first edition text bites the prophesy off ('Then – but enough!'), removing, or rather, disguising *Sordello*'s claim to hegemony. Browning seems to have perceived that 'the perfect nature', precisely because of its union of power and love, would need to renounce power in the same gesture which affirmed it. But then the problem of *Pauline* reappears: if power and love are opposites, they cannot coexist, or rather, can do so only in a kind of formal pun by which the poem at once invokes and dissolves its own textual substance. The rows of stars which irregularly dot the text of *Pauline* form the sign – a crude enough one, eventually abandoned – of the text's dissolution, as, in a subtler way, does the constant difficulty of determining the time and place of the utterance, or its written or spoken status;[29] the Preface to *Paracelsus* requires the structure of that poem to be understood as likewise dissolved, or in process of dissolution:

It is certain [. . .] that a work like mine depends more immediately [than acted drama] on the intelligence and sympathy of the reader for its success – indeed were my scenes stars it must be his co-operating fancy which, supplying all chasms, shall connect the scattered lights into a constellation – a Lyre or a Crown.

Penguin i 1030

Traditional drama, with its narrative continuities, has developed 'chasms' which disintegrate its parts into 'scattered lights'; the invocation of the reader's 'co-operating fancy' marks the début of the possibility, constantly developed and refined in Browning's subsequent career, that shifting the ontological site of the poem from the *text* to the *mind* of its *reader* might reverse the entropy of the text and reintegrate its fragmented forms without the dangerous assistance of the poet's will-to-power.

2
The Problem of Audience

Goethe had a strong liking for the Enigmatical, which frequently interferes with the enjoyment of his works. I have often heard him maintain that a work of art, especially a poem, which left nothing to divine, could be no true, consummate work; that its highest destination must ever be to excite to reflection; and that the spectator or reader could never thoroughly enjoy and love it, but when it compelled him to expound it after his own mode of thinking, and to fill it up out of his own imagination.

Müller's Characteristics of Goethe, trans. S. Austin (1833) iii 324

I

In the *Essay on Shelley*, Browning defines an 'objective poet' as one who works 'with an immediate reference . . . to the common eye and apprehension of his fellow men', careful 'to supply [them] with no other materials than [they] can combine into an intelligible whole'.[1] This definition both typifies Browning's commitment to his public, and foreshadows its central problem. The poet will write only what his audience will find 'intelligible'. The audience will take responsibility for combining the 'materials' into a 'whole'. Each proposition represents a means by which the writer can abdicate from dominance over his reader. Ready intelligibility in a poem allows the reader to feel that its language corresponds to his own and is therefore not a foreign, 'poetic' idiom; reader-creativity completes the process by enthroning the reader in the author's vacant seat. But however desireable in themselves, the two programmes proved inordinately difficult to combine. The story of Browning's relation to the public of his period is the story of his struggle to get the reader to contribute to his poetry without sacrificing intelligibility, as he admits in a rather rueful letter of 1868:

> I can have but little doubt but that my writing has been, in the main, too hard for many I should have been pleased to communicate with; but I never designedly tried to puzzle people, as some of my critics have

28

supposed. On the other hand, I never pretended to offer such literature as should be a substitute for a cigar, or a game of dominoes, to an idle man.

To W. G. Kingsland 27 Nov. 1868; *LH* 128–9

The desire to 'communicate' with 'many' makes Browning regret that he has been 'too hard' for them; the difficulty arises, however, not from his reputed wish to 'puzzle' people, but his desire to produce a literature in relation to which they cannot be 'idle', but must *work*: 'as Wordsworth says (a little altered) "you must like [a new book] before it be worthy of your liking"' (ibid., *LH* 128). The reference to Wordsworth is particularly significant, since it was from Wordsworth that Browning, and the Victorian period as a whole, inherited their theory of audience. The controversy as to what he meant by 'the language really used by men' has sometimes obscured Wordsworth's concern with the writer-reader relationship; in fact it was this relationship, and Wordsworth's desire to revolutionise it, that was itself responsible for the famous phrase. Wordsworth's attack on 'Poetic Diction' dramatises his claim that the poet is not a privileged, exceptional being but 'a man speaking to men'; it produces four revolutionary poetic principles:

1. Poetry must please.
2. Poetry must be written in ordinary language.
3. Poetry should deal with 'common life'.
4. Poetry must elicit a contribution from its reader.

The first of these is the least controversial, echoing as it does the Horatian 'teach by delighting'. Wordsworth states it with, however, unprecedented passion. The 'necessity of giving immediate pleasure to a human being' is not 'a degradation of the poet's art':

It is an acknowledgement of the beauty of the universe, an acknowledgement the more sincere, because it is not formal, but indirect; it is a task light and easy to him who looks at the world in a spirit of love: further, it is a homage paid to the native and naked dignity of man, to the grand elementary principle of pleasure, by which he knows, and feels, and lives, and moves.

Preface to 'Lyrical Ballads' (1802); *Poems*, ed. J. O. Hayden (Harmondsworth, Middx, 1977: hereafter *Hayden*) i 879–80

The last sentence makes it clear that for Wordsworth the 'delight' of

poetry was not sugar coating on a didactic core, but itself a worthy end for
the poet who acknowledges 'the native and naked dignity of man'. This
humanistic position directs him to the second stage of his manifesto:

> The Poet thinks and feels in the spirit of the passions of men. How,
> then, can his language differ in any material degree from that of all
> other men who feel vividly and see clearly? It might be *proved* that it is
> impossible. [. . . For] Poets do not write for Poets alone, but for men.
> Unless therefore we are advocates for that admiration which depends
> upon ignorance, and that pleasure which arises from hearing what we
> do not understand, the Poet must descend from this supposed height,
> and in order to excite rational sympathy, he must express himself as
> other men express themselves.
>
>   883

Poetic diction, Wordsworth believed, presupposes that the poet is *a
superior being*. Acknowledgement of 'the native and naked dignity of
man', a dignity proper to *all* men, commits the poet, therefore, to using
other men's language to symbolise their equality with him. The third
principle, that poetry should deal with 'common life' follows, for
Wordsworth, fairly directly from the second, though other motives for
the choice of such subjects intermingle: 'Humble and rustice life was
generally chosen, because, in that condition, the essential passions of the
heart find a better soil in which they can attain their maturity, are less
under restraint, and speak a plainer and more emphatic language'.

The logical next step, for Wordsworth as later for Browning, was to
open the poem to the reader's contribution. Wordsworth took it,
however, not in the *Preface to the Lyrical Ballads* but in the Preface to the
Poems of 1815, where it appears as an extension of the earlier Preface's
attack upon 'Taste'. Where in 1800, Wordsworth merely expressed his
scorn for those 'who will converse with us . . . gravely about a *taste* for
poetry, as they express it, as if it were a thing as indifferent as a taste for
Rope-dancing, or Frontiniac or Sherry' (879), in 1815 he explains that his
objection to the word 'Taste' arises from its being 'a metaphor, taken
from a *passive* sense of the human body, and transferred to things which
are in their essence *not* passive, – to intellectual *acts* and *operations*'
(Essay, Supplementary to *Preface to 'Poems'* [1815]: *Hayden* ii 945).
Appreciation of 'the profound and exquisite in feeling, the lofty and
universal in thought and imagination' cannot be brought under any
metaphor implying passivity, '[b]ecause without the exercise of a
cooperating *power* in the mind of the Reader, there can be no adequate
sympathy with either of these emotions' (946). Creation becomes co-

creation, completing the programme of poetic humanism under the political rubric which for Wordsworth, as later for Browning, placed it on a democratic basis.

The writers of the early Victorian period pursued Wordsworth's programme with fervour. A pioneer statement appeared in Henry Taylor's Preface to *Philip van Arteveldte* of 1834, which contained a fierce attack on the second generation of Romantic poets, especially Byron and Shelley, for having, in Taylor's view, betrayed Wordsworth's principles by departing from 'life' and 'common sense':

> Spirit was not to be debased by any union with matter, in their effusions; dwelling, as they did, in a region of poetical sentiment which did not permit them to walk upon the common earth, or to breathe the common air.
>
> p. xiii

Of Byron's works Taylor complains, '[t]here is nothing in them of the mixture and modification, – nothing of the composite fabric which Nature has assigned to Man' (xvii), of Shelley's, that 'there seems to have been an attempt to unrealise every object in nature, presenting them under forms and combinations in which they are never to be seen through the mere medium of our eyesight' (xxii). Works such as E. S. Dallas's study of the history of literary criticism, *The Gay Science* (1865), extend Taylor's principle that poetry should possess 'relevancy to [the reader's] life' by setting out to prove that all the best critics in history have insisted on the pre-eminence of pleasure in poetry. 'The true judges of art', Dallas concludes,

> are the much despised many – the crowd – and no critic is worth his salt who does not feel with the many. There are, no doubt, questions of criticism which only few can answer; but the enjoyment of art is for all[.] . . . In one word, the pleasure of art is a popular pleasure.
>
> i 127, 130

Most mid-Victorian critics accepted this view. According to Richard Simpson, '[t]he seal of the poet is popular acceptation';[2] G. H. Lewes expressed the same view in his prefatory remarks to *The Principles of Success in Literature*:

> In how far [sic] is success a test of merit? Rigorously considered it is an absolute test. . . . We may lay it down as a rule that no work ever succeeded, even for a day, but it deserved that success; no work ever

failed but under conditions which made failure inevitable. . . . The instinct which leads the world to worship success is not dangerous. The book which succeeds accomplishes its aim. The book which fails may have many excellencies, but they must have been misdirected.

Fortnightly Review i (May–August 1865) 89, 91

Trollope, in his *Autobiography* (1882), comes even closer to Wordsworth, arguing that since 'it is the first necessity of [the novelist's] position that he make himself pleasant', 'the writer of stories must please, or he will be nothing' (*Autobiography* [Leipsig 1883] 206, 218). Discussing Dickens, Trollope even accepts numerical sales as sufficient evidence of public pleasure:

There is no withstanding such testimony as this. Such evidence of popular appreciation should go for very much, almost for everything, in criticism on the work of a novelist. The primary object of a novelist is to please; and this man's novels have been found more pleasant than those of any other writer.

229

Dickens himself, writing to an aspiring author, tersely assumed that 'you write to be read, of course' (*Letters*, ed. W. Dexter [1938] ii 679), and the genesis of *The Old Curiosity Shop* illustrates how profoundly this dictum shaped his own work:

The first chapter of this tale appeared in the fourth number of *Master Humphrey's Clock*, when I had already been made uneasy by the desultory character of that work, and when, I believe, my readers had thoroughly participated in that feeling too. The commencement of a story was a great satisfaction to me, and I had reason to believe that my readers participated in that feeling too.

Preface

In his anxiety to couple his audience with himself, Dickens imagines 'a dialogue of one' in which his own aesthetic instincts are ratified by their mirror-image in public taste. Thackeray noted that in the event Dickens really did achieve a 'communion between the writer and the public' which was 'continual, confidential, something like personal affection' ('A Box of Novels' in *Barry Lyndon* etc, Oxford n.d. 413).

The effect of such a philosophy, naturally enough, was an anxiety, still periodically condemned as commercial rather than principled, to shape the work of literature according to popular demand. The above quotation shows that at the prompting of the public's approval of a short story, Dickens expanded *The Old Curiosity Shop* into a full-length novel, as later he married off Pip to Estella when Bulwer Lytton expressed his dismay over the original unhappy ending of *Great Expectations*. Dickens exploited serialisation of his novels (a practice he himself had revived) to extend this intimacy, since the reception of each particular serial episode could, and often did, provide a basis for the conception or modification of the next. Martin Chuzzlewit could be packed off to America, or Miss Mowcher transformed from procuress into saint, in response to external approval or disapproval. Poets too were affected: Tennyson's serial publication of *The Idylls of the King*, and deference to critical opinion when revising poems, Elizabeth Barrett Browning's imitation of the plot of the best-selling *Jane Eyre* for her own best-seller *Aurora Leigh* (1856), are only the most conspicuous examples of an almost envious attempt by poets in search of popularity to take over part of the novelist's terrain.

It is perhaps not surprising, after these examples, to find some disquiet being expressed. Thackeray noted that pressure of production might have caused Dickens' works to have 'lost in art', and wondered whether they were 'written for future ages'; Matthew Arnold was less hesitant:

> [T]he *Times* tells us day after day how the general public is the organ of all truth, and individual genius the organ of all error; nay, we have got so far, it says, that the superior men of former days, if they could live again now, would abandon the futile business of running counter to the opinions of the many, of persisting in opinions of their own: they would sit at the feet of the general public, and learn from its lips what they ought to say. . . . But it is a doctrine which no criticism that has not a direct interest in promulgating it can ever seriously entertain. The highly-instructed few, and not the scantily-instructed many, will ever be the organ to the human race of knowledge and truth.
>
> 'The Bishop and the Philosopher', *Macmillan's Magazine* vii (1863) 241–56, 243; *The Complete Prose Works of Matthew Arnold*, ed. R. H. Super (11 vols, Ann Arbor 1960–77) iii 43–4

Though Arnold was not the first to take this view, there can be no doubt that his articulation of it as part of the wider aesthetic polemic of the first series of *Essays in Criticism* did much to detach late-Victorian aestheticians from the mid-Victorian preoccupation with popularity. The plunge of Trollope's, and later Dickens's reputation during the 1890s reflected, in part at least, the belief that their unabashed concern with the

reception of their works was intellectually disreputable.[3] Yet it was a
deeply serious concern. Ruskin – hardly a cynical hack – had hoped that
his period might include 'painters labouring in the midst of [society],
more or less guided to the knowledge of what is wanted by the degree of
sympathy with which their work is received' (*The Works of John Ruskin*
ed. Cook and Wedderburn [39 vols 1903–12] xvi 81), and asserted
elsewhere that '[a] great painter's business is to do what the public ask of
him, in the way that shall be helpful and instructive to them . . . not to
consult their pleasure for his own sake, but to consult it much for theirs'
(xxii 88). Another statement links this position to Wordsworth's:
'Perfectly beautiful art can only be produced by the help of sympathy and
with the reward of giving pleasure' (xxi 105). Ruskin was consistent
enough to employ the tools by which novelists had engaged and measured
that 'sympathy'. Three of his most important works, *Modern Painters*,
The Stones of Venice and *Fors Clavigera* were produced – and indeed,
written – as serials, with a full commitment to the principle of reception as
the dominant control over production. In the Preface to the first volume
of *Modern Painters*, for instance, Ruskin remarks, 'Whether I ever completely fulfill my intention [of continuing the work] will partly depend
upon the spirit in which the present volume is received' (iii 6). Many of
his later works took the form of lectures – lectures in which he expresses a
passionate craving for immediate and reciprocal communication with his
hearers:

> I begin, accordingly, tonight low in the scale of motives; but I
> must know if you think me right in doing so. Therefore, let me ask
> those who admit the love of praise to be usually the strongest motive in
> men's minds in seeking advancement, and the honest desire of doing
> any kind of duty to be an entirely secondary one, to hold up their hands.
> (*About a dozen hands held up – the audience, partly, not being sure the
> lecturer is serious, and, partly, shy of expressing opinion.*)
>
>   xviii 57

This kind of interdependence between speaker and audience was what
Dickens too sought in the public readings of his works, telling one
audience,

> Let me assure you that whatever you have accepted with pleasure,
> either by word of pen or by word of mouth, from me, you have greatly im-
> proved in the acceptance. . . . You have, and you know you have, brought to
> the consideration of me that quality in yourselves without which I

should but have beaten the air. Your earnestness has stimulated mine, you laughter has made me laugh, and your tears have overflowed my eyes.

Speeches, ed. R. H. Shepherd (1884) 289

All these examples, and the entire phenomenon of Victorian popular literature, may be seen as a manifestation of the humanism which on the political level inspired the period's series of Reform Acts: to bring literature to a newly-widened and newly-literate electorate was to act upon a belief in the principle of political equality, and on the local level that same principle inspired writers to seek popularity as a demographic extension of the principle governing literary production.

It was this concept of interaction which dictated the Victorian response to Wordsworth's other two cardinal principles of literary humanism. For Trollope, the criterion of intelligibility followed directly from the pleasure-principle: 'It is the first necessity of [the novelist's] position that he make himself pleasant. To do this, much more is necessary than to write correctly. . . . [He] must be intelligible, – intelligible without trouble' (*Autobiography* 218). Ruskin also connected the two elements, in a criticism of his own style:

> Were I writing it now I should throw it looser, and explain here and there, getting intelligibility at the cost of concentration. Thus when I say – 'Luxury is possible in the future – innocent and exquisite – luxury for all and by the help of all –' that's a remains of my old bad trick of putting my words in braces, like game, neck to neck, and leaving the reader to untie them. Hear how I should put the same sentence now: – 'Luxury is indeed possible in the future – innocent, because granted to the need of all; and exquisite, because perfected by the aid of all.' You see it has gained a little in melody in being put right, and gained a great deal in clearness.
>
> xxii 515

In another lecture he apologises, in quoting 'a portion of the series of notes published some time ago in the *Art Journal*' for their being 'written obscurely', his current ideal being to write 'with the single view of making myself understood' (xix 408). Note that there has been a change of emphasis during this adaptation of Wordsworth's idea. For Wordsworth, the essential criterion was that poetry should be written in 'a selection of the language really used by men', intelligibility being assumed to be a natural property of such language; Victorian theorists separated intelligibility from the conception of a natural language, and made it a separate aim. Naturalness becomes for them a criterion for *subject-matter*, introducing a distrust of unfamiliar or exotic themes which is very much a secondary issue with Wordsworth (see, however, the Prologue to *Peter Bell*).

This stress upon intelligibility creates problems in the implementation of Wordsworth's fourth principle, the need to compel the reader to supply some element of the text's meaning. Ruskin, perhaps the most sensitive and refined Victorian critic of Romanticism, himself adopted Wordsworth's position in a passage urging that '[t]he right point of realisation, for any given work of art, is *that which will enable the spectator to complete it for himself*'. For '[i]t is not enough that it be well imagined, it must task the beholder also to imagine well; and this so imperatively, that if he does not choose to rouse himself to meet the work, he shall not taste it, nor enjoy it in any wise' (xi 213–4). Again, Ruskin deduces the principle directly from a humanistic premise ('that in which the perfect being speaks must also have the perfect being to listen'). With the criterion of intelligibility, equally humanistic in origin, it has however no necessary connection. Trollope, indeed, states the latter in a form which virtually excludes the former: 'It is not sufficient that there be a meaning that may be hammered out of the sentence, but that the language should be pellucid that the meaning should be rendered *without an effort to the reader*' (*Autobiography* p. 201: m. i.), and Ruskin himself notes a conflict between intelligibility and reader-creativity: 'I write in words you are little likely to understand, because I have no wish (rather the contrary) to tell you anything that you can understand without taking trouble' (xxvii 98). In adding, 'I neither wish to please, nor displease you', he further separates the principle of reader-dependence from the pleasure-principle.

These conflicts, very important in the case of Browning, were supplemented by another within the principle of reader-dependence itself. I have related reader-dependence to the principle of abdication, the writer's renunciation of his poetic ego in recognition of the claims of others. By suggesting that an art which does not elicit a contribution from its reader thereby 'insult[s]' him, Ruskin implies that an art which abdicates from the tyranny of the discursive and invites the reader's participation pays an indirect tribute to the essential nobility of man. But it is only a partial abdication. Ruskin's reader-dependence is hardly aleatoric. Once his reader has fully 'rouse[d] himself', 'the guidance which the artist gives him should be full and authoritative: the beholder's imagination should not be suffered to take its own way, or wander hither and thither' (xi 214). Ruskin puts it elsewhere that he wants 'to lead you [the reader] to think *accurately*' i.e. to reach a conclusion already pre-determined by the author. In terms of the model of poetic creation I proposed in the last chapter, such a restoration of the author's didactic hegemony amounts to a resumption of power over the reader. I shall show that in Browning's case this equivocation forms the core of an almost intractable problem of audience.

II

Browning's opinion, given to two correspondents, of Tennyson's 1842 collection, hardly seems to encourage the view that he accepted popularity as a measure of literary merit:

> I send with this Tennyson's new vol. and, alas, the old with it – that is, what he calls old. You will see, and groan! The alterations are insane. *Whatever* is touched is spoiled. There is some woeful mental infirmity in the man . . . [Moxon] tells me that he is miserably thin-skinned, sensitive to criticism (foolish criticism), wishes to see no notices that contain the least possible depreciatory expressions – poor fellow!
>
>   to Alfred Domett 13 July 1842; *RB & AD* 40–1

But a letter to E.B.B. gives a more ambiguous account. Early in their correspondence, she wrote to ask 'whether you are liable to be pained deeply by hard criticism and cold neglect', pre-emptively commenting:

> It appears to me that poets who, like Keats, are highly susceptible to criticism, must be jealous, in their own persons, of the future honour of their works. Because, if a work is worthy, honour must follow it – though the worker should not live to see that following or overtaking. Now, is it not enough that the work be honoured – enough I mean, for the worker?
>
>   3 Feb. 1845: *LK* 14

Such earnest, rather hectoring high-mindedness must have made anything but simple agreement rather difficult; but in fact Browning in his reply goes a good deal further. The letter is important enough to quote at length:

> Then you inquire about my "sensitiveness to criticism," and I shall be glad to tell you exactly, because I have, more than once, taken course [sic] you might else not understand. I shall live always, – that is for me –

I am living here this 1845, that is for London. I write from a thorough
conviction that it is the duty of me, and with the belief that, after every
drawback & shortcoming, I do my best, all things considered – that is
for *me*, and, so being, the not being listened to by one human creature
would, I hope, in nowise affect me. But of course I must, if for merely
scientific purposes, know all about this 1845, its ways and doings, and
something I do know, as that for a dozen cabbages, if I pleased to grow
them in the garden here, I might demand, say, a dozen pence at Covent
Garden Market, – and that for a dozen scenes, of the average goodness,
I may challenge as many plaudits at the theatre close by; and a dozen
pages of verse, brought to the Rialto where verse-merchants most do
congregate, ought to bring me a fair proportion of the Reviewers' gold-
currency, seeing the other traders pouch their winnings, as I do:* well,
when they won't pay me for my cabbages, nor praise me for my poems,
I may, if I please, say "more's the shame," and bid both parties
'decamp to the crows' in Greek phrase, and YET go very lighthearted
back to a garden-full of rose-trees, and a soul-full of comforts; if they had
bought my greens I should have been able to buy the last number of
"Punch", and go thro' the toll-gate of Waterloo Bridge, and give the
blind clarionet-player a trifle, and all without changing my gold – if
they had taken to my books, my father and mother would have been
proud of this and the other 'favourable critique,' and . . at least so
folks hold . . I should have to pay Mr. Moxon less by a few pounds –
whereas . . but you see! Indeed, I force myself to say ever and anon, in
the interest of the market-gardeners regular and Keats's proper, – "It's
nothing to *you*, – critics & hucksters, all of you, if I *have* this garden and
this conscience, – I might go die at Rome, or take the gin and the
newspaper, for what *you* would care"! So I don't quite lay open my
resources to everybody. But it does so happen, that I have met with
much more than I could have expected in this matter of kindly and
prompt recognition. I never wanted a real set of good hearty praisers –
and no bad reviewers – I am quite content with my share. No – what I
laughed at in my "gentle audience" is a sad trick the real admirers have
of admiring at the wrong place – enough to make an apostle swear. *That*
does make me savage, – *never* the other kind of people; why, think now:
take your own "Drama of Exile" and let *me* send it to the first twenty
men & women that shall knock at your door to-day and after – of whom
the first five are – the Postman, the seller of cheap sealing-wax, Mr.
Hawkins Junr, the Butcher for orders, and the Tax gatherer – will you
let me, by Cornelius Agrippa's assistance, force these five and their
fellows to read, and report on, this drama – and, when I have put these

faithful reports into fair English, do you believe they would be better than, if as good, as, the general run of Periodical criticisms? Not they, I will venture to affirm. But then, – once again, I get these people together and give them your book, and persuade them, moreover, that by praising it, the Postman will be helping its author to divide Long Acre into two beats, one of which she will take with half the salary and all the red collar, – that a sealing wax-vendor will see red wafers brought into vogue, and so on with the rest – and won't you just wish for your Spectators and Observers and Newcastle-upon-Tyne – Hebdomadal Mercuries back again! You see the inference – I do sincerely esteem it a perfectly providential and miraculous thing that they are so well-behaved in ordinary, these critics; and for Keats and Tennyson to "go softly all their days" for a gruff word or two is quite inexplicable to me, and always has been. Tennyson reads the "Quarterly" and does as they bid him, with the most solemn face in the world – out goes this, in goes that, all is changed and ranged. . Oh me! –

11 Feb. 1845: *LK* 18–19

[*I have preserved the original reading: Browning inserted 'see' after 'as I do' before sending the letter, thus subtly – and defensively – changing his point.]

Browning here divides himself into two halves. The first in its 'garden-full of rose-trees' is absolutely immune to criticism because it writes out of a pure, disinterested sense of duty. But the poem, produced, is sent to market by the other half, which cares so passionately about its reception as to go into a fit of rage if 'the Reviewers' gold-currency' is not forthcoming. Browning is trying to convince E.B.B. that it is possible to be 'sensitive to criticism' without thereby proving oneself 'jealous . . . of the future honour of [one's] works'. He then advances the supporting argument that he has, after all, not been too badly mauled, and in any case prefers blame in the right places to praise in the wrong ones; a position allowing him to ridicule those who, like Keats and Tennyson, are prostrated by the first harsh word, or, worse, willing to alter the offending poems. What Browning has not done is to explain what 'course you might . . . not understand' he has actually taken. This must refer to a *result* of his 'sensitiveness to criticism', not such sensitiveness in itself (the latter could hardly be called a 'course' he has taken 'more than once'), and can only be some specific action in response to criticism. At the same time, such action clearly must differ from Tennyson's. All the evidence suggests he means that he had set out to produce work in what he believed would be a popular form and style. In a letter to Alfred Domett he admitted to publishing *Dramatic Lyrics* 'for popularity's sake' (*RB & AD* 36), a remark paralleled in a slightly later letter to E.B.B.:

> I don't even care about reading now – the world, – and pictures of it, rather than writings about the world! but you must read books in order to get words and forms for "the public" if you *write*, and *that* you needs must do, if you fear God.
>
> 11 Mar. 1845; *LK* 39

Again, he divides himself into two halves, the one pleasantly watching the world while the other performs its duty to God by writing poetry. But in writing that poetry, this second half works 'for "the public"' and casts about for acceptable 'words and forms'.

A survey of Browning's career up to the time of his correspondence with Elizabeth Barrett suggests that at that time he was very much engaged in a search for 'words and forms' with which to attract a widespread audience.

The story of John Stuart Mill's unpublished review of *Pauline*, and Browning's embarrassment and withdrawal of the poem, is famous; if, as some scholars have concluded, his embarrassment directly caused the poem's withdrawal, then this episode would constitute a first evidence of Browning's subservience to the opinions of those 'very few, who react upon the rest' (the identity of Mill, and his intellectual eminence, were known to him). It has even been suggested that his subsequent practice of using only dramatised speakers, rather than authorial 'confession', was a reaction to Mill's accusation of 'morbid self-consciousness'.[4] More substantial is the evidence that *Paracelsus*, his next work, was moulded partly in response to, not Mill's unpublished notice of *Pauline*, but another, much more favourable review by W. J. Fox, Browning's friend and the editor of the *Monthly Repository*. Just before the publication of *Paracelsus*, Browning sent, with defensive jokiness, a request to Fox for another helping hand:

> You will 'sarve me out'? – two words to that; being the man you are, you must need very little telling from me, of the real feeling I have of your criticism's worth[;] . . . not a particle of your article has been rejected or neglected by your observant humble servant, & very proud shall I be if my new work bear in it the marks of the influence under which it was undertaken.
>
> to Fox, 16 Apr. 1835; *Correspondence* iii 134

Even allowing for the touch of flattery in this passage, Browning is quite clearly declaring his willingness to accept advice from critics, and a comparison between Fox's article and Browning's poem suggests that he really had done so. Fox *approved* of what Mill condemned as the 'morbid self-consciousness' of *Pauline*, and in effect advised Browning that this introspection was the only valid subject for a modern poet:

> There is an art, not less felicitous than that which produces characters like a Creator, and links events together like a providence, and makes its combinations tend to the premeditated result like an overruling fate or destiny, in that which traces the growth of an individual mind, the influence upon it of things external, the powers unfolding themselves within it with all their harmonies and discords, the ties of association flowing hither and thither like the films of a spider's web, yet strong as iron bands, its prevailing tendencies and frequent irregularities, with all that makes it a microcosm, if it be not rather the world of matter that is the microcosm, and that of the mind, the true and essential universe alone worthy of observation and interest.
>
> *Monthly Repository* n.s. vii (1833) 252–62: 252

In the Preface to the first edition of *Paracelsus* Browning correspondingly claims, 'I have ventured to display somewhat minutely the mood itself in its rise and progress'; his 1863 prefatory letter to *Sordello*, with its assertion that 'little else is worth study' than the 'incidents in the development of a soul', comes even closer to Fox's wording.

Fox does, however, offer an implicit objection to what Mill called the 'egotism' of *Pauline*, by praising other poets' capacity to project themselves outwards into the identity of invented characters:

> They felt *their* feelings, thought *their* thoughts, burned with *their* passions, dreamed *their* dreams, and lived their lives, or died their death. In relation to his creations, the poet is the omnific spirit in whom they have their being.
>
> 253

The unfelt paradox here (are the poet's character in him or he in them?) reappears in Aprile's determination to dedicate his art to mankind:

> common life, its wants
> And ways, would I set forth in beauteous hues:
> The lowest hind should not possess a hope,

A fear, but I'd be by him, saying better
Than he his own heart's language. I would live
For ever in the thoughts I thus explored[;]
. . . they should be mine henceforth,
Imbued with me, though free to all before[.]

iii 556–61, 563–4

Clearly, Browning had taken Fox's hint, at least to the extent of having a character paraphrase it; and the egotism curled up inside Aprile's altruistic programme is no less present in Fox's. Nevertheless, the decision to adopt a historical personage as the 'individual mind' to be explored may well have been inspired by the criticism faintly implied.

On one aspect of *Pauline*, however, Fox was almost severe:

[H]e has not given himself the chance for popularity which Tennyson did, and which it is evident that he easily might have done. His poem stands alone, with none of those slight but taking accompaniments, songs that sing themselves, sketches that every body knows, light little lyrics, floating about like humming birds, around the trunk and foliage of the poem itself[.]

259

Browning seems to have taken this criticism quite literally, for the blank verse of *Paracelsus* is regularly interrupted, after Pt. i, by 'slight little lyrics'. And not content with merely taking Fox's hint, he enlarged it into a thematic motif. It is only after he has met Aprile and learnt the value of human love that Paracelsus begins to sing lyrics; these therefore take on the double character of a thematic motif in the growth of his mind and a gesture towards the 'popularity' which Fox had assured him they would produce. It is clear that in attaching Fox's demand for lyrics to Aprile's love of mankind Browning was associating the quest for popularity with a Wordsworthian humanism: in that sense, he had absorbed Fox's 'influence' at the deeper level where it became part of his poetic programme. *Pippa Passes*, where the utterance of 'slight lyrics' becomes even more markedly a moral and thematic concern, illustrates the durability of the lesson.

Browning's next work, *Strafford*, was equally influenced by external guidance. In a favourable review of *Paracelsus*, John Forster noted in it what he termed 'Evidences of a New Genius for Dramatic Poetry'; shortly afterwards he got William Macready, the leading actor of the day, to ask Browning to 'write [him] a play'. That *Strafford*, Browning's next publication and first acted drama, was a result of this double pressure is apparent in Browning's choice of a subject which Forster was concurrently engaged with,[5] and in his statement in its preface that he had been '*induced* to make the present attempt'; that he yielded to such inducement in the belief that popularity would follow emerges from a reference to *Strafford* in the Preface to the first number of *Bells and Pomegranates*, the series begun immediately after the débâcle of *Sordello*:

> two or three years ago I wrote a Play, about which the chief matter I much care to recollect at present is, that a Pit-full of goodnatured people applauded it: – ever since, I have been desirous of doing something in the same way that should better reward their attention. What follows I mean for the first of a series of Dramatical Pieces, to come out at intervals, and I amuse myself by fancying that the cheap mode in which they appear will for once help me to a sort of Pit-audience again. Of course, such a work must go on no longer than it is liked[.]
>
> *Penguin* i 1070

The character of *Bells and Pomegranates*, as here described, was clearly determined by what Browning took to be the popularity of drama, combined with an astute awareness of the growing importance of the serialised novel: simultaneously, the phrase 'something . . . that should better reward their attention' betrays his covert didacticism. The co-presence of these two aims emerges more clearly still in Browning's explanation of the title of *Bells and Pomegranates* to E.B.B.:

> The Rabbis make Bells & Pomegranates symbolical of Pleasure and Profit, the Gay & the Grave, the Poetry & the Prose, Singing and Sermonising – such a mixture of effects as in the original hour (that is quarter of an hour) of confidence & creation, I meant the whole should prove at last[.]
>
> to E.B.B. 18 Oct. 1845: *LK* 241

III

Browning accepted then, though in a modified form, his period's insistence upon popularity as a legitimate test of poetic merit. He also accepted the key tenets of populist aesthetics:

(i) *Egalitarianism*. Here he directly echoes Wordsworth:

[Wordsworth:] Among the qualities I have enumerated as principally conducing to form a Poet, is implied nothing differing in kind from other men, but only in degree.

Preface to 'Lyrical Ballads', Hayden i 882

[Browning:]   the finest mind,
All in degree, no way diverse in kind
From minds about it[.]

Sordello v 561–3

(ii) *Intelligibility*. To use his own words, '*clear expression* should be [the poet's] only work and care': indeed, 'from the beginning I have been used to take a high ground, and say, all endeavour elsewhere is thrown away' (*RB & AD* 127).

(iii) *Reader-dependence*. Again the influence of Wordsworth is apparent, when in the Preface to *Paracelsus*, his first acknowledged publication, he half-echoes Wordsworth's 'co-operating power':

It is certain . . . that a work like mine depends . . . immediately on the intelligence and sympathy of the reader for its success – indeed were my scenes stars it must be his *co-operating fancy* [m.i.] which, supplying all chasms, shall connect the scattered lights into one constellation – a Lyre or a Crown.

Penguin i 1030

Sordello was the work intended as the climax of Browning's earliest attempts to translate his humanistic ideology into stylistic terms. The failure of *Pauline* – Browning was later bitterly to note that 'not one copy' of his 'Fragment of a Confession' was sold – had led to his conceiving *Sordello*, in 1833–34, as a deliberately 'marketable' work; the Preface to *Paracelsus* promises the reader 'other productions which may follow in a more popular, and perhaps less difficult form' (*Penguin* i 1030). *Strafford* was described, again in a preface, as a holiday from the major task of *Sordello*, as indeed *Paracelsus* had been. *Sordello* was to be the *magnum opus*, the perfect poem which would bring together the democratic and reader-dependent elements of his creative philosophy by turning writer and reader into 'brothers':

Yourselves effect what I was fain before
Effect, what I supplied yourselves suggest,
What I leave bare yourselves can now invest.

> How we attain to talk as brothers talk,
> In half-words[.] . . . Leave the mere rude
> Explicit details! 'tis but brother's speech
> We need, speech where an accent's change gives each
> The other's soul – no speech to understand
> By former audience: need was then to expand,
> Expatiate – hardly were we brothers!
>
> v 622–6, 635–40

The last three lines describe an undesirable 'former' state when because the poet would 'expand, expatiate' from a position of implied superiority, the audience could not be his 'brothers'. In the ideal poem, poet and reader cohabit in a state of quasi-domestic intimacy in which words are simply the catalysts, not the substance, of sympathetic communication. A revision Browning made in the 1863 text (quoted above, p. 27) makes it clearer that this description was intended to apply to *Sordello* itself, making it the epic of brotherly love between the poet and his readers.

It is hard to believe that any intention in literary history has ever failed so badly. It was not just that the poem was received with incredulous ridicule, and thereby missed its primary aim of popularity. It was that he was held to have had the arrogant effrontery to *seek* failure. One critic put it:

> the author who chooses deliberately to put 'his light under a bushel' of affectations, must not be surprised if men refuse the labour of searching it out, and leave him to the peaceable enjoyment of that obscurity which he has courted.
>
> *Athenaeum*, 30 May 1840 431–2, 431: *Browning: the Critical Heritage*,
> eds Boyd Litzinger and Donald Smalley (1970: hereafter *CH*) 63

The irony is intensified by the fact that the offending features of the poem are those which for Browning would make his reader his 'brother'; the *Athenaeum* reviewer actually uses Wordsworthian phrasing to emphasise his point: 'It might be worth Mr Browning's while to *use the language of ordinary men*, and to *condescend* to be intelligible' (ibid. 432: m. i.). The phrases I have italicised make it quite clear that Victorian reviewers interpreted Wordsworth's principles as enjoining simple intelligibility, where Browning had taken them to involve primarily the recruitment of the reader's 'cooperating power'. Other critics itemised the stylistic features to which they took exception:

The story is most elliptically constructed, full of breaks and leaps; the
syntax of quite an unusual character, a mass of perplexity and
obscurity; the versification is harsh and knotty; the language, instead of
being throughout 'English undefiled', is larded with many fantastic
and arbitrary invertions, and the whole set together in a ricketty,
hysterical, capricious style, producing the most startling and repulsive
effect.

Dublin Review viii (May 1840): 551–3, 552: *CH* 64

Thus the *Dublin Review*; the *Metropolitan Magazine*, making the parallel
claim that *Sordello* consists of 'unintelligible oozings of nonsense'
illustrated its point with an admittedly well-chosen specimen:

"–Meantime, just meditate my madrigal
O' the mugwort that conceals a dewdrop safe!'
What, dullard? We and you in smothery chafe,
Babes, baldheads, stumbled thus far into Zin
The Horrid, getting neither out nor in,
A *hungry* sun above us, sands *among*
Our throats, – each dromedary lolls a tongue,
Each camel churns a sick and frothy chap,
And you, 'twixt tales of Potiphar's mishap,
And sonnets on the *earliest ass that spoke*,
Remark you wonder any one needs choak
With founts about! Potsherd him Gibeonites,
While awkwardly enough your Moses smites
The rock, though he forego the Promised Land
Thereby, have Satan claim his carcass, and
Dance, forsooth, Metaphysic Poet . . . . ah
Mark ye the dim first oozings?"

iii 815–32: quoted *Metropolitan Magazine*
(literary suppl.) xxvii (Feb. 1840) 108–9: *CH* 66

Yet this passage is concerned with the contrast between a nature poet
whose self-absorption causes him to ignore the real-life predicament of
his readers, and another (Browning himself) who is vitally aware of their
needs and as committed to their welfare as Moses was to that of the
Israelites. Secure in the confidence that this is the proper role for the
poet, he invites the common people ('Gibeonites') to express their
approval by stoning his rival for his apostacy. This passage anticipates his

claim, in Book v, that in its involvement of the reader *Sordello* is the climax of poetic development; appropriately, it draws in the reader by concealing its discursive meaning beneath a surface made up of 'breaks and leaps'. But for the critic, it illustrates the 'premeditated, wilful and incurable' 'sins of his verse' which demand its immediate and indignant rejection.

I dwell upon Browning's discomfiture not as a good joke but because it marked the inception of a problem that was to bedevil his entire career. The charges against *Sordello* were renewed at regular intervals for the next fifty years. Browning's relations with both his critics and his public suffered damage which even his later popularity could not altogether repair. It seems worthwhile, therefore, to explore the related questions: what caused the failure of *Sordello*? and what effect did this have on Browning's conception and practice of his art?

IV

I have already noted that in private descriptions of his attitude to his audience, Browning characteristically divides himself into two parts, the first a poet whose allegiance is to the public, the second a completely self-sufficient being, unconcerned with the reception of his work. This distinction corresponds to that made, in both *Sordello* and the *Essay on Shelley*, between the 'objective' and the 'subjective' poets. It is the objective poet who is concerned with his auditory. The subjective, on the contrary, dedicates himself and his work directly to God, drawing inspiration from 'his own soul', in which he finds 'the nearest reflex of that divine mind', and making no concession to contemporary taste: indeed, the sublimity of his habitual concerns leaves no room for such compromise.

Sordello is a poet of the subjective type, and his career illustrates the difficulties inevitable when such a poet enters into relations with an audience. In Mantua, on the crest of a wave of popularity founded on a single poem, Sordello sets about the attempt to put his transcendent vision into language, to forge, in his own words, an 'armour' to contain it: only to meet inevitable failure, 'Because perceptions whole . . . reject so pure a work of thought / As language'. The failure is a double one: in the poem, which in using language at all ties infinity to its opponent, time, and in his audience, who, because they 'lack . . . perception' cannot 'clutch / And reconstruct' the infinite behind its treacherous words. Two options remain. The first, which Sordello seriously entertains, and which his historical obscurity suggests (for Browning) that he partially adopted, is to give up writing and rest content with the perfection preserved unsullied by his silence. The second is outlined as Browning's explanation, in Book iii, of the qualities of Sordello's few extant pieces. These are, he claims, radically flawed in art. But that is only to be expected in a poet of his type, and is indeed a kind of virtue. For these very flaws are the only possible sign that he recognises the incommensurability between vision and language, and refuses the disastrous attempt to put one inside the other. Unfortunately, such a poet's readers interpret this gesture as indicating either incompetence or, as the reception of *Sordello* suggests, arrogance; and the close resemblance between this aspect of Browning's poetics and what Friedrich von Schlegel called 'Socratic Irony' suggests that the latter interpretation was not entirely inapposite. 'Socratic Irony', as Schlegel defined it, involved the poet not only in a rejection of language as a medium for his vision, but also in a repudiation of his audience:

There are ancient and modern poems which breathe, in their entirety and in every detail, the divine breath of irony. In such poems there lives a real transcendental buffoonery. Their interior is permeated by the mood which surveys everything and rises infinitely above everything limited, even above the poet's own art, virtue and genius[. Socratic irony] contains and incites a feeling of the insoluble conflict of the absolute and the relative, of the impossibility and necessity of total communication. It is the freest of all liberties, for it enables us to rise above our own self; and still the most legitimate, for it is absolutely necessary. It is a good sign if the harmonious dullards fail to understand this constant self-parody, if over and over again they believe and disbelieve until they become giddy and consider jest to be seriousness and seriousness to be jest.

Lyceum-Fragments nos 42 & 108 in *Friedrich Schlegel: Dialogue on Poetry and Literary Aphorisms*, trans. E. Behler and R. Struc (Pennsylvania, 1968) 126 & 131[6]

I take Schlegel to mean that self-parody, by allowing the writer to reject both his own literary product and himself as its producer, becomes a means of indicating 'the insoluble conflict of the absolute and the relative' (the relative here including 'the poet's art, virtue and genius', the absolute being what Schlegel elsewhere calls 'the spirit of universality', or God). This kind of self-parody is rife in *Sordello*:

Potsherd him, Gibeonites!
While awkwardly enough your Moses smites
The rock, though he forgo his Promised Land
Thereby, have Satan claim his carcase, and
Figure as Metaphysic Poet . . . ah,
Mark ye the first dim oozings? Meribah!

iii 825-30 (1888 text)

The rollicking style here, with its airy allusions to both canonical and apocryphal Bible leaves the reader unsure whether to unravel the allusions and seriously take Browning for Moses, or to laugh at a comic display climaxing in the author's ludicrous claim to the status of prophet and lawgiver. 'Transcendental buffoonery' seems to me exactly to describe this tone, and its effect, as we have seen, was undeniably to confuse 'harmonious dullards' into 'fail[ing] to understand this constant self-parody'.

But *this* view of poetry creates a disparity rather than an equality between the poet and his reader. Incompleteness, far from inviting us, in a democratic spirit, to help complete the poem, now symbolises the poet's despair before the task of expressing the magnitude of his own being through the flawed materials at his disposal to an audience made up of what Schlegel called 'harmonious dullards'. And it is this attitude which dominates Browning's restatement of his aesthetics to Ruskin in a letter of 1855. The occasion for this episode was the publication of Browning's *Men and Women* in 1855. Ruskin received a copy, and under pressure from Dante Gabriel Rossetti, already a proselyte, sent Browning a letter containing his comments:

[W]hen I take up these poems in the evening I find them absolutely and literally a set of the most amazing Conundrums that ever were proposed to me . . . I would pray you, faith, heartily, to consider with yourself, how far you can amend matters, & make the real virtue of your work acceptable & profitable to more people.

2 Dec. 1855; in D. DeLaura, 'Ruskin and the Brownings: twenty-
five unpublished letters', *Bulletin of the John Rylands Library* liv
(1972) 314-46, 324, 326

This unintelligibility results from Browning's insistence that the reader contribute to the poem:

[Y]our Ellipses are quite Unconscionable: before one can get through ten lines, one has to patch you up in twenty places, wrong or right, and if one hasn't much stuff of one's own to spare to patch with! You are worse than the worst Alpine Glacier I ever crossed. Bright, & deep enough truly, but so full of Clefts that half the journey has to be done with ladder & hatchet.

326–7

Browning replied at great length, particularly in response to this objection:

For your bewilderment . . . – how shall I help *that*? We don't read poetry the same way, by the same law; it is too clear. I cannot begin writing poetry till my imaginary reader has conceded licences to me which you demur at altogether. I *know* that I don't make out my conception by my language, all poetry being a putting the infinite within the finite. You would have me paint it all plain out, which can't be; but by various artifices I try to make shift with touches and bits of outline which *succeed* if they bear the conception from me to you. You ought, I think, to keep pace with the thought tripping from ledge to ledge of my 'glaciers', as you call them; not stand poking your alpenstock into the holes, and demonstrating that no foot could have stood there; – suppose it sprang over there?

Ruskin, *Works* xxxvi p. xxxiv

What is striking about this passage – and indeed the whole letter – is that in it Browning nowhere restates the humanistic reader – dependence announced in *Sordello*. Instead, he arrogantly declares his own infinite superiority to his readers:

Do you think poetry was ever generally understood – or can be? Is the business of it to tell people what they know already, as they know it, and so precisely that they shall be able to cry out – 'Here you should supply *this* – *that*, you evidently pass over, and I'll help you from my own stock'? . . . A poet's affair is with God, – to whom he is accountable, and of whom is his reward; look elsewhere, and you find misery enough.

xxxv–vi

Browning's 'my own stock' mocks Ruskin's 'stuff of one's own', he accuses Ruskin of being one of those who ask the poet to 'tell people what they know already'. Denying his reader the partnership he had accorded him in *Sordello*, Browning resumes his didactic hegemony in self-sufficient isolation, declaring himself answerable to God alone.

However, two significant qualifications prevent us from interpreting this letter as involving a full Socratic Irony. For in one passage, Browning makes it clear that not *all* his readers are to be considered 'harmonious dullards'. Instead, he distinguishes between the average spectator of *Hamlet*, who worships Macready's histrionics rather than Shakespeare's genius and is accordingly happy to let Macready suppress 'certainly a third of the play, with no end of noble things', and the intelligentsia ('a very few, who react upon the rest') who can be welcomed as the poet's 'brothers' when they correctly apreciate the 'reality' which lies behind the disruptions and buffooneries which repel the rest.

A possible source for this revision of Socratic Irony is the similar revision proposed by Friedrich Schlegel's brother, August Wilhelm. Shakespearian Irony, suggests August Wilhelm, was not designed to repel *all* the poet's readers, since with its help the poet can 'make, as it were, a sort of secret understanding with the select circle of the more intelligent of his readers or spectators'. Browning echoes this passage when he makes Sordello describe how, during the performance of his imaginary drama he himself, though ostensibly absent from the proceedings, will in fact remain 'implied / Superior now' and can therefore 'circumvent / A few, my masque contented, and to these / Offer unveil the last of mysteries' (v 614–6). The same distinction between 'harmonious dullards' and 'the more intelligent of his readers' is made in *The Essay on Shelley* when Browning identifies 'spirits of a like endowment with [the poet's] own, who, by means of his abstract, can forthwith pass to the reality it was made from' (*Penguin* i 1001). These passages do much to explain why Browning was so preoccupied with the critical reception of his poetry; professional reviewers, he hoped, belonged to that privileged category of the 'very few, who react upon the rest'; and when, as typically happened, they proved recalcitrant, he found himself being pushed, to his evident alarm, towards the full Romantic Irony of a poet whose transcendent vision was inaccessible to *all* his readers. Ruskin's bewilderment was especially wounding in that Browning saw Ruskin as one of the foremost minds of his age, and one, furthermore, who had come very close to Browning's own aesthetic position.

The second qualification in Browning's Romantic Irony was the survival in his aesthetics of a didactic element which Schlegel effectively excludes. Indeed, it is the didacticism of his work that he preferred to blame for its unpopularity:

It is all teaching, on the contrary, and the people hate to be taught.
They say otherwise, – make foolish fables about Orpheus enchanting
stocks and stones, poets standing up and being worshipped, – all
nonsense and impossible dreaming.

xxxvi

This argument brings Browning very close to the position Ruskin himself
had adopted, in which reader-dependence was designed to elicit, not an
idiosyncratic or fanciful contribution, but an 'accurate', that is, a
prescribed one. Indeed, Ruskin's objection to *Men and Women* was not, as
Browning appears to have supposed, for its adherence to the principle of
reader-dependence itself, but for what he regarded as the lack in
Browning's work of adequate guidance to the reader. The clue is found in
Ruskin's use of the phrase 'wrong or right' in his objection to Browning's
'Ellipses'. This clearly suggests that Browning's reader-dependence is
culpable because his guidance to his reader is insufficient to compel him
to 'think *accurately*'. And in his reply, Browning in effect admits that he
does want to limit his reader's creative space. To ask Ruskin to 'keep pace
with the thought' of a poem is clearly to forbid him to 'take [his] own way,
or wander hither and thither'.

V

Does this mean that Browning's conception of his relation to his audience
is self-contradictory? Can the reader be simultaneously his 'brother' and
his immeasurable inferior? Not simultaneously, perhaps; but there is in
Sordello an account which by viewing the writer–reader relationship as an
evolutionary process, produces a formula for reconciling the polarities.
Since it provides also a description of Browning's creative strategy – a
strategy that he seriously endeavoured to implement in the works which
follow *Sordello* – it is worth describing in some detail.

In Book iii of *Sordello* (862–1022), Browning posits three distinct kinds
of poet. All are concerned to communicate what Browning calls
'perceptions whole' from the visionary plane at which the poet functions.
The difference lies in the procedure they adopt. The first category, 'the
worst of us', can only '*say* they so have seen' (i.e. verbally lay claim to
experiences they cannot transmit). The second, 'the better', get as far as
describing 'what it was they saw'. But they in turn are surpassed by the
third and 'best', who 'impart the gift of seeing to the rest'. In the passage
that follows, Browning gives a practical demonstration of the work of
each kind in turn. The first two ('worst' and 'better') simply describe a

reality which their reader passively accepts as 'true'; the third ('the best') poses an enigma which obliges the reader to seek a meaning beneath its surface. We then discover that the same meaning underlay the first two examples: what all three 'say' is that the significance of experience is to be found in its depths rather than on its surface, matching up the text's message with its procedures. In recognising this the reader is finally congratulated on 'having seen too what I saw', i.e. having acquired and used a 'gift of seeing'. In effect, the audience is being *educated* by being taken through kinds of poetry it already likes to a more abstract kind which, in the process, it has learnt to construe and prefer. After which,

> Thus far advanced in safety then, proceed!
> And having seen too what I saw, be bold
> And next encounter what I do behold
> (That's sure) but bid you take on trust!

iii 912–15

Having been made to 'see', the reader is at last prepared for the poet's true teaching, which concerns things which, even with the help of his new 'gift of seeing', he could scarcely 'see' unaided. Having abdicated his poetic authority in order to train others to use their powers, the poet exploits those powers by resuming his own didactic authority at the higher level to which he has introduced his readers. But the educative process was itself didactic, in that the reader, though 'free' to reach his own conception of the meaning of what the poet gave him, was constantly guided by cryptic hints towards his apotheosis of understanding.

I believe that this passage reveals Browning's overall poetic strategy. He would begin by working within existing popular forms. His audience, from their initial inertia, would gradually be drawn into supplying, or rather detecting, a transcendent significance behind the surface display. Then it would be ready for the ultimate occult, the subjective poet's vision of the absolute. Along the way, however, it would be constantly behind the point which ideally it should have reached, and in the very process of calling upon his readers' powers, the poet might occasionally mock their dilatoriness – playfully, as in the passage I have cited from *Sordello*, or irritably, as in the significantly-named *Popularity* from *Men and Women*. This was the poem selected for comment in Ruskin's letter, with the remark, 'yes, that touches the matter in hand'. It certainly does. *Popularity* echoes E.B.B.'s claim that the truly original poet can hardly expect contemporary recognition, but must await 'the coming age' for his due acclaim. But in the meantime . . .?

Meantime, I'll draw you as you stand,
  With few or none to watch and wonder;
I'll say – a fisher, on the sand
  By Tyre the old, with ocean-plunder,
A netful, brought to land.

21–5

This extraordinary conceptual leap, by which the 'true poet' is replaced by – or compared with? – a 'fisher on the sand', presumably illustrates how the poet imparts 'the gift of seeing' by making his reader bridge the semantic chasm; but the context also suggests that he expects *un*popularity to follow the attempt and therefore that 'the rest' will *not* learn to 'see'. In which case the poem does become the act of defiance and contempt which Browning's contemporaries – including Ruskin – so frequently suspected him of intending. *Popularity* ends with a contrast between the 'true poet' and second-raters who follow and exploit his innovations, figured as the contrast between the discoverer of a new and beautifully-coloured dye, who is condemned to go hungry, and those who get hold of it to exploit it and make their fortunes:

Hobbs hints blue, – straight he turtle eats:
  Nobbs prints blue, – claret crowns his cup:
Nokes outdares Stokes in azure feats, –
  Both gorge. Who fished the murex up?
What porridge had John Keats?

61–5

Ruskin's comments typify the contemporary reaction:

[W]as this what God kept [Keats] *safe* for? To feed Nobbs with Turtle. Is this what you call Accepting the future ages duty. – I don't understand.
  "What porridge"? Porridge is a Scotch dish, I believe; typical of bad fare. Do you mean that Keats had bad fare? But if he had – how was he kept safe to the worlds end? I don't understand at all!!!!!!!

326

Browning defended himself by claiming (consistently with his general theory) that if 'the jump [is] too much', it is because 'The whole is all but a simultaneous feeling with me' Ruskin, *Works*, xxxvi p. xxxv. It is true that the meaning of the passage is not *that* hard to work out, but there was surely a touch of provocativeness in writing so obscurely in a poem on popularity, especially when he also speaks of 'turn[ing] to the bystanders and tell[ing] them a bit of my mind about their own stupid thanklessness and mistaking'. In a kind of sarcastic hara-kiri the poem which attacks their mistaking also furnishes them with a capital opportunity of mistaking its own meaning.

Popularity illustrates, I think, Browning's yielding to a constant temptation to desert his educative strategy with a gesture of despairing contempt for his uncomprehending readers. However, I am not suggesting that this was his usual intention and thus the sign of his abandonment of his creative programme. Rather, his career consists of a constant oscillation between the democratic and the élitist, the humanistic and the ironic attitudes to his audience. Browning's comment to his friend Joseph Milsand about *Men and Women* suggests that that collection too was to epitomise his dialectic:

> I am writing, a *first step towards popularity for me* – lyrics with more music and painting than before, *so as to get people to hear and see.* [m.i.]
> 24 Feb. 1853: 'Deux lettres inédites de Robert Browning à Joseph Milsand', *Revue Germanique* xii (1921) 253

Again, the step towards popularity masks the desire to develop his audience's power to 'see what I have seen'. The presence of *Popularity* in *Men and Women*, however, indicates the presence of the ironist whose bitterness was hardly likely to be assuaged by the failure, in its turn, of *Men and Women*. The cumulative effect of these reversals emerges in Browning's explanation, in *The Ring and the Book* (1869), of his decision again to use 'art' to 'teach [his] lesson':

> Because, it is the glory and good of Art,
> That Art remains the one way possible
> Of speaking truth, to mouths like mine, at least.
> How look a brother in the face and say
> 'Thy right is wrong, eyes hast thou yet art blind,
> Thine ears are stuffed and stopped, despite their length:
> And, oh, the foolishness thou countest faith!'
> Say this as silverly as tongue can troll –
> The anger of the man may be endured,
> The shrug, the disappointed eyes of him,
> Are not so bad to bear – but here's the plague

That all this trouble comes of telling truth,
Which truth, by when it reaches him, looks false,
Seems to be just the thing it would supplant,
Not recognisable by whom it left –
While falsehood would have done the work of truth.
But Art, – wherein man nowise speaks to men,
But only to mankind, – Art may tell a truth
Obliquely, do the thing shall breed the thought,
Nor wrong the thought, missing the mediate word.
So may you paint your picture, twice show truth,
Beyond mere imagery on the wall, –
So, note by note, bring music from your mind,
Deeper than ever the Andante dived, –
So write a book shall mean, beyond the facts,
Suffice the eye and save the soul beside[.]

                                      xii 838–63

The last nine lines once again acclaim a reader-dependent art for its power to breed 'the thought' in the reader's mind without the risk of being misunderstood through a direct 'mediate word'. But the first seven lines suggest that the 'truth' of 'Art' will be a denial that the reader can really acquire this power! He cannot be got to 'hear and see' because his 'eyes' are 'blind', his 'ears' 'stuffed and stopped', and though Browning *may* mean that the transmission of such a message by 'oblique' means will serve to unclog these organs, this is a logical impossibility. The desire to insult rather than to instruct certainly appears to have chosen Browning's words for him. His explicit repudiation of Wordsworth's belief that the poet is 'a man speaking to men' in 11.16–17 confirms that his attitude had hardened since *Sordello*.

The peculiarities of Browning's style seem to be explicable in terms of two quite separate philosophies. For one, the democratic, his 'Ellipses' intend to recruit the reader's cooperating fancy into the process of creation. The other, the ironic, uses these same features to encrypt a meaning too high and precious for exposure to the uninitiated. Once again Browning abdicates and resumes power, forswears and exercises tyranny, with the same gesture, and thus rehearses in his philosophy of audience the primal duality of his political beliefs.

3
The Problem of Form

I

While trying to persuade the soldier Salinguerra to support his programme for liberal reform, Sordello links it with what he anticipates will be the historical evolution of poetry. As the 1863 running-titles make clear, this evolution falls into three stages: the first, epic; the second, drama; the third not named but clearly presaging the dramatic monologue.[1] The grounds on which Sordello distinguishes these, and mounts them into an ascending series, is their sensitivity to the morality of the reader-writer relation. In epic, the earliest form, the poet controls the reader's response by telling him what to think about the action:

> Apprehend
> Which sinner is, which saint, if I allot
> Hell, Purgatory, Heaven, a blaze or blot,
> To those you doubt concerning!
>
> v 588–91

In drama, the next genre, the poet removes himself from the work, and presents his characters directly to an audience, which is commanded to

> behold
> How such, with fit assistance . . . disengage
> Their forms, love, hate, hope, fear, peace make, war wage,
> In presence of you all!
>
> v 607–8, 609–11

However, the use of the imperative ('behold') implies that the poet maintains his presence through the very virtuosity with which he conceals it, and Sordello confirms that though ostensibly absent, the dramatist remains

57

> implied
> Superior now, as, by the platform's side,
> [He] bade them do and suffer[.]

v 611–13

There is a need, then, for a further stage in which the subject-matter changes from 'external things' to 'man's inmost life', and the style to a reader-dependent one. Between 1833 and 1855, Browning passed through all these three stages in his own development.

Sordello itself was designed as an epic, the form, Browning claims, he was forced into by his audience:

> Never, – I should warn you first –
> Of my own choice had this, if not the worst
> Yet not the best expedient, served to tell
> A story I could body forth so well
> By making speak, myself kept out of view,
> The very man as he was wont to do,
> And leaving you to say the rest for him.
> . . . But it seems
> Your setters-forth of unexampled themes,
> Makers of quite new men, producing them,
> Would best chalk broadly on each vesture's hem
> The wearer's quality; or take their stand,
> Motley on back and pointing-pole in hand,
> Beside him. So, for once I face ye, friends[.]

i 11–17, 25–31

This passage makes it clear that Browning's reluctance to use the epic form was caused by the problematic relation of its narrator to the subject and the audience. It is therefore the role of narrator and the act of narrating that he sets about subverting. The result was what his friend Richard Henry Horne described as the

> confused 'story', and broken, mazy, dancing sort of narrative no-outline, which has occasioned so much trouble, if not despair, to [Browning's] most patient and painstaking admirers.
>
> *A New Spirit of the Age* (repr. 1907) p. 374

In the last chapter I explained the ambivalence of Browning's attitude to his audience; here we encounter features which reflect a different problem, the problem of narrative as a medium for the poet. Browning inherited from Shelley a profound distrust of narrative:

> There is this difference between a story and a poem, that a story is a catalogue of detached facts, which have no other connexion than time, place, circumstance, cause and effect; the other is the creation of actions according to the unchangeable forms of human nature, as existing in the mind of the Creator, which is itself the image of all other minds.
>
> *Shelley's Prose*, ed. D. L. Clarke (Albuquerque, 1954) 281

The business of narrating is made impossible by the combined impossibility and necessity of thereby 'putting the infinite into the finite', reducing the timeless to the temporal. Browning's solution in *Sordello* – a catastrophic one as far as his contemporary audience was concerned – was to invert the problem by erasing time itself from the narrative process.

Rather than being narrated in a straight line, *Sordello* is built round a series of cardinal moments, each of which finds Sordello alone and deep in thought. His thoughts *contain* narrative, in that he reflects upon and thus indirectly narrates the events which have brought about the current crisis. But the story-line exists to service his wider metaphysical and political speculations, and is therefore of an embedded and secondary character. Browning emphasises the point by having Sordello go over the same sequence of events on each occasion, as if they were a puzzle to be solved rather than transparent in meaning; furthermore, Sordello treats certain episodes of his life, in particular his childhood at Goito and his poetic apprenticeship at Mantua, as representative stages of the poet's development, or symbols of the eternal dialectic of human existence, rather than phases of his own personal development. As the narrative thickens with repetition, variation and digression, it begins to lose its forward momentum and to solidify, so to speak, into a construct not in time, but in space (or time-made-space). The peculiar arrangement of the time-sequence has the same effect. After beginning *in medias res*, with his hero in Mantua in the thick of war and intrigue, Browning plunges into a gigantic flash-back which occupies the remainder of the first two-and-a-half books, to surface again in the vicinity of its inaugural scene – but only in the *vicinity*, for the moment itself remains elusive and unrecovered – only to break off with a long digression on a parallel moment of decision in

Browning's own life when, on the steps in Venice, he determined to dedicate his poem to 'suffering humanity'. By breaking his narrative apart, and revealing himself in the act of composing it, Browning issues the loudest possible proclamation of its artificiality, and to make sure the point is not missed, he opens his digression with his statement that Sordello's work, and by extension his own, is to be viewed as ironic rather than realistic. The more straightforward narrative of the last three books never quite abolishes the memory of this alienative episode, and therefore never makes of itself a narrative of the traditional kind.

II

Because the dramatist has no choice but to remain 'out of view' leaving his characters to act out their story for themselves, drama would seem to release Browning from the problem of narration. However, his stated motive for making it the staple of his published output in the years immediately following the failure of *Sordello* was, as we saw in chapter two, its *popularity*. But the form also had moral implications. Romantic critics had stressed the *selflessness* and therefore the moral rectitude of drama, normally through the example of Shakespeare, who in Coleridge's words 'darts himself forth, and passes into all the forms of human character and passion', and whose Protean versatility underlies Keats's characterisation of the 'camelion poet' who possessing 'no self' of his own is always 'in for and filling some other body'.[2] A. W. Schlegel, whose *Lectures on Dramatic Poetry*, translated into English in 1815, did much to extend and emphasize this conception of drama, speaking again apropos Shakespeare, put it that

> the distinguishing property of the dramatic poet who is great in characterisation ... is the capability of transporting himself so completely into every situation, even the most unusual, that he is enabled, as plenipotentiary of the whole human race, without particular instructions for each separate case, to act and speak in the name of every individual.
>
> A. W. Schlegel, *Lectures* ii 128

Behind these accounts lies the Platonic doctrine of Love, in which the lover, loving in the other the 'beauty' he lacks in himself, strives to unite himself with and become the other. The structural peculiarity of drama, its repression of the author, made it a natural illustration of this doctrine.

When, therefore, Browning's Aprile in part ii of *Paracelsus* cries out, 'I would LOVE infinitely, and be loved', his ambition to write in a dramatic mode is seen as a logical corollary. In Browning's own cycle of plays this self-abnegation is thematised in the action: as the dramatist has abdicated in favour of his characters, so those characters are made to rehearse the corresponding moral and political gestures before an audience whose applause completes the circle and ratifies the poet's humanistic claims.

If drama fulfilled his formal/moral requirements so well, why did Browning abandon drama after 1846? Why was *Luria* (1846) his last full-length play?

The answers are indicated in the preface to his first play *Paracelsus*. Browning admits that as a closet-drama it deviates from the conventional canons of acted drama:

[I]t is an attempt, probably more novel than happy, to reverse the method usually adopted by writers whose aim it is to set forth any phenomenon of the mind or the passions, by the operation of persons and events; and . . . instead of having recourse to an external machinery of incidents to create and evolve the crisis I desire to produce, I have ventured to display somewhat minutely the mood itself in its rise and progress, and have suffered the agency by which it is influenced and determined, to be generally discernable in its effects alone, and subordinate throughout, if not altogether excluded; and this for a reason. I have endeavoured to write a poem, not a drama; the canons of the drama are well-known, and I cannot but think that, inasmuch as they have immediate regard to stage representation, the peculiar advantages they hold out are really such only so long as the purpose for which they were at first instituted is kept in view. I do not very well understand what is called a Dramatic Poem, wherein all those restrictions only submitted to on account of compensating good in the original scheme are scrupulously retained, as though for some special fitness in themselves[.]

Penguin i 1029–30

Browning is arguing, reasonably enough, that unacted drama is under no obligation to follow the rules (unity of time and place, physical actability) which govern stage drama. It is suggestive, however, that he interprets such rules as 'restrictions'. His implied attitude became explicit when he described *Strafford*, his next – and definitely acted – play as 'one of Action in Character, rather than Character in Action' (1st edn Preface). Such a reversal of Aristotle's terms seems to make stage drama indistinguishable from closet-drama; both display 'the mood itself in its rise and progress': the application of such a formula to a stage play can only mean that Browning's 'reservations' about the value of the 'peculiar advantages' of 'an external machinery of incidents' extended a good deal further than he admitted in the preface to *Paracelsus*. This is so. Browning never accepted that 'any phenomenon of the mind or passions' could really be portrayed by 'the operation of persons or events'. Truth, Paracelsus argues, 'is within ourselves', it 'takes no rise / From outward things'; and the closeness of 'outward things' here to the Preface's 'external machinery of events' strongly suggests that he voices some version of Browning's own belief. Confirmation is found in the form of the poem, in which the hectic activity of Paracelsus's life vanishes into five quiet interviews with a friend. History itself dissolves before the process of inner development whose apotheosis, the great death-bed speech in which Paracelsus finally 'Attains', arrives at the point where, in every 'outward' sense, he would be consigned to the oblivion of failure.

A similar contrast pervades the historical plays. They too, in defiance of the traditional configuration, promote the secret, inner histories of the characters' souls into priority over the gross activity of external events. Strafford's outward self-seeking proves to conceal his actual devotion to the king, and Browning reinforces his point by giving the play an unhistorical ending: *his* Charles I appears at Strafford's jail and, in contrition to his own complicity in Strafford's ruin, vows to ransom him by granting the Long Parliament's demands. Strafford's refusal to accept this generosity – which ironically 'might' have averted the Civil War – is in one sense Browning's tacit admission that it *is* unhistorical, but the rhetoric suggests equally that Browning wanted to rescue a moment of true inner sentiments – Charles's love for Strafford now at last openly manifested – from the distortions of real history, or at least from the cynicism implicit in history's recorded action. The unhistorical ending of *King Victor and King Charles*, in which Charles restores the crown to his dying father, likewise appears a revelation too precious for historical record. In a daring gesture, Browning even has Victor offer the 'real' historical ending as a face-saving legend to Charles, in token of the love which history-books cannot credit:

> Charles – how to save your story? Mine must go!
> Say – say that you refused the crown to me!
> Charles, yours shall be my story! You immured
> Me, say, at Rivoli. A single year
> I spend without a sight of you, then die –

That will serve every purpose – tell that tale
The world!

ii 326–32

By an extraordinary inversion, actual history, composed of the 'external machinery of incidents', usually supposed to be the determinant of individual psychology, dwindles to the status of legend while the inner movements of passion usurp its status as fact.

And in their individual relationships in turn, characters experience action – the individual equivalent to general history – not as a means of self-expression but as an impenetrable barrier to mutual comprehension. Strafford agonises that the King cannot know his love and loyalty:

What shall convince you? What does Savile do
To prove him. . . . Ah, one can't tear out one's heart
And show it, how sincere a thing it is!

1 ii 201–3

and this passage might serve as a motto for the misunderstood protagonists – King Charles, Djabal, Valens, Luria – who find, as Arnold later put it, 'no vent in action' for their infinite desires, and as a result can only act ambiguously and be misunderstood. Browning's plays study the misinterpretations which result from the semiotic poverty of action. As Browning later put it,

Along with every act – and speech is act –
There go, a multitude impalpable
To ordinary human faculty,
The thoughts which give the act significance.

Red Cotton Night-Cap Country (1873) 3277–80

Though action *is* significant, its meaning is obscured by the intricacy and subtlety of the informing thoughts. Protagonists are periodically immobilised and rendered dumb by a fatal inner excess of motive. Mildred, in *A Blot in the 'Scutcheon*, accused by Tresham of the loss of virginity which she has certainly experienced but feels more than simple guilt for, stands silent while he accuses her. The Queen (in *In a Balcony*), confronted by the revelation that Norbert and Constance have deceived her, convulsively 'grasp[s] . . . the balcony' in a gesture whose meaning the play's truncated ending teasingly witholds. (Browning did suggest, when asked, that she might perhaps be expected to have died, joining Djabal, Luria, Mildred, Tresham and the many others for whom the inadequacy of external action can be overcome only through the 'internal' act of self-inflicted or spontaneous death.)

Nor does the problem end there. For if 'truth is within ourselves', the commitment of drama to 'the combination of humanity in action' – and therefore in principle to a common or neutral world as its arena – becomes philosophically questionable. In a passage in *La Saisiaz* (261–4) Browning claims that, having only 'the knowledge that I am', he can have no idea 'If my fellows are or are not, what may please them and what pain.' And if, as he goes on to claim, God has given 'his own world to every mortal', what is left of the common world posited by drama? As if this ontological onslaught were not enough, drama is simultaneously subjected to a moral attack, similar to Mill's argument that

> different persons . . . require different conditions for their spiritual development; and can no more exist healthily in the same moral, than all the variety of plants can in the same physical, atmosphere and climate.
> *Essay on Liberty* in *Works*, ed. J. M. Robson xviii (Toronto, 1977)
> 270

Mill's conception of 'Liberty', which Browning shared, included giving each individual moral authority over himself by reducing society to the role of liberty's mere custodian. Browning's plays press a parallel polemic by depicting situations in which one character undermines another's liberty through an insistence that the 'conditions . . . for spiritual development' are the same for both. I have illustrated the use of this theme in *Pippa Passes* (Chapter one), but it is just as strongly present in the other plays: Tresham wants to impose his lugubrious, cobwebbed morality on a sister emancipated from it by sexual passion; Constance, arch-manipulator in Browning's comic masterpiece *In a Balcony*, ruthlessly exploits Norbert's love for her as a means of enslaving him:

> then, you take my way? . . .
> Work out my thought, give it effect for me[? . . .]
> Help me to pay her! Stand upon your rights?
> You, with my rose, my hands, my heart on you?
> Your rights are mine – you have no rights but mine.
>
> 330, 332, 336–8

– Relationship itself becomes an instrument of enslavement once a common world of action is posited as its medium. Significantly, Browning develops this argument, in *In a Balcony*, by writing a satire on drama itself. The play involves a complex intrigue: Constance loves Norbert, but in order to gain permission from the Queen to marry him, forces him into an equivocal statement which the Queen interprets as indicating that he loves *her*. Constance's manoeuvres are accompanied and paralled by a constant use of dramaturgical language: she is in effect trying to take over the composition of Browning's play, and continually writes, revises and updates parts for herself and others within it. Hence when, at the end, the Queen finds Constance and Norbert kissing, Constance instantly improvises a scenario to whitewash the transgression. 'Hist, madam! So I have performed my part', she begins, and theatrical metaphors proliferate as she outlines Norbert's 'part' as that of the Queen's true lover who, having used Constance as confidante in his long struggle to win the Queen, is too decent to dismiss her without 'the first – which is the last – rewarding kiss'. And so –

> So, now his part being properly performed,
> Madam, I turn to you and finish mine . . .
> Enough, my part is played. . . . For him –
> For him, – he knows his part!

> 758–61

Unfortunately, Norbert leaps to the conclusion that the Queen and Constance are in league to test his love *for Constance*, and therefore adopts a completely different 'part':

> So – back again into my part's set words –
> Devotion to the uttermost is yours,
> But no, you cannot, madam, even you,
> Create in me the love our Constance does[.]

> 830–3

In other words, his 'part' consists of his own sincere self uttering the truth which Constance's masquerades have strangled. Browning emphasises the point by having Norbert instinctively reject the 'play' and resist the plotting that besets it. Instead, Norbert proposes infinity as the 'place' where the lovers ought to meet. And eventually, when all the plotting has finally thwarted itself, infinity is the only place left:

Constance: It is one blaze
About me and within me.
Norbert: Oh, some death
Will run its sudden finger round this spark
And sever us from the rest!

                                                      915–18

Climaxing the play as it does, such a moment negates both the action by
which the drama unfolds, and the time – Constance's 'Not now!' – within
which that action endures.

   In all the plays Browning makes an attempt, parallel to the handling of
epic narrative in *Sordello*, to collapse dramatic time into *coups de théâtre*,
epiphanic moments – the moment at which, in each scene of *Pippa Passes*,
the protagonists' tangled destinies are unravelled by her song; the
moment at which, in *Luria*, Braccio announces Florence's vindication of
Luria to a Luria who is dead because Florence doubted him. It is
suggestive, in this context, that so many of the plays are compressed into a
single day. Yet even that is not enough, each individual scene is then
severed from the rest and encircled in its own peculiar intensities,
characters' speeches turn away from each other inwards towards the
'truth' which 'abides in fulness' inside every soul. By the time he wrote
Luria in 1846 Browning had confessedly abandoned the attempt to
construct a common world:

> It is all in long speeches – the *action, proper*, is in them – they are no
> descriptions, or amplifications – but here . . . in a drama of this kind, all
> the *events*, (and interest), take place in the *minds* of the actors . . .
> somewhat like Paracelsus in that respect[.]
>
>   to E.B.B. 11 Jan. 1846: *LK* 381

The next step would be to detach these 'long speeches' from the
problematic context of 'humanity in action' and unequivocally locate the
events 'in the *mind* of the actor' at the centre of 'his own world'. The
dramatic monologue, which was the form that, following the experiment
with drama, Browning began to exploit as his central genre, resembles
drama in allowing the poet to abdicate in favour of others, 'being, though
often Lyric in expression, always Dramatic in principle, and so many
utterances of so many imaginary persons, not mine'. Yet simultaneously,
the poet resumes power by claiming the kind of implicit superiority
which in *Paracelsus* Aprile had ascribed to the dramatist:

> common life, its wants
> And ways, would I set forth in beauteous hues:
> The lowest hind should not possess a hope,
> A fear, but I'd be by him, saying better
> Than he his own heart's language. I would live
> For ever in the thoughts I thus explored,
> As a discoverer's memory is attached
> To all he finds; they should be mind henceforth,
> Imbued with me, though free to all before[.]

> ii 556–64

The humanistic urge to abdicate in favour of 'the lowest hind' is countered by the wish to say *'better /* Than he his own heart's language', making his thoughts *'mine* henceforth, / Imbued with me'. The act which forfeits the poet's power is said to resume it, a paradox also argued by the double reading of 'I would live / For ever in the thoughts I thus explored', as either the poet's eternal subservience to his creatures (abdication) or his personal immortality (resumption). My concern in the remainder of this chapter is with the structures Browning built round the basic concept of the dramatic monologue in the effort to make it responsive to his creative metaphysics.

III

> . . . making speak, myself kept out of view,
> The very man, as he was wont to do,
> And leaving you to say the rest for him.

> *Sordello* i 15–17

The problem with epic and drama, for Browning, was twofold. First, the position of the poet was unsatisfactory to the extent that in both genres he proved, directly or implicitly, to be in absolute control, compromising the 'independence' of his creatures; secondly, the reader too was deprived of freedom by the lack of any space for his independent work. The dramatic monologue, as Browning defines it in the passage quoted above, solves both those problems. The speaker is put in command of the space of the text by being permitted to speak without interruption either from the poet or from other *dramatis personae*; the reader remains in control of

interpretation by being invited to 'say the rest for him'. But that very
interpretative margin creates a potential point of re-entry for the poet,
inasmuch as the reader will inevitably seek to reconstruct that poet's
supervisory perspective, and match his own contribution to it.
Abdicating power jointly to the character and the reader, Browning
simultaneously resumes it through the reader's appeal to him for
corroboration of his (the reader's) interpretation. It is hardly surprising
that dramatic monologue should be so inseparably associated with
Browning: the centrality given to the form by its consonance with his
aesthetics made it dominate his work as it has in no other author's case.

Robert Langbaum's famous analysis of the dramatic monologue in *The
Poetry of Experience* arrives at a similar conclusion. He dismisses on the
one hand such blandly pan-historical definitions as that of B. W. Fuson,
who in *Browning and his Predecessors in the Dramatic Monolog* seems
prepared to call *any* poem with a dramatised speaker a dramatic
monologue, and on the other hand strictly generic descriptions which
reduce the form to an array of structural features.[3] In place of this,
Langbaum, taking his cue from Macallum's claim that 'the object [of the
dramatic monologue] is to give facts from within',[4] arrives at a position in
which dramatic monologue springs out of a tension between 'sympathy'
and 'judgment'.

Langbaum argues that as it develops in the work of Browning and
Tennyson, dramatic monologue is essentially a Romantic genre, arising
from a combination of the Romantic interest in consciousness, and the
Romantic ethic of *Einfuhlung* (sympathy or empathy). He is right. But in
seeking to derive the form *exclusively* from Romantic sources,
Langbaum, I believe, upsets the very balance he sets up, the balance
between 'sympathy' and 'judgment'. Judgment, for him, is only
important 'as the thing to be suspended', as a preliminary framework
which melts away in the heat of the persona's utterance of what in a later
chapter Langbaum calls 'his song, his life's meaning'.[5] Given his earlier
argument that Romantic writers invariably suspend or modify traditional
moral standpoints in order to gain an 'extraordinary perspective', such a
conclusion is hardly surprising; but Browning's own account of the form,
in so far as we can reconstruct it, suggests that judgment plays a role at last
equal to that of sympathy. That role is defined for him by the ironic
techniques of Augustan satire, with which he combines, in the dramatic
monologue, the Romantic impulse towards sympathy.

Browning's acquaintance with Augustan satire dates from early youth.
'My father', he wrote inside his copy of Dryden's translation of Juvenal's
satires, 'read the whole of the Dedicatory Preface aloud to me as we took a

walk together up Nunhead Hill, Surrey, when I was a boy'. This preface contains Dryden's major statement of the principles governing his satiric practice:

> How easy it is to call rogue and villain, and that wittily! But how hard to make a man appear a fool, a blockhead, or a knave, without using any of those opprobrious terms! To spare the grossness of the names, and to do the thing yet more severely, is to draw a full face, and to make the nose and cheeks stand out, and yet not to employ any depth of shadowing.
>
> > 'A Discourse Concerning Satire', *Of Dramatic Poetry and other Essays*, ed. G. Watson (1962) ii 136–7

One of Browning's most extended critical comments on *his* art, already quoted on pp. 55–6, contains clear echoes of this passage. Dryden believes that the best satire will 'spare the grossness of the *names*, and . . . do the *thing* yet more severely', Browning that art itself 'may tell a truth / Obliquely, do the *thing* shall breed the thought, / Nor wrong the thought, missing the mediate *word*' (m.i.). For both, the 'thing' is a meaning implicit in the art but absent from its verbal surface. Browning adds that, as a result, the receiver of art in effect *creates* it – paints the picture, makes the music, writes the book – by inverting the writer's manifest 'falsehood' – a process best described in the words in which the Strattis, in *Aristophanes' Apology*, celebrates 'the Comic Muse':

> Hail who accepted no deformity
> In man as normal and remediless,
> But rather pushed it to such gross extreme
> That, outraged, we protest by eye's recoil
> The opposite proves somewhere rule and law!

> 1375–9

This 'opposite' is 'the fine form, the clear intelligence' which the reader infers in the process of 'recoil' from the portrait of 'body uncouth, halt and maimed . . . soul grotesque, corrupt or blank'. Essentially, the method is satiric.

A comment by Browning on his presentation of the lawyers in *The Ring and the Book* illustrates the way in which the implied author hints at his presence:

I hate the lawyers: and confess to tasting something of the satisfaction, as I emphasise their buffoonery, which was visible (they told me at Balliol, the other day) on the sour face of one Dr Jenkins, whileome Master of the College, when, having to read prayers, he would of a sudden turn and apostrophize the obnoxious Fellows, all out of the discreet words of the Psalmist, "As for liars, I hate and abhor them!" – then go on quietly with his crooning.

1 Feb. 1869: *LJW* 177

To translate into the terms of the dramatic monologue: the persona's words remain, as they must, apparently his own and free of registered intrusion from outside; but the delivery of those words by the poem establishes an emphasis which may reverse or deflect his intention. That emphasis obliges the reader to become aware that the poet's viewpoint differs from his character's. Such implicit presence provides another sense in which dramatic monologue was suitable to Browning's aesthetics. By allowing the persona to speak, the poet abdicates a power which his reappearance as implied author allows him to resume; the fact that that implied author is contructed by the reader, allows the poet again to abdicate while the reader determines the poetic meaning.

It does not follow, however, that the inferred meaning will take the satirical form of an adverse judgment. A reversed judgment, by which the reader determines on sympathy, is equally possible, and Browning characteristically inserts clues which point in both directions. Thus in describing the effect upon her of Browning first blank-verse dramatic monologue, *The Bishop Orders his Tomb*, E.B.B. in one place singled out the most overtly satirical passage of the poem for approving comment, only to conclude that 'You force your reader to sympathize positively in his glory in being buried!',[6] which indicates her recognition that the portrait is more than a simple satire on Catholic materialism. Browning's own comments on *Prince Hohenstiel-Schwangau, Saviour of Society* (1871) illustrate the co-presence of the two poles in his own conception of the form:

I don't think, when you have read more, you will find I have 'taken the man for any Hero' – I rather made him confess he was the opposite, though I put forward what excuses I thought he was likely to make for himself, if inclined to try. I never at any time thought much better of him than now; and I don't think so much worse of the character as shown us in the last few years, because I suppose there to be a physical and intellectual decline of faculty, brought about by the man's own faults, no doubt – but I think he struggles against these; and when that is the case, depend upon it, in soliloquy, a man makes the most of his good intentions and sees great excuse in them – far beyond what our optics discover!

to Edith Story 1 Jan. 1872: LH 152

Accused of having 'taken the man for any Hero', that is, of having lavished an uncritical sympathy on him, Browning momentarily affirms that he has done 'the opposite', that is, satirised him, only to qualify that remark in turn. What follows is a delicate balance of sympathy and judgment whose reflection in the poem itself is implied by the fact that while one reviewer called it a 'eulogism on the Second Empire' another found it 'a scandalous attack on the old constant friend of England'.[7] Such double readings were exceedingly common – the endless controversy as to whether the Duke in *My Last Duchess* is to be considered 'shrewd' or 'witless' is a case in point[8] – and in them we surely find evidence that the dynamic of the dramatic monologue form, as Browning practised it, was *indeterminacy of interpretation*. His poems are full of interpretational clues, but these point in different directions, and the net result is that while we remain aware that the persona's viewpoint is not the same as the poet's, we can never be certain whether sympathy or judgment predominates in the latter's standpoint.

It would clearly be possible to argue that the reader need not interrogate the text for evidence of the author's conception of it, and it was in order to prevent, or at least control this possibility, I believe, that Browning developed the feature which represents his most decisive innovation in dramatic monologue form, the use of an interacting interlocutor or *second-consciousness*. This feature seems to me, indeed, so crucial to the form that only poems which include a second-consciousness, I would argue, ought to be called dramatic monologues. Those which lack this feature are dramatic *lyrics*.

Browning himself never made this distinction, and Langbaum considers it unnecessary:

We are told, for instance, that the dramatic monologue must have not only a speaker other than the poet but also a listener, an occasion, and some interplay between speaker and listener. But . . . a classification of this sort does not even cover all the dramatic monologues of Browning and Tennyson.

The Poetry of Experience (repr. 1972) 76

Langbaum is undoubtedly right to attack naive genre formalism. But his last sentence comes dangerously close to circularity, and I would claim that a call *Childe Roland to the Dark Tower Came*, one of the exceptions he cites, a dramatic lyric is to mark an important difference between it and, say, *The Bishops Orders his Tomb*. Essentially, the presence of an interlocutor prompts a 'realist' reading of the monologue as genuine speech, which in turn promotes or even determines that alienation of reader from persona which preserves our consciousness of an implied author. Dramatic lyrics are altogether less certain to involve either 'natural' speech or alienation. Since Langbaum's argument is precisely that readers never really are alienated from monologue personae, it is not surprising that he should avoid or minimise this distinction.

Dramatic lyrics use a dramatised speaker, but because he addresses the reader directly, it is impossible to regard his utterance as a natural speech-event; he speaks a *poem*, and Browning's invariable use of lyric metres and rhyme-schemes for monologues of this kind reinforces the point. Such poems, however 'dramatic in principle' (to use Browning's own phrase) are simultaneously 'lyric in expression'; their persuasion is directed at the reader, and though the reader can refuse to be persuaded, he cannot be certain that this is the appropriate response. Dramatic monologues, conversely, because addressed to an interlocutor are immediately understood as 'real speech' occupying a dramatic situation which is as it were overheard by a reader detached from the speaker's rhetorical purpose.

There is of course one 'naturalised' form of self-address, the soliloquy, and Browning used the word for at least one of his dramatic monologues, *Prince Hohenstiel-Schwangau, Saviour of Society* (letter quoted pp. 70–1 above). But that poem is a special case, in that it is discovered to be soliloquy only when, towards the poem's close, it turns out that the Prince, for rhetorical purposes, has *invented* the interlocutor who up to that point had appeared to be listening to and questioning him. Few of the poems I call dramatic lyrics turn out to be soliloquies in even this Pickwickian sense. In a play the soliloquiser has to be given a fragment of the dramatised space-time in which to speak, which in turn means that he must be plausibly uncoupled from the dramatic action for the duration of his solo. But Browning's dramatic lyricists frequently 'speak' during moments of action, describing events in which they simultaneously participate. The most extreme case is *The Patriot*, whose speaker describes his journey to the scaffold; Childe Roland, who narrates, in the past tense, the experiences leading up to what most readers take to be *his* death, provides an extension of this motif. A less extreme case, *The Last*

Ride Together, illustrates the non-naturalistic convention of utterance adopted in dramatic lyric by foregrounding the possibility of a natural speech, but refusing to supply it. The speaker narrates how he embarks on a ride with his mistress, and the poem delivers his reflections during that ride; they are not, however, spoken to her, the opportunity for natural speech is refused, and the resulting utterance has either to be construed as transcribed soliloquy or as retrospective lyric. The existence of a parody of the poem spoken by the mistress indicates, though playfully, a possible dissatisfaction with this convention.[9]

A good illustration of the difference made by a dramatised interlocutor is what I regard as one of Browning's earliest dramatic monologues, the cameo in *Sordello* dramatising how the critic Naddo admonished Sordello's over-intellectual approach to poetry:

> Would you have your songs endure?
> Build on the human heart! – why, to be sure
> Yours is one sort of heart – but I mean theirs,
> Ours, everyone's, the healthy heart one cares
> To build on! Central peace, mother of strength,
> That's father of . . . nay, go yourself that length,
> Ask those calm-hearted doers what they do
> When they have got their calm! And is it true
> Fire rankles at the heart of every globe?
> Perhaps. But these are matters one may probe
> Too deeply for poetic purposes:
> Rather select a theory that . . . yes,
> Laugh! what does that prove? – stations you midway
> And saves some little o'er-refining. Nay,
> That's rank injustice done me! I restrict
> The poet? Don't I hold the poet picked
> Out of a host of warriors, statesmen . . . did
> I tell you? Very like!

ii 797–814

There is no chance of our taking the speaker of these words for the poet, and this is because the dramatic occasion of his utterance is so precisely specified, not by allusions to fictional circumstances (a device which Browning did use on occasion) but by his constant interaction with an auditor who, though inaudible to us, is understood to react to, comment on, even laugh at what Naddo says to him. His interruptions form a series of comic deflections which convince us that Naddo's discourse is improvised rather than composed and therefore occupies a real occasion; Naddo's self-induced hesitations, as when he fails to perorate his invocation of 'Central peace', have a similar effect. But Naddo is interrupted, and hesitates, because the second consciousness, unlike the interlocutor of such prototypes as the Horation Ode or the Romantic 'conversation poem', *opposes* the persona. Sordello is Naddo's opposite. Naddo believes that poetic theory comes a long way second to the prime duty of gratifying the contemporary public by sticking to a worn *via media* of poetic subject-matter and expression. Sordello spends most of his time speculating on whether he should write at all – a scruple incomprehensible to Naddo, as we see when he toys cautiously with Sordello's comment that 'fire rankles at the heart of every globe' only to drop it with a pert 'perhaps'. The comedy of this warns us that Naddo is hardly a reliable aesthetician; yet its effect of embedding within the statement of his case trace-elements of the opposite case is a serious gain, both in inclusiveness for the speaking voice and in formal balance. The second-consciousness here helps to focus doubts felt by the reader concerning the words which appear on the page, and its fragments of reported speech become the framework out of which the reader constructs the implied author. Naddo's speech forms the 'thing' that 'breeds the thought', 'the successive and the many' by which the 'simultaneous and sole' is represented.

The fact that, as its name implies, the dramatic monologue remains a monologue – that the second-consciousness never speaks – complicates matters, however. At one level, this extraordinary device represents a refusal directly to compromise the power and autonomy of the persona; simultaneously, it points, in the most radical fashion possible, to meaning as being or including *absence* or *silence*. To complete the construal of a dramatic monologue's meaning, we require access to the response of the person to whom it is addressed, and for whom its rhetorical manoeuvres are intended. In witholding that response Browning forces the reader himself to provide it, and thus compels him to hypostasise a meaning beyond the periphery of the persona's intention.

It does not follow, however, that the second-consciousness represents the implied author, or that the outcome of its presence is necessarily satiric. In *Bishop Blougram's Apology* we have a second-consciousness who indeed claims to sit in judgment upon the persona; but by the end of the poem we are well aware of the spuriousness of that claim. Indeed, in a gesture that becomes increasingly pervasive in Browning's dramatic monologues, Blougram attacks the very idea of judgment implied by

Gigadibs', and by extension our, silent presence. 'Even your prime men who appraise their kind', he argues, 'confuse themselves' before the perplexing multiplicities of human action; and because 'our interest's on the dangerous edge of things' we are moreover instinctively attracted to cases which cross and confuse moral boundaries: 'The honest thief, the tender murderer,/The superstitious atheist' and so on. As 'an unbelieving priest', Blougram himself belongs to such a category, and it enables him to 'keep the line/Before your sages', to erase or complicate the process of judgment. And in many other poems, the position of the second-consciousness as representative of a superior judgment is likewise questioned or annulled.[10] Resistance to judgment – resistance to the very ironic possibilities of the form in which they are portrayed – proves to be a constant possibility for Browning's dramatic monologuists; but it is a possibility always advanced in counterpoint to its opposite.

It seems to me that the persona-second-consciousness relation is crucial in guaranteeing the radical instability of dramatic monologue form, its cycles of sympathy and judgment, of authorial abdication, reader-dependence and authorial resumption of power. Thus when, as I shall argue in a later book, Browning became worried about the satiric element of his form, it was by revising the relation between speaker and interlocutor that he sought to rectify the situation.

4

The Structured Collection

I

Robert Browning is a name which will serve the future historian of the English literature of the nineteenth century to point the moral of genius unfaithful to its trust.

> G. Brimley in *Fraser's Magazine* liii (Jan. 1856) 105–16 (hereafter *Brimley*): 105; *CH* 165

[*Men and Women*] is by many degrees more eccentric, affected, resolutely strange, and in parts deliberately unintelligible, than its predecessors[.]

> *Christian Remembrancer* xcii (1856) 281–94; 281

All these faults seem to us attributable to either the low vanity of attaining the praise of originality by the cheap method of being different from other people, or the inexcusable laziness of not choosing to take the trouble to correct his first rough thoghts.

> *Spectator* 1434 (22 Dec. 1855) 1346

Men and Women, published in 1855, represents Browning's public commitment to the dramatic monologue form. In *Christmas-Eve and Easter Day* (1850), he had endeavoured to move in the opposite direction, writing a poem of direct vision and personal statement, and as far as popular success was concerned, had failed completely. It is evident that the example of his wife's work, with its spontaneous subjectivity and widespread popular appeal, had moved him to emulation: this is suggested very strongly by passages in their letters. But the experiment proved, at least as far as he was concerned, abortive or premature; neither reviews nor sales were anything to boast of, and Browning himself, dismissing the work as 'that poor "Christmas Eve" that hasn't paid printing yet,'[1] turned back to dramatic lyric and dramatic monologue in putting together a collection designed, as he told his friend Joseph Milsand, as 'a first step towards popularity'. This statement indicates that he believed that dramatic monologues were what the age demanded, at least from him, and that obtaining contemporary success remained a prime motive in his poetic career.

But the event hardly matched his expectations. As 'a first step towards popularity' *Men and Women* was an almost total failure. The murmur of complaint which had greeted *Christmas Eve and Easter-Day* became, as the quotations at the head of this section indicate, a chorus of abuse. Though not all critics were so severe, Browning's reaction reveals that he at least considered that he had suffered yet another *débâcle*:

> I have read heaps of critiques at Galignani's, mostly stupid and spiteful, self-contradicting and contradictory of each other. What effect such "rot" . . . [has] with the reading public, you must tell me if I am ever to know.
>
> to Edward Chapman, 17 Jan. 1856: *NL* 87

Such violence of language is something new in his reaction to criticism, and marks the inception of a hostility which was never to be completely appeased. He was clearly concerned that such a reception might endanger the book's chance of popularity, believing as he did that critics constituted 'a very few, who react upon the rest'. His fears were justified. *Men and Women* sold no better than 'that poor Christmas Eve'.

It is not hard to understand Browning's concern. He was in his forties. In *Christmas Eve and Easter-day* and *Men and Women* he had tried the experiment, outlined in the *Essay on Shelley*, of producing 'successive perfect works' in the subjective and objective modes: both had failed. His strategy seemed exhausted, leaving him at a creative impasse.

For five years at least, he remained in that impasse. There is no evidence that he wrote any significant poetry between 1855 and 1860.[2] He experimented instead with drawing and sculpture, arousing apprehensions that he might actually abandon poetry altogether. Some such fear is audible behind the relief with which his wife greeted his renewed creativity when, in 1861, she told her sister-in-law that after a long period of working 'by fits and starts' and 'getting out of spirits' he had at last produced 'material for a volume'.[3] That the cause of his moodiness had been 'his treatment in England' – treatment which she denounces as 'an infamy of that public' – E.B.B. openly admits. The contrast between his position and hers, after the hyperbolic acclaim which greeted her *Aurora Leigh* in 1856, had been noted by them both, and probably contributed an edge of guilt to her natural concern at his depression.

It is rare, however, for such moratoria to be nothing but the blank interludes they seem, and in this chapter I shall suggest that Browning spent as much of those nine years in creative rethinking of his poetic strategy as in what E.B.B. called 'chewing bitter cud'. The two major works which he produced in the 1860s, *Dramatis Personae* (1864) and *The Ring and the Book* (1869), can both be seen in relation to the reception of *Men and Women* – specifically, as attempts to meet some of his critics' objections by evolving a new structural principle. Significantly, it was in a revision of the offending *Men and Women*, made for the *Collected Poems* of 1863, that this principle was first put into practice.

II

In order to understand Browning's development in the 1860s it is first necessary to examine the complaints of 1855. Browning himself read all the reviews within his reach, and filled his letters with aggrieved references to them, so clearly the possibility, at least, of his having responded to them is there.

He heard, as he himself noted, a great variety of complaints, 'many self-contradicting and contradictory of each other'. But two in particular stand out:

> the work does not, indeed, exhibit Mr Browning's powers at the same continuous stretch of exercise as such previous works as *Paracelsus*, *Sordello*, or *Christmas Eve and Easter-Day*.
>
> *British Quarterly Review* xxiii (Jan. 1856) 151–80; 158

> The love-poems, as might be expected, are the most difficult to understand; they are also the worst.
>
> *Guardian* xi (Jan. 1856) 34–5: 35[4]

These two quotations are at once characteristic of the 1855 reviews of *Men and Women* and more generally symptomatic of problems central to Victorian aesthetics. They point on the one hand to a demand for long or epic poems, and on the other hand to a defition of poetry which is essentially small-scale and lyric. On both criteria Browning is found guilty of dereliction of 'duty' (the word appears in more than one review); that they flatly contradict each other goes generally unnoticed.

In the literary criticism he wrote in the 1830s,[5] John Stuart Mill anticipated the privileging of lyric in mid-Victorian aesthetic theory, and his essays provide us with the most coherent and consistent justification for that bias. The axiom from which it derives is that poetry is concerned with *feeling*, 'the delineation of the deeper and more secret workings of the human heart' (105). In this, Mill echoes Wordsworth's definition of poetry as 'the spontaneous overflow of powerful feelings', but he casts aside Wordsworth's careful qualifications, in particular his claim that the poet must, to write with 'a worthy purpose', have 'thought long and deeply'. At best, Mill is prepared to concede, as he does in *The Two Kinds of Poetry* (117–30), that there may be people called 'poets of culture', who write a didactic poetry derived from reflection or ratiocination; but these remain generically inferior to the 'poets of nature', in whom

> Thoughts and images will be linked together, according to the similarity of the feelings which cling to them. A thought will introduce a thought by first introducing the feeling which is allied to it. At the centre of each group of thoughts or images will be found a feeling; and the thoughts or images are there only because the feeling was there. All the combinations which the mind puts together, all the pictures which it paints, all the wholes which Imagination constructs out of the materials supplied by Fancy, will be indebted to some dominant *feeling*, not as in other natures, to a dominant *thought*, for their unity and consistency of character.
>
> 120–1

E. S. Dallas's 1852 definition of poetry as 'poetic feeling' (*Poetics* 83) is characteristic of his period's general decision to make feeling the criterial property of poetry. It was a decision that could do no service to Browning. *His* forte, as his critics noted, 'really lies rather in exhibiting the intellectual and moral characteristics of a man or an age, than in giving expression to the affections and the passions' (*Brimley* 114). Brimley goes on to suggest that he would consequently make 'a fine biographer or essayist' but his very phrasing implies a categorical distinction between such talents and those proper to the poet. As a less hostile critic put it in 1864, 'The mind with which language is a "pure work of thought", as our author confesses it to be in his own case, can scarcely find its full play in the lyric form' (M. D. Conway, *Victoria Magazine* ii [1864] 298–316, 312). Conway's phrasing draws attention to the fact, already noted by James Martineau in 1859, that the definition of poetry shared between Mill and mid-Victorian reviewers in effect restricts it to the lyric kind:

> Mr Mill's poet must be all loneliness and intensity, – a kind of special firework going off itself in infinite night. So isolating a definition would in no case apply to other than lyric poetry; and our author has

the courageous consistency to adopt the limitation, and to consider the
drama and the epic redeemed from prose only by the intermixture of
lyrical elements.

'John Stuart Mill', *National Review* ix (1859) 495

Mill himself had conceded that 'if the view we are now taking of poetry be
correct', 'lyric poetry . . . is . . . more eminently and peculiarly poetry
than any other' (123); actually, as Martineau points out, his position is
more extreme than that phrasing implies.

This is partly because while restricting poetry to the lyric, Mill
simultaneously redefined the lyric to fit his theoretical priority of feeling.
Traditionally, the lyric was regarded as a poem sung to accompaniment,
and Conway's suggestion that a lyric poem ought to 'chant itself' (ibid.)
shows the durability of this association. Browning's mid-Victorian critics
regularly castigated his inattention to the musical aspect of poetic writing,
his coarseness of diction and abrupt, unrelaxed style – objections
summarised by William Stigand's assertion that 'Mr Browning has an ear
and a taste incapable of distinguishing sufficiently the delicacies of rhyme
and rhythm to become a lyric poet'.[6]

For Mill, however, there was more to lyric than qualities of sound. In
his essay on Alfred de Vigny (1838) he began to explore the relation
between his own criterion of feeling, and the traditional one of musicality
or euphony, and came up with the following line of argument:

All emotion which has taken possession of the whole being – which
flows unresistedly and therefore equably – instinctively seeks a
language that flows equably like itself[.] . . . Hence, ever since man has
been man, all deep and sustained feeling has tended to express itself in
rhythmical language; and the deeper the feeling, the more
characteristic and decided the rhythm; provided always the feeling be
sustained as well as deep; for a *fit* of passion has no natural connection
with verse or music, a *mood* of passion has the strongest.

236

The innovations here are, first, the discovery of an equation between 'a
mood of passion' and poetic musicality, on the basis that under the
dominion of such a mood the mind naturally expresses itself
rhythmically; and secondly, the restriction of each poem to, in effect, the
expression of a *single* mood.[7] The second point emerges obliquely, from
Mill's objection to 'fits of passion'. A fit of passion is presumably a state of
feeling which has a beginning and an end, and is thus integrated into a

continuum of changing emotional states. A mood, conversely, neither begins nor ends, but subsists in a perpetual *medias res*. Hence Mill's tendency, in his early essays, to ignore the plural in Wordsworth's 'powerful feeling*s*', substituting phrases like 'some dominant feeling', 'state of mind', or, speaking of Wordsworth himself, 'he never seems *possessed* by a feeling; no emotion seems ever so strong as to have entire sway, for the time being, over the current of his thoughts' (122). Such language suggests, first, that Mill invariably thought in terms of *single* emotions, and secondly, that he conceives of such emotions as temporarily abolishing the poet's personality, and converting him into the abstract expression of 'exultation, or grief, or pity, or love, or admiration, or devotion' (122–3). 'It is only when under the overruling influence of some one state of feeling', therefore, that Shelley 'is a great poet'; for

> States of feeling, whether sensuous or spiritual, which thus possess the whole being, are the fountain of that poetry which we have called the poetry of poets; and which is little else than the utterance of the thoughts and images that pass across the mind while some permanent state of feeling is occupying it.
>
> 124

It is because of Wordsworth's resistance to such possession, Mill concludes, that his genius 'is essentially unlyrical' (123). But Mill has refashioned the idea of lyric, converting its conventional generic definition into a psychological one: lyric is the utterance of a poet in the grip of an overmastering mood, not a poem in such and such a metre, or having a recognisable musicality. Or rather, musicality is an involuntary *result* of the poet's psychological state, not of his decision to write in a certain genre.

What Mill says of Wordsworth is said of Browning by one of the acutest mid-Victorian critics, Richard Holt Hutton, who remarked, 'his mind seldom or never seems to fall under the dominion of a single sentiment or passion, without which poetry cannot properly be called lyric', and again, more forcibly, 'Mr Browning has no moods'.[8] Browning agreed with him. In the *Essay on Shelley* (written just before *Men and Women*), he explicitly rejects 'a kind of poetry which shows a thing not as it is to mankind generally, nor as it is to the particular describer, but as it is supposed to be for some unreal neutral mood, midway between both and of value to neither' (*Penguin* i 1005). This description pinpoints what might be called the idealising aspect of the aesthetics of mood: that the poet must cease to be a distinct individual or 'particular describer' and surrender himself to a pseudo-universality which Browning denounces as 'unreal'. Browning thereby exposes and repudiates the mid-Victorian use of Mill's argument as the ground of a demand for ideal or spiritual utterance.

Thus E. S. Dallas who, as we have seen, follows Mill in defining poetry as 'poetic feeling', and likewise accords primacy to lyric among the genres, feels able to assert that 'the divine and all that is not *Me* triumphs in the lyric' (83). And he compounds this somewhat bizarre assertion with its logical corollary, that drama, traditionally the opposite genre to lyric, represents the triumph of 'personality or self-hood'.[9] These statements make sense only if it is assumed that the 'mood' recorded by lyric is essentially extra-personal, which it becomes negatively by the exclusion of idiosyncrasy, and conversely that the display of character and individuality, even when not the author's, represents the intrusion of personality into a poetry which ought to have got rid of such features. Bagehot put it that in lyric the poet 'describes, not himself, but a distillation of himself', that is, 'such of his moods as . . . typify certain moods . . . of all men'.[10]

The reviews of *Men and Women* provide evidence that this curious inversion had widespread currency. The fact that that collection, like Browning's earlier one, is 'dramatic in principle' did not prevent critics from labelling it, or rather its author, as 'selfish' and 'personal': 'The riches and the ability are there, but the employment and the expression of them seem to us, on the whole, more perverse, personal, and incomplete than they were formerly' (*Athenaeum* 1464 [17 Nov. 1855] 1327–8). Again,

> Writer of plays, of philosophical poems, of dramatic lyrics, he has in each class given evidence of strong natural powers weakened by self-indulgence, by caprice, by hankering after originality, by all the mental vices which are but so many names of vanity and self-seeking. Instead of looking on his gifts of imagination and of intellect as entrusted to him for the benefit of others, and of imposing on him the duty of training their rude forces into a perfect faculty of song, he has just got out of them the utmost personal pleasure that they would yield with the least possible trouble.
>
> *Brimley* 105

Of course, one aspect of what these writers label as 'personal' is Browning's idiosyncratic style, his 'mannerism'. But that is part of the equation which identifies the perfect lyric as non-individual and 'therefore' ideal.

Mill was well aware that his theory had formal consequences. In *What is Poetry?* he notes that his neurological definition of the poem as coextensive with a 'mood' or 'state of excitement' logically excludes narrative: indeed,

> So much is the nature of poetry dissimilar to the nature of fictitious narrative, that to have a really strong passion for either of the two, seems to presuppose or to superinduce a comparative indifference to the other.
>
> 104

He adds, 'an epic poem . . . is so far as it is epic (i.e., narrative), . . . is not poetry at all', though it will normally *include* poetry. In this, he is recalling Coleridge's remark that 'a poem of any length neither can be, nor ought to be, all poetry' in the light of Shelley's distinction, in the *Defence of Poetry*, between a 'story' and a 'poem':[11] in *What is Poetry?* Mill however maintains that a long poem, presumably organised on a non-narrative basis, remains possible, and half-blames Shelley himself for not having 'acquired the consecutiveness of thought necessary for a long poem' (123-4). The essay on Vigny, however, abolishes even this vestigial concession to the tradition of poetic genres. Having restricted the poet to the depiction of 'moods of passion', Mill goes on to note the logical corollary that such an account of the poetic process

> naturally demands *short* poems, it being impossible that a feeling so intense as to require a more rhythmical cadence than that of ordinary prose should maintain itself at its highest elevation for long together.
>
> 237

His conclusion that 'a long poem will always be felt to be something unnatural and hollow' is echoed by other critics. Edgar Allan Poe contends that 'the phrase "a long poem" is a flat contradiction in terms', and attacks epic, specifically *Paradise Lost*, for attempting length; Walter Bagehot defines poetry as 'memorable and emphatic, intense, and *soon over*'.[12]

A similar addiction to lyric did not however stop some of Browning's critics from complaining that 'the work does not exhibit Mr Browning's powers at the same continuous stretch of exercise as . . . previous works'. 'There is no getting through the confused crowd of Mr Browning's *Men and Women*',[13] is a typical grumble. Nor was Browning the only sufferer from this complaint. A reviewer of Tennyson's *The Princess* asked 'who has not known Tennysonians, who were living in full and confident expectation of a coming *opus magnum*?'.[14] *Maud*, published in the same year as *Men and Women*, was 'as a whole, incomplete and unsatisfying', 'not to be accepted as 'an equivalent for that great master-work . . . which the world expects from him';[15] Tennyson must 'do the duty which England has long expected of him, and . . . give us a great poem on a great subject'.

One reviewer used the publications of 1855, including *Maud* and *Men and Women*, as the text of a weighty sermon against the general failure by Victorian poets in their 'duty' to write long poems:

> Modern poets . . . are too prone to dissipate their strength in evanescent trifles[.] Poetic genius, according to them, seems to consist in the power of throwing off at random the phantoms which rise up uncalled in the imagination, without regard to their connexion or congruity.
>
> *Guardian* xi (Jan. 1856) 34–5: 34

The last sentence of this comment extends the objection by associating the failure to write substantial works with fragmentariness or arbitrariness of progression at the local level, a point also made by Richard Simpson in his review of 'Festus' Bailey's *The Mystic*:

> When he has found a suitable epithet, or a convenient paraphrase, or a striking characteristic to attach to each name, he thinks he has done all that is required. There is no arrangement, nor can there be; there is no particular reason why any one thing should be named before any other.
>
> *Rambler* n.s. iv (1855) 460–6: 466

It is probable that these objections derive from that put forward by Matthew Arnold in his Preface of 1853, during a comparison between the classics, who 'regarded the whole', and the moderns, who only 'regard the parts': 'We have poems which seem to exist merely for the sake of single lines and passages; not for the sake of producing any total impression' (*Poems*, ed. Allott [1965] 598). If the general aesthetic of the time virtually forbade long poems, why did critics nevertheless demand them? Arnold's campaign against the fragmentariness of modern writing was clearly influential; that in turn, however, owes much to Carlyle's polemics of the 1830s.

Where Mill psychologised the poetic genres, Carlyle socialised them.

His early writings amount to a jeremiad against his own period for being jittery, feeble, hypochondriac;[16] and a potent weapon in his attack is the absence of significant long poems. For epic, in his view, demand an equivalent spiritual magnitude in its historical period, a cardinal sign of which is 'Belief' ('the end of Understanding is not to prove and find reasons, but to know and believe' [*Misc.* iii 5]). Only when an epic, with its accompanying religious mythology, is 'understood to be [a] narrative of *facts*', says Carlyle, is it possible to take it seriously: but

> none but the earliest Epic Poems can claim this distinction of entire credibility, of Reality. . . . [T]he farther we recede from those early days, when Poetry, as true Poetry is always, was still sacred or divine, and inspired (what ours, in great part, only pretends to be), – the more impossible becomes it to produce any, we say not true Poetry, but tolerable semblance of such; the hollower, in particular, grow all manner of Epics; till at length, as in this generation, the very name of Epic sets men a-yawning, the announcement of a new Epic is received as a public calamity.
>
> 'Biography', *Misc.* iii 51

In 1853 E. S. Dallas refined Carlyle's point by arguing that 'to unfold the reality of things' the poet must assign causes to the phenomena he represents, and 'not . . . content with pointing out their second causes, . . . will mount up to the great First Cause'. This is why 'the Deity is systematically introduced into the highest epic'.[17] The problem, as Richard Simpson pointed out in his review of *The Mystic*, is that whereas 'in the infancy of culture the people attribute personal causes to all phenomena', that is, ascribe them to anthropomorphic deities, for nineteenth-century man causation is 'merely mathematical or material'; the modern poet, therefore, rather than giving, as his predecessors could and did, 'a lesson in the causes of things',

> has either to confine himself to descriptions of scenery, to pathetic histories, or the excitement of passion and feeling; or if he strives to sit in the seat of the ancient *vates*, he has to enunciate what neither he nor his hearers believe[.]
>
> op. cit. 461

The sensible modern poet will therefore 'not seeks to teach' because he 'knows better than to ascribe things to such causes as the poet must introduce, if he wishes to be a poet'. Epic, because of its background in a no longer credible animistic theology, is an absurdity in an atheistic or agnostic age.

But this argument was not universally accepted. Elizabeth Barrett Browning protests against it in *Aurora Leigh*:

> The critics say that epics have died out
> With Agamemnon and the goat-nursed gods –
> I'll not believe it. . . . [E]very age,
> Heroic in proportions, double-faced,
> Looks backwards and before, expects a morn
> And claims an epos.
>
> *Aurora Leigh* (1856) 186

Accepting Carlyle's premise but denying his conclusions, E.B.B. contends that an epic remains possible, and indeed necessary, for a *heroic* age. This claim lies behind the constant demand from critics that poets should 'leave the exhausted past, and draw [their] subjects of present import', using materials 'got out of the time in which we live'.[18] Epic treatment of such materials will then constitute the desired 'epos'.

There is however a telltale note of hysteria in these demands for a modern 'epos' which betrays how much those who make such demands covertly recognise the opposite argument that the absence of epic necessarily accuses the age of *not* being heroic. So Arnold for one felt. 'Poets are told', he commented in 1853,

> that [this] is an era of progress, an age commissioned to carry out the great ideas of industrial development and social amelioration. They reply that with all this they can do nothing; that the elements they need for the exercise of their art are great actions[;] that so far as the present age can supply such actions, they will gladly make use of them; but that an age wanting in moral grandeur can with difficulty supply such[.]
>
> *Allott* 605

Underlying the demand for long poems in the mid-Victorian period is the fear that without them the age stands condemned to littleness, coupled with the irrational hope that poets might be *persuaded* to produce something which could only arise spontaneously from a sound and unselfconscious social climate.

Carlyle himself illustrates all the inconsistencies I have identified in this chapter. In the 1830s he apparently lamented the demise of the epic, yet his definition of poetry in *The Hero as Poet* insists upon its 'being *metrical*, having music in it, being a Song' (83), and he was never reconciled to what he regarded as the lack of 'melody' in Browning's work, asking him, during a meeting of 1845, 'Did you never try to write a *Song?*' (*LK* 26). In 1856, however, he too, like the reviewers, begged Browning to work on 'one great subject', explicitly dropping his previous stipulation that this should be treated in prose.[19] Browning had the unenviable task of making sense of instructions which were simultaneously universal and self-contradictory.

<h2 align="center">III</h2>

The problem of extracting long poems from short-poem experiences had also faced Wordsworth, when his insistence that 'all good poetry is the spontaneous overflow of powerful feelings' encountered his resolve 'to compose a philosophical poem, containing views of Man, Nature and Society'. This was *The Recluse*. The pressure to write it came from Coleridge rather than reviewers;[20] but Wordsworth faced essentially the same problem as the Victorian poets, of constructing a continuity of discourse against which his aesthetic was actually in rebellion. This emerges from his description of *The Recluse* as a record of 'the sensations and opinions of a poet living in retirement'.[21] The word 'sensations' takes primacy over 'opinions', which itself hardly suggests the continuity implicit in the idea of 'a philosophical poem', but rather a scrapbook of notions recorded as they rise spontaneously to consciousness, before being marshalled into a logical array. De Quincey acutely noted that because in *The Excursion*, the only part of *The Recluse* actually to be published, 'the narrative is not of a nature to be moulded by any determinate principle of controlling passion', the poem cannot avoid 'a desultory or even incoherent character' in its 'train of philosophic discussions'.[22]

It is hardly surprising, therefore, that the main body of *The Recluse* remained unwritten. In its place Wordsworth put forward, in the Preface to *The Excursion* (1814), two strategies for achieving a similar result by different means:

> Several years ago, when the Author retired to his native mountains, with the hope of being enabled to construct a literary Work that might live, it was a reasonable thing that he should take a review of his own mind, and examine how far Nature and Education had qualified him

for such employment. As subsidiary to this preparation, he undertook
to record, in verse, the origin and progress of his own powers[.]

Hayden ii 36

Here he describes the work which was published after his death as *The
Prelude*. Its autobiographical nature enables Wordsworth to sidestep the
problem of thinking in verse by taking as his subject the development of
his powers of thought from contact with environment and circumstances.
His train of reflections thus remains organic to the experiences which
nurtured it, and can 'spontaneously' arise from them in a continuity
governed by biographical sequence rather than logical necessity. Even
then, however, there remains a certain irreducibility in those experiences,
the 'spots of time' which as they brought it into being, constitute the
poem's *raison d'être*. They remain disturbingly 'untranslated'; the poem
is arranged round them with great skill, yet their intensity in the
pedestrian narrative surroundings produces an effect like that noted by
De Quincey in *The Excursion*, the effect of a long poem 'virtually
dismembered into many small poems'. Wordsworth perhaps implicitly
recognised this fact in publishing several of these episodes as single
poems in 1815. They can stand lone.

The second of Wordsworth's two strategies follows his description of
The Recluse as 'the body of a Gothic church', with *The Prelude* as its 'ante-
chapel'. He adds,

> that his minor Pieces, which have been long before the Public, when
> they shall be properly arranged, will be found by the attentive Reader
> to have such a connexion with the main Work as may give them claim to
> be likened to little cells, oratories, and sepulchral recesses, ordinarily
> included in those edifices.

Hayden ii 36

This 'arrangement' of 'his minor pieces' is what Wordsworth undertook
in the 1815 edition of his poems. In the Preface to that collection, he
enlarges upon the principle behind this proceeding:

> [P]oems, apparently miscellaneous, may with propriety be arranged
> either with reference to the powers of mind *predominant* in the
> production of them; or to the mould in which they are cast; or, lastly, to
> the subjects to which they relate. . . . My guiding wish was, that the
> small pieces of which these volumes consist, thus discriminated, might
> be regarded . . . as composing an entire work within themselves[.]

Hayden ii 909–10

This device can be seen as a tactic for procuring a surrogate long poem. In a period deprived of the example of *The Prelude* (it is arguable that literary history would have been rather different if Wordsworth had published that poem in 1805), such a tactic took primacy in poets' attempts to write long poems, producing the form which I call the 'structured collection'.

The structured collection involves assembling separate poems into a larger design. In some cases the poems would have been originally published separately, in others, composed so as to fit their places in the collection; either way, an absence of formal continuity makes the 'connection' between poems the responsibility of the reader. Three principal varieties of structured collection emerged during the nineteenth century, the *generic*, the *biographical* and the *thematic*. The generic type of structured collection consists of poems of the same form. The biographical type is organised around the experiences of a single protagonist, usually also the speaker, and frequently identified with the voice of the poet himself. The thematic type is based upon a concept, or string of concepts, and might involve a variety of speakers, or no foregrounded speaker at all.

The generic structured collection is the simplest and most precedented form of the genre: Horace's *Odes*, Virgil's *Eclogues* and Spenser's *Complaints* are examples taken at random from earlier literatures. Nineteenth-century examples are comparatively rare, as might be expected in a period dominated by the Romantic antipathy to genre; the title of Landor's *Heroic Idyls* (1863) proclaims his self-consciously atavistic allegiance to older traditions. Other Romantic and Victorian examples usually involve some element of generic innovation, as most famously the Wordsworth-Coleridge *Lyrical Ballads* and Browning's own *Dramatic Romances and Lyrics* and *Dramatic Idyls*. But generic similarity is not enought to turn a collection into 'one whole work' in Wordsworth's sense, and a collection needs to involve one or both of the other two principles to become structured in the sense I intend here.

The centrality of the biographical type of structured collection in nineteenth-century poetry is emphasised by Langbaum: '[T]he narrative or drama of experience can be said to approach in its structure a series of dramatic lyrics connected in biographical sequence' (*Langbaum* 58). Tennyson's *In Memoriam* (1849) and *Maud* (1855), Coventry Patmore's *Angel in the House* (1854–62) and Meredith's *Modern Love* exemplify this type. In these cases, there is an obvious affinity with the sonnet-sequence (a form significantly resuscitated during the nineteenth century, notably by Wordsworth in his *Ecclesiastical Sonnets*, Elizabeth Barrett Browning in *Sonnets from the Portugese*, and Dante Gabriel Rossetti in *The House of*

Life). Some European examples are both earlier in date and larger in scope: Heine's *Buch der Lieder* (1828) and Hugo's *Les Contemplations* (1856) form, in one sense, much looser autobiographical ensembles than Tennyson's, but that very eclecticism brings them closer to Wordsworth's ambition to compose *all* his shorter poems into 'one whole work'.[23] Hugo's description of *Les Contemplations* as 'les mémoires d'une âme' succinctly describes the essential aim of this group of works as a whole.

The thematic type of structured collection is rarer in nineteenth-century English poetry, after its spectacular inception in Blake's *Songs of Innocence and Experience* (I exclude the use of fanciful titles for collections, such as Byron's *Hours of Idleness* or Coleridge's *Sybilline Leaves*). Coleridge claimed that *Lyrical Ballads* was of this type,[24] and it is probable that Wordsworth's interest in thematic ordering began with that collection: its political emphasis heralds and probably influenced that of later examples such as Ebenezer Elliot's *Corn-Law Rhymes* (1831), Elizabeth Barrett Browning's *Poems before Congress* (1860) and Swinburne's *Songs before Sunrise* (1871). However, it is not obvious, in these cases, that the *sequence* of poems has been influenced by their thematic affinity. Two collections in which the thematic principle is carried to a higher level of organisation appeared in the 1850s: Gerald Massey's *Craigcrook Castle* (1856) and Victor Hugo's *La Légende des Siècles* (1859).

'CRAIGCROOK CASTLE', according to a note on the contents page, 'may be read as a continuous Poem, or divided into separate Poems'. Reviewers were struck, or rather bewildered by the novelty of what one called 'this curious alternative', and complained that 'in throwing the design of his work open to the fancy of the reader, Mr Massey confesses his great defect as an artist – the want of constructive power'. Another described the poems as having been 'artificially woven into close contact'.[25] In one sense, this is fair comment. *Craigcrook Castle* opens with a frame resembling the Prologue to the *Canterbury Tales*, in which a group of people plan a Symposium; the six 'chapters' which follow are the stories told by various members of the group. As reviewers remarked, this is a rather lax principle of unification. However, each individual 'chapter' contains, not a connected story, but a series of separate lyrics which do indeed combine into implicit narrative. The influence of Tennyson's *The Princess* and *Maud* is very apparent, and it would be a mistake to underrate Tennyson's contribution to the thematic structured collection, even though neither of those works strictly belongs to that category. Massey himself, in his dedicatory letter, confessed however that

Craigcrook Castle 'falls short of what I had thought to accomplish in my plan': its principal interest is in mentioning a 'plan' at all.

Much more grandiose, both in plan and in confession of failure, was Hugo's *La Légende des Siècles*. The work as a whole, according to Hugo, is no more than the 'commencement': 'Il existe solitairement et forme un tout, il existe solidairement et fait partie d'un ensemble'. It is not, however, 'un fragment'. Il existe en part. . . . L'arbre, commencement de la forêt, est un tout. . . . A lui seul, il ne prouve que l'arbre, mais il annonce la forêt'. And as this inaugural volume, so the individual poems of which it is composed. Hugo's 'ensemble' is 'Exprimer l'humanité dans une espèce d'oeuvre cyclique'; 'les poèmes qui composent ce volume', therefore, 'ne sont donc autre chose que des empreintes successives du profil humain'; and, 'divers par le sujet' are 'inspirés par la même pensée', namely, 'le Progrés'. In sum,

> Comme dans une mosaïque, chaque pierre a sa couleur et sa forme propre; l'ensemble donne une figure. La figure de ce livre, on l'a dit plus haut, c'est l'Homme.
>
> *La Légende des Siècles* (Paris 1962) 60

Like *Les Contemplations* and *Craigcrook Castle*, *La Légende des Siècles* is divided into titled chapters; it professes however a much broader and more intensive principle of unification between its parts, and constitutes the most ambitious structured collection of the 1850s. It is organised as a historical sequence, beginning with the Creation, moving to the Christian and Islamic inceptions, followed by a series on the Renaissance, the seventeenth century, the present, and, in a magniloquent gesture, 'Vingtième Siècle' and 'Hors du Temps'.

It is clear, then, that the structured collection principle was available to Browning from many sources; indeed, it would not be too much to say that the 1850s saw it emerge into something like cultural predominance. *In Memoriam*, a prototype biographical structured collection, seems to usher in a whole series of imitations and parallels. To those which I mentioned (*Maud*, *Craigcrook Castle*, *The Angel in the House*, *Les Contemplations*, *La Légende des Siècles*) should be added Whitman's *Leaves of Grass*, the first edition of which (1855) refused even to give separate titles to its poems, emphasising their unity within the personality of 'Walt Whitman, one of the roughs, a Kosmos'. Heine's *Buch der Lieder* was translated into English by J. E. Wallis in 1856, exciting comparisons with Tennyson,[26] and contributing to the revival of interest in Heine which his death in the same year helped to consolidate. Major articles by

George Eliot, Monckton Milnes and Julian Fane[27] contributed to the growth of 'the mid-Victorian Heine-legend', one of whose results, as Sol Liptzin notes, was that 'Elizabeth Barrett Browning, who had never risked translating from the German, . . . attempted a rendering of six Heine poems in 1860'.[28] Her effort may reflect the influence of Julian Fane's friend Robert Lytton, who was a constant visitor and correspondent of both Brownings during the late 1850s, and whose *The Wanderer* (1859), a substantial and ambitious structured collection of the biographical type, forms a kind of imitative tribute to Heine's *Buch der Lieder*. Lytton said of it to his (and the Brownings') friend John Forster:

> I should wish the book to be regarded less as a collection of detached lyrics than as a single and prolonged love-poem, varied only in form and treatment by the varieties of experience and emotion.
>   3 Apr. 1858: *Letters*, ed. Lady Betty Balfour (1906) i 88

Browning could have read any, and probably read all of these works. Tennyson he read automatically. Patmore presented complimentary copies of *Angel in the House* as its parts came out. Meredith did the same with *Modern Love*. The 1871 edition of *Leaves of Grass*, like the works just mentioned, was in Browning's library, suggesting that he might well have encountered either the 1855 or the 1860 editions. Lytton discussed *The Wanderer* with him. And in *Dis Aliter Visum*, a poem of 1864, a passing reference ('Heine for songs') shows that he was aware of the popularity of Heine, and the foundation of that popularity in the *Book of Songs*.

The most convincing evidence, however, relates to Victor Hugo, who was also, after Wordsworth, probably the most important influence on Browning's development of the structured collection form. In a letter, written early in his career to his friend Amedée de Ripert-Monclar, Browning remarked, 'I admire his Lyrics exceedingly' (5–7 December 1834: *Correspondence* iii 109). He owned a print of Hugo in 1846 (see *LK* 886, 898), and, according to Mrs Orr, 'much wished to know' him, to the extent of obtaining a letter of introduction to him from Lord Houghton in 1866 (*NL* 177). E.B.B. greatly admired Hugo, writing to Mrs Jameson: 'Have you read Victor Hugo's "Contemplations"? We are doing so at last. As for *me*, my eyes and my heart melted over them' (9 Apr. 1857: *Kenyon* ii 260). She drafted an appeal to Napoleon III to rescind Hugo's exile from France at about the same time (see *Kenyon* ii 261–2).

It is quite possible that both Browning and E.B.B. learnt – or relearnt – the structured collection principle from Hugo's *Les Contemplations*. E.B.B.'s *Poems before Congress* was both the first collection she produced after reading *Les Contemplations*, and her first approach to a structured collection (its poems are all about the liberation of Italy). That some internal organisation was involved is suggested by the precision with which Browning asked their publisher Chapman to insert a new poem into the volume 'immediately *after* the "Tale of Villafranca" and before the "August Voice" ' (31 Jan. 1860: *NL* 126–7). And E.B.B.'s *Last Poems*, which Browning published after her death, were 'given as they occur on a list drawn up last June', according to Browning's prefactory note. So E.B.B. may have been the first to respond to Hugo.

It was presumably the Brownings' known interest in Hugo which led their friend Isa Blagden to send them a copy of *La Légende des Siècles* when it came out in 1859. Browning's comment (one of his longest on a comtemporary work) was dominated, after some mainly complimentary remarks about particular poems, by Hugo's preface:

> The most absurd thing, however, is the magniloquent preface – all the vast plan that was in the poet's mind, and all his humility about the little of it he has been able to accomplish, and all his modest confidence in the efficaciousness of that little – and the whole, one big bubble of mere breath which a touch breaks – in turning over the leaves of the book itself: for any of his former collections of miscellaneous poetry would just as exactly answer to this particular plan as the present. But he can't let truth be truth, or a number of remarkable poetical pieces speak for themselves, without assuring you that he meant them to join Man to God, with the like pleasant practicalities.
>
> (30 Nov. 1859: *DI* 48–9

Significantly, Browning's complaint is directed not against Hugo's adoption of a structured collection principle, but against what Browning sees as the needless pretentiousness of Hugo's cosmic design, and an element of generality or cloudiness in a 'plan' which would allow it to accommodate almost any of Hugo's poems. The evidence that Browning was not hostile to the use of a plan as such is to be found in his adoption, in the 1860s, notwithstanding his ridicule of Hugo, of precisely the same principle for the posthumous *Selections* from his wife's poetry:

> It has been attempted to retain and dispose the characteristics of the general poetry according to an order which should allow them the prominency and effect they seem to possess in the larger . . . works of the poet. A musician might say, such and such chords are repeated, others made subordinate by distribution, so that a single movement may initiate the progress of the whole symphony.

– that is, E.B.B's shorter poems (the 'general poetry') have been placed in an order which allows them implicitly to echo the thematic concerns of her 'larger . . . works', making them, in effect, another long poem growing out of the same concerns. A thematic link between two such poems will give their theme predominance over the more isolated topics of others, forming an architecture equivalent to that which in music holds together the various movements of a symphony. Hugo's influence on this statement emerges from a comparison of Browning's final sentence with one from the *Preface* to *La Légende*: 'Ce volume d'ailleurs . . . est à l'ouvrage dont il fait partie, . . . ce que serait à une symphonie l'ouverture' (op. cit.). Browning later repeated the procedure for his own *Selected Poems* in 1872:

> In the present selection from my poetry, there is an attempt to escape from the embarrassment of appearing to pronounce upon what myself may consider the best of it. I adopt another principle; and by simply stringing together certain pieces on the thread of an imaginary personality, I present them in succession, rather as the natural development of a particular experience than because I account them the most noteworthy portion of my work. Such an attempt was made in the volume of selections from the poetry of Elizabeth Barrett Browning: to which – in outward uniformity at least – my own would venture to become a companion.

A comment in a letter to his friend Alfred Domett amplifies this statement:

> I went through the business . . . with reference to the imaginary life of a sort of man, beginning with one set of likings and fancyings, and ending with another[.]
> Domett, *Diary*, ed. E. A. Horsman (Oxford 1953) 51

(There may be an echo, here, of Robert Lytton's description of *The Wanderer* as being spoken by 'an imaginary individual' [*Letters* i 87]).

All this suggests that at some point between 1855 and 1865 Browning became aware of the possibility of rearranging poems into some kind of significant sequence, and at first sight he would appear to have preferred the biographical type. However, these statements are confused, to say the least: note how belatedly the concept of 'an imaginary personality' is ascribed to the E.B.B. *Selections*, for instance. It is necessary to turn to the collections themselves to see how they are structured. I shall discuss here the 1865 *Selections* from E.B.B., since the 1872 set was produced *after* the first period of experiment with the form in the 1860s.

The E.B.B. *Selections* amount to a covert memoir. Browning did his best to prevent any formal biography of his wife from being written;[29] but he was prepared to hint at her characteristic life-experiences and attitudes in arranging her poems. The *Selections* narrate her life as a sequence of aspirations and disappointments arising from a Wordsworthian sense of childhood as enshrining a perfection which adulthood irrecoverably forfeits. The principal elements of her existence, love, poetry and politics are all coloured by a recurring pattern of disillusion, which announces that life after childhood will invariably disappoint a woman's chimerical hopes, and turn out a sad and perplexing business, to which death might well be preferable. The presentation of these materials follows a roughly chronological order. The first three poems deal with childhood as an extraordinary perfection, the 'lost bower' of the second poem whose loss deposits the poet ill and exhausted on her 'couch'. The next 'chapter' deals with love as entailing the pain of self-sacrifice mingled with the consolation of death. The next shows the poet as ravaged and neglected by her contemporary world. Next, Browning juxtaposes two sequences of E.B.B's sonnets; those written before she knew him, in which anguish and desire for death predominate, and the *Sonnets from the Portuguese*, her tribute to his action in redeeming her from despair and marrying her to himself and the world. But in the following sequence, again concerned with love, imperfection and betrayal mingle with affirmation, until the sequence reaches *My Heart and I*, with its refrain, 'Enough! we're tired, my heart and I', as though the sheer variety of worldly and erotic experience had proved intolerably wearisome. There follows, as in life, a vehement engagement with Italian politics, with the poems however carefully ordered to conclude on a preference for simple love in *Mother and Poet* and *Nature's Remorses*; and after that, *A Musical Instrument*, reiterating the poet's sense of suffering a gloomy election. The sequence ends with the last poem she wrote. *The North and the South.*

A useful illustration of the *Selections'* repeating pattern, and of Browning's method of weaving originally disparate poems into it, is the 'section' concerned with the poet's relation to classical myth and art. This begins with two contrasting images of the poet; as the 'early rose' which blossoms before its time, and the libation-bearer who 'pour[s] us wine' (*A Lay of the Early Rose; Wine of Cyprus*). The first is clearly E.B.B. herself, as Romantic poet; the second the classical writers, whom she lists and reveres: 'Can I answer the old thinkers / In the forms they thought of, now?' (35-6). This self-doubt is echoed in the fact that the following three poems are translations from the Greek, and the second of them, *Song of the Rose*, reiterates the two images with which the sequence began: 'Ho! the rose breathes of love! ho, the rose lifts the cup / To the red lips of Cypris invoked for a guest!' (*Song of the Rose* 9–10). The fact that the translation is of a poem ascribed to Sappho suggests that the classical woman poet seems to offer a haven of secure identity for E.B.B. herself, but the sequence concludes on the disillusioned palinode of *The Dead Pan*, in which the death of Pan brings about the dereliction of Olympus and the repudiation of the 'chalice' of classical poetry:

> O ye vain false gods of Hellas,
> Ye are silent evermore!
> And I dash down this old chalice
> Whence libations ran of yore.

> 211–14

The rebellion against Pagan culture, while clearly part of E.B.B.'s individual development, simultaneously reflects a more general intellectual debate, suggesting that a conceptual organisation has superseded the biographical.

IV

From the start, Browning's aesthetics had included a contradiction between the desire to grant his characters the independence demanded by a democratic humanist philosophy, and the need to express some sense of the whole in which they were contained; to hold, and at the same time abjure power over them. As God to his creation, so, argues Aprile, the poet to the 'mimic creation' he governs:

> His sprites created,
> God grants to each a sphere to be its world,
> Appointed with the various objects needed
> To satisfy its own peculiar wants;
> So, I create a world for these my shapes
> Fit to sustain their beauty and their strength!

> *Paracelsus* ii 444–9

The parallel between God and the human artist is, however, incomplete. God, for whom no paradox presents a problem, furnishes a separate 'sphere' for each of his 'sprites': Aprile proposes to place his 'shapes' within a *single* world. But how can this be done without compromising their God-given independence? In Browning's last play, *In a Balcony*, Norbert voices a similar desire to combine individuality and association:

> This eve's the time,
> This eve intense with yon first trembling star
> We seem to pant and reach; scarce aught between
> The earth that rises and the heaven that bends;
> All nature self-abandoned, every tree
> Flung as it will, pursuing its own thoughts
> And fixed so, every flower and every weed,
> No pride, no shame, no victory, no defeat;
> All under God, each measured by itself.

244–52

Norbert establishes a common world by the mere co-presence of various elements within the arrested moment, yet simultaneously emphasizes their separateness, both physically ('*every* tree . . . *every flower* . . . *every* weed') and morally ('no pride, no shame etc'), instigating a rebellion against any kind of supervisory system or order. The paradox climaxes in the final line, where the 'all' of 'All under God' proposes a mutuality which is immediately contradicted by the stubborn individuation of 'each' within a renewed declaration of independence.

As a form, the dramatic monologue satisfied the first demand – for an anarchic independence of characters – at the expense of the need for a unified scheme within which to view them. Browning's doubts about the danger of a disintegrative particularity in his view of things were voiced to E.B.B. in 1845:

> that is a way of mine which you must have observed; that foolish concentrating of thought and feeling, for a moment, on some one little spot of a character or anything else indeed . . . taking away from the importance of the rest of the related objects which, in truth, are not considered at all . . . or they would also rise proportionally when subjected to the same (. . . that is, correspondingly magnified and dilated.) light and concentrated feeling[.]

25 Dec. 1845; *LK* 343

The word 'foolish' implies dissatisfaction, and 'related' links this discontent to his recognition that the phenomena which his art separates are in reality interconnected.

The structured collection represents a way of restoring authorial control without trading away the 'independence' of individuals. The separate monologues remain separate. But their participation in a larger structure guarantees that they will be seen as parts of a whole, not each separately as a whole. Simultaneously, the fact that that larger structure remains implicit ensures both that their freedom is not compromised by the collection's plan, and that the reader in turn remains free to perceive or not to perceive the general order, becoming himself a participant in, indeed a constituter of, the dialectic of structure and randomness. Again, Wordsworth provided a precedent. In the Preface to *The Excursion*, in which he argued that all his works, 'when properly arranged', would be perceived as forming parts of a unified whole, he concluded,

> It is not the Author's intention formally to announce a system: it was more animating to him to proceed in a different course; and if he shall succeed in conveying to the mind clear thoughts, lively images, and strong feelings, the Reader will have no difficulty in extracting the system for himself.
>
> *Hayden* ii 37

In that abstract sense, the structured collection represented the perfect solution to Browning's formal and moral dilemmas. There remained the question, how was it to be structured? on what principle? I have suggested that two options presented themselves in Browning's period, the biographical and the thematic, representing on the one hand, a *chronological*, and on the other hand a *conceptual* method of perceiving or organising the materials of experience. It was the schism between these two methods that Browning inherited from early-Victorian aesthetics and healed in his own version of the structured collection form.

5

The Structure of the Revised *Men and Women*

I

In 1862, in response to what one reviewer was to call 'a sufficient demand on the part of the public', Browning produced a collected edition of his poems to date, the first since 1849. Several important changes of editorial policy become apparent when the two collections are compared. In many ways, *1849* was the more radical: its exclusion of *Sordello* announces Browning's intention of propitiating an unsympathetic public, and the same conciliatory spirit directs his revision of other poems. With *Paracelsus* and *Pippa Passes* in particular, he went to the length of interpolating substantial clarificatory passages. *1863* openly repudiates this willingness to revise. In reissuing *Sordello*, Browning noted that his attempts to revise it in the spirit of 1849 had proved unsuccessful, if not misguided: 'after all, I imagined another thing at first, and therefore leave as I find it'. And other poems too were left as found, even, in many instances, reverting to a pre-*1849* reading.

What is innovatory in the 1863 edition, however, is the way the poems are grouped and arranged. *1849* had simply reprinted the two previous collections of shorter poems, *Dramatic Lyrics* and *Dramatic Romances and Lyrics* under the collective title *Dramatic Romances and Lyrics*. In *1863* these poems were redistributed into collections called *Dramatic Romances* and *Dramatic Lyrics*. The rationale of this distribution is that *Dramatic Lyrics* consists of poems in which the intensity of the speaker's ruling passion is paramount, *Dramatic Romances* of narratives. That this reorganisation constituted a conscious approach to a genre-based principle of arrangement is suggested by Browning's decision to dismantle the 1855 *Men and Women*. In a footnote (to *One Word More*) in the 1863 *Poems* he explains that 'the greater portion' of the original fifty poems of *Men and Women* have been 'more correctly, distributed under the other titles in the volumes'.

The title *Men and Women* remains in the *1863* edition, but it refers to a mere twelve poems instead of fifty, and of these only eight appeared in the 1855 version. These are:

> '*Transcendentalism*'
> *How It Strikes a Contemporary*
> *Karshish*
> *Fra Lippo Lippi*
> *Andrea del Sarto*
> *Bishop Blougram's Apology*
> *Cleon*
> *One Word More*

Interestingly enough, groupings very like this were suggested by two of the critics of 1855. George Brimley 'excepted from the general censure passed up on these volumes . . . *Fra Lippo Lippi, The Epistle of Karshish, How it Strikes a Contemporary, Bishop Blougram's Apology, Andrea del Sarto, Cleon*' (114–15). Richard Simpson selected *Fra Lippo Lippi, How It Strikes a Contemporary, Bishop Blougram, Andrea del Sarto, Cleon* and *One Word More*. But although they offer similar lists, Brimley and Simpson were working from a different rationale. What Brimley has distinguished is a new genre to set alongside the dramatic lyric and the dramatic romance. Brimley gropes around for a title for 'compositions in which the exhibition of character is effected by a single discourse – soliloquy, conversation or epistle'; the name by which we now designate the form, dramatic monologue, was later suggested by William Stigand, in his review of *Dramatis Personae* for the *Edinburgh Review* in 1864. What Richard Simpson discerned, by contrast, was a thematic link:

> [T]he poems that have had the most attraction for us form a series on the different phases of artist-life, and the comparison of it with that of the unartistic portion of mankind. . . . Together these poems may be said to form, not a philosophy of art, but a philosophy of artists.
>
> *The Rambler* n.s. v (1856) 54–71: 59

These were major reviews, and Browning certainly read them. He refers testily in a letter to 'some grimley or whatever the name is' (see *CH* 165), and is reported to have taken a particularly keen interest in Simpson's review, believing it to be the work of Cardinal Wiseman, on whom he had modelled Bishop Blougram (see *LH* 195). The coincidence between their selections from *Men and Women* and his own in 1863 suggests that he may have been influenced by their view of what constituted the core of collection; but if he was acting on their suggestion he was also refining on it, since the rationale of the 1863 *Men and Women* is something rather more complex than either Brimley or Simpson had in mind. This becomes clear when one considers the poems from earlier collections which he added to those retained from *1855*:

Artemis Prologuises
Pictor Ignotus
The Bishop Orders his Tomb at St Praxed's Church
Rudel to the Lady of Tripoli

Immediately, one notes that the last three of these poems are concerned, like Simpson's selection, with art; however, *Artemis Prologuises* is not; nor is *Karshish* from *1855*. *1863* cannot be called, therefore, a straightforward 'philosophy of artists'. Nor, however, is it straightforwardly a generic collection as Brimley advocated, for *Rudel to the Lady of Tripoli* is a lyric poem, 'giving expression to the affections and the passions' and thus violating Brimley's preference for poems 'exhibiting the intellectual and moral characteristics of a man or an age'.

I shall argue in this chapter that the revised *Men and Women* (hereafter *2M&W*) is actually a thematic structured collection, which subsumes Simpson's scheme for it into a broader design.

II

In order to piece together Browning's scheme for *2M&W* it is essential to consider the order in which he placed its poems. This is as follows:

Prologue	1. 'Transcendentalism' – a Poem in Twelve Books	No. 49	*1855*
	2. How It Strikes a Contemporary	no. 22	*1855*
	3. Artemis Prologuises	no. 7	*1849**
	4. Karshish	no. 10	*1855*
	5. Pictor Ignotus	no. 16	*1849**
Main	6. Fra Lippo Lippi	no. 6	*1855*
Part	7. Andrea del Sarto	no. 28	*1855*
	8. The Bishop Orders his Tomb	no. 23	*1849**
	9. Bishop Blougram's Apology	no. 26	*1855*
	10. Cleon	no. 41	*1855*
Epilogue	11. Rudel to the Lady of Tripoli	no. 9	*1849**
	12. One Word More	no. 51	*1855*

In the right-hand column, I have indicated the collections from which the poems, the 'Epilogue' in my scheme. *One Word More* had been quite What emerges is that both sets of poems – from the *Men and Women* of 1855 and from the *Dramatic Romances and Lyrics* of 1849 – have been comprehensively re-ordered, making 2*M&W* an entirely new sequence. In the left-hand column I have indicated what I think was the motive of this revision: to produce 'one whole work' with, as Wordsworth required, 'a beginning, a middle and an end'.

The simplest rationale underlies the juxtaposition of the last two poems, the 'Epilogue' in my scheme. *One Word More* had been quite explicitly the Epilogue of *1855*. In it Browning, for once in his own voice, dedicates his collection of 'fifty men and women' to his wife, speaking of a personal love which is concealed behind the public self of his poetry:

> God be thanked, the meanest of his creatures
> Boasts two soul-sides, one to face the world with,
> One to show a woman when he loves her!

>   184–6

In *Rudel to the Lady of Tripoli* a poet again worships his mistress, this time as a sun which a sunflower pursues in its course across the sky; again, this devotion is at once the secret motive for poetic utterance, and an inner haven from the celebrity attending that utterance:

>   Say, men feed
> On songs I sing, [but] men applaud
> In vain this Rudel, he not looking here
> But to the East – the East!

>   30–1, 34–6

In juxtaposing these two poems, then, Browning was, on one level, simply reinforcing the act of dedication already performed by *One Word More*. There is a difference, however. Rudel worships his lady from afar, with a devotion that is both hopeless and, technically, adulterous. Browning lives with his in domestic bliss. The progression represents at once the shift from courtship to marriage and a historical development from medieval cults of frustrated or illegal love, to the Victorian domestic ideal. As I shall show, this kind of implicit historiography is central to the collection as a whole.

The 'Prologue' group also possesses a reasonably clear rationale. In the light of his decision to group E.B.B.'s shorter poems, for the 1865 *Selections*, 'according to an order which should allow them the prominency and effect they seem to possess in the larger . . . works of the poet', it becomes significant that while he was revising *Men and Women* for 1863, Browning was also working on *Sordello* for the same edition, and, according to one report, on the first book of *The Ring and the Book* as well. Both those poems open with a discussion of aesthetic theory. And this is precisely what we find in *Transcendentalism* and *How It Strikes a Contemporary*; the nature and even the order of their discussion closely parallels that in book i of *The Ring and the Book*.

At the beginning of *The Ring and the Book* Browning claims that its composition involved two separate stages. The first was his exultant recognition of the moral power and beauty of the contents of 'the old yellow book' which he found in Florence, and used initially as an after-dinner tale with which to turn 'gay to grave', adding an 'alloy' of imagination to lend it narrative pungency. But the next stage involved the 'evaporation' of the alloy under the heat of the self-posed question: 'How much of the tale was *true*?' (m.i.). He embarked on a long programme of study to verify and supplement his original documents, correcting his first intuitive, imaginative apprehension of the story by a scrupulous search for its historical reality. In this account of the creative process, then, inspiration gives way to research: another version of the subjective-objective dichotomy that runs through Browning's thought. A similar shift takes place in the 'Prologue' to 2*M&W*. The speaker of *Transcendentalism* defines poetry as simply the act of making the reader share the poet's perceptions, like 'John of Halberstadt' who 'with a "look you!" vents a brace of rhymes, / And in there breaks the sudden rose herself' (39–40); the poet of *How It Strikes*, conversely.

> took such cognisance of men and things,
> If any beat a horse, you felt he saw;
> If any cursed a woman, he took note;
>   . . . then went home,
> And wrote it fully to our Lord the King[.]

30–2, 43–4

Here the positioning of inspiration and research in separate, successive poems points up the incompatibility of the two viewpoints. This problem is also confronted in *The Ring and the Book*. If 'there's nothing . . . good except truth', how, Browning asks, can he justify his use of imagination, 'which proves good yet seems untrue'? The answer offered there is that the poetic process is essentially one of *resurrection*. The poet must by diligent research excavate his materials from reality; then he must provide them with life from his own imagination. As a parallel, Browning instances a 'Mage' who detaches 'half of [his] soul', which

> in its pilgrimage
> O'er old unwandered waste ways of the world,
> May chance upon some fragment of a whole,
> Rag of flesh, scrap of bone in dim disuse,
> Smoking flax that fed fire once: prompt therein
> I enter, spark-like, put old powers to play,
> Push lines out to the limit, lead forth last
> (By a moonrise through a ruin of a crypt)
> What shall be mistily seen, murmuringly heard,
> Mistakenly felt: then write my name with Faust's!

i 750–9

Resurrection is correspondingly the subject of the third poem in 2*M & W*, *Artemis Prologuises*. Aesculepius, ordered by Artemis to piece together the butchered fragments of Hippolytus, has

> soothed
> With lavers the torn brow and murdered cheeks,
> Composed the hair and brought its gloss again,
> And called the red bloom to the pale skin back,
> And laid the strips and jagged ends of flesh
> Even once more, and slacked the sinew's knot
> Of every tortured limb – that now he lies
> As if mere sleep possessed him[.]

105–12

This is strikingly similar to the passage from *The Ring and the Book*, and the word 'composed' quietly allows us to compare Hippolytus' resuscitation, like the Mage's, to an act of literary creation.

In both cases, however, Browning appears to have found the act of resuscitation problematic. He describes the 'Mage' as 'stopping midway short of truth / And resting on a lie'; *Artemis Prologuises* breaks off before the moment of Hippolytus' resurrection. Browning's account of his composition of the poem is revealing:

> I had another slight touch of something unpleasant in the head . . . [and] wrote in bed such a quantity of that "Hippolytus", of which I wrote down the prologue, but forgot the rest, though the resuscitation-scene which was to have followed, would have improved matters[.]
>   to Julia Wedgwood 17 Oct. 1864: *LJW* 102

The resemblance to Coleridge's account of his composition of *Kubla Khan* is unmistakeable, and Browning's inability or unwillingness to complete *his* poem records, I think, a hesitation parallel to Coleridge's. It was not so much that he too felt estranged from his own creativity, but that the image introduced to describe that creativity proved unacceptable on the conscious level. For in *Sordello* he had expressed a deep guilt about 'catching the dead' be reviving old and forgotten stories and men; the truncation of *Artemis Prologuises*, leaving Artemis to 'await, in fitting silence, the event' of the climactic 'resuscitation' of Hippolytus reflects a similar qualm (itself figured in the continuation of the original myth when Zeus kills the resuscitator Aesculapius for his presumption). When, therefore, Browning confronts, in the 'Mage', a further occasion for such guilt, he feels obliged to offer the supplementary instance of Elisha, who like the Mage resurrected a man, but in the name, this time, of God. The central subject of *Karshish*, the next poem in 2*M&W* is Christ's resurrection of Lazarus, which, placed where it is, both provides the resurrection-scene missing from *Artemis Prologuises*, and casts Aesculepius' feat as, like the Mage's, the minor imitation of a divine action.

The parallel with *The Ring and the Book* suggests that *Karshish* does indeed fit Simpson's conception of *Men and Women* as adumbrating a philosophy of artistic creation; confirmation is to be found in the similar sequence in the E.B.B. *Selections* in which a progression from Pagan to Christian conceptions of art takes place. I have already noted how *The Dead Pan* concludes a section exploring the power and potential of classic art; the poem also introduces Christianity as the successfully competing aesthetic doctrine. In her introductory note E.B.B. remarked that the poem was 'partly founded on a well-known tradition mentioned in a treatise of Plutarch (*De Oraculum Defectu*), according to which, at the hour of the Saviour's agony, a cry of "Great Pan is dead!" swept across the waves in the hearing of certain mariners, – and the oracles ceased'. The poem contrasts what is figured as the desuetude and desiccation of the Olympic pantheon with the vitality implicit in Christ's redeeming death and resurrection: 'By the love He stood alone in / His sole Godhead rose complete, / And the false gods fell down moaning'. E.B.B.'s attempt to connect this religious revolution to a change in aesthetics is less than convincing. Christian writers are described as committed to 'the truth', Pagan to 'falsehood': no attempt is made to explain or justify the assertion. Browning's version is a good deal subtler.

III

Both Prologues – to 2M&W and *The Ring and the Book* – argue that art is a dual process, initiated by inspiration but compelled to devote that inspiration to materials supplied by the world. An existential version of the same dialectic dominates the Main Part of 2M&W, in the form of a meditation on the balance of spirit and flesh in man. As the spiritual essence of art should bring 'scraps of flesh' to life, so ideally man's spirit informs and vivifies his body, receiving in return the sense-impressions which give it substance and delight. Browning's earlier preference for the word 'perceptions' over, say, 'conception', to describe the poet's subject-matter confirms the centrality of this interdependence in his thought: the fact that the poems of the Main Part are all spoken by producers or connoisseurs of art and thus form what Simpson rightly called 'a philosophy of artists' completes the equation between the two domains, and the integration of the Prologue with the collection's Main Part.

In its manifestation as an aesthetic theory in 2M&W, Browning's humanism closely resembles the argument put forward in Ruskin's *The Nature of Gothic*. Ruskin divides artists into 'Purists', 'Naturalists' and 'Sensualists'. The Purists are those who, confronted with a world which inevitably 'has good and evil mingled in it', 'perceive, and pursue, the good and leave the evil'. The Sensualists 'perceive and pursue the evil, and leave the good'. The Naturalists are 'those in the centre, the greatest', who 'perceive and pursue the good and evil together, the whole thing as it verily is' (x 221). It is not specifically Ruskin's purpose to trace a historical pattern, yet his examples inevitably suggest one. His Purists are 'the early Italian and Flemish painters'; his Naturalists, 'Michael Angelo, Leonardo, Giotto, Tintoret, and Turner'. His Sensualists include Salvator Rosa, Caravaggio, and the Italian and Flemish masters of the 17th and 18th centuries. Apart from Turner, with his messianic status in Ruskin's thought, these artists historicise Ruskin's dialectic as a progression from Purism (medieval and early Renaissance) through

Naturalism (high Renaissance) to Sensualism (late Renaissance). A similar pattern emerges in the Main Part of 2*M&W*.

The integration of spirit and flesh is projected as an artistic ideal in the first poem of the Main Part, *Pictor Ignotus*:

> – Never did fate forbid me, star by star,
>   To outburst on your night with all my gift
>   Of fires from God: nor would my flesh have shrunk
>   From seconding my soul, with eyes uplift
>   And wide to heaven, or, straight like thunder, sunk
>   To the centre, of an instant; or around
>   Turned calmly and inquisitive, to scan
>   The license and the limit, space and bound,
>   Allowed to truth made visible in man.

4–12

The dual movement upwards to 'heaven' or downwards 'to the centre' establishes a polarity between 'soul' and 'flesh', but Pictor conceives a mid-point at which the artist stands 'calmly' to comprehend the dualities – 'license' and 'limit', 'space' and 'bound' – which combine to make up 'truth made visible in man'. This balance is reflected in the art itself, which, striving to render his own spirit tangible to other men, seeks reciprocally to translate their flesh into spirit by depicting 'human faces' and then abstracting from such faces the ideal towards which each tends: 'Whether Hope rose at once in all the blood. . . . Or Rapture drooped the eyes. . . . Or Confidence lit swift the forehead up' (17, 19, 21). But such abstractions are in turn representations of actual human passions, thus again accomplishing the synthesis that is then completed by approbation from those same faces:

> Oh, thus to live, I and my picture, linked
>   With love about, and praise, till life should end,
> And then not go to heaven, but linger here,
>   Here on my earth, earth's every man my friend[!]

36–9

His programme for art, then, proposes that it should (1) represent Man; (2) represent him individually; and (3) represent him to himself. In this way, the origin of art in a balance of spirit and flesh is reflected in the complex of its subject-matter and reception. The date given as the poem's subtitle, 'Florence 15––', gives this ideal a posited historical realisation, as the inception of the Italian Renaissance, which proves to be the subject-matter also of the following three poems.

But Pictor himself has, in the event, refused to produce art of this kind. Instead of 'human faces' he paints, from within the cloister that fences him from the outside world, always 'The same series, Virgin, Babe and Saint, / With the same cold calm beautiful regard'. The reason he gives for this betrayal – it is no less – of his earlier ambition is that the fulfilment of his humanistic ideal must have embroiled his pictures in the low traffic of the market-place:

> These buy and sell our pictures, take and give,
> Count them for garniture and household-stuff,
> And where they live needs must our pictures live
> And see their faces, listen to their prate,
> Partakers of their daily pettiness[.]

50–4

But such a rejection of the commercialising of art is inconsistent, since the siting of art within the market is no more than the economic corollary of his art's need to represent man to himself. Pictor's rejection of it, therefore, is as illogical as his neurotic loathing of the very 'faces' which his paintings would theoretically celebrate. To immure himself in a cloister and reproduce liturgical formulae is to accept defeat not merely for himself as artist, but for the humanist conception of art, and in principle for art itself, as he admits in his exhortation, 'So, *die* my pictures! surely, gently die!'[m.i.]. This is in one way ironic, since, as the adjectives argue, the 'endless cloisters and eternal aisles' form precisely an *immortal* setting for the art bestowed on them; but shut away from the nurture of 'human faces', that art dies under the weight of its own refusal to be *seen*. His art is that of a Ruskinian 'Purist'; his motives, however, reveal that a belated Purism is no more than the cowardly evasion of the artist's new duty to embrace Naturalism as the necessary goal of art (the 'youth men praise so' whom he envies is clearly Raphael, one of Ruskin's Naturalists).

*   *   *

The relation between *Pictor* and *Fra Lippo Lippi* resembles that between *Artemis* and *Karshish*, and that between *Rudel* and *One Word More*: the second poem successfully consummates the action – resurrection, love – left incomplete or frustrated in the first. Like Pictor an artist-monk, Lippi translates *his* humanism into his art spontaneously and directly: 'First, every sort of monk, the black and white, / I drew them, fat and lean: then, folk at church etc' (145–6). And, as Pictor wished to do, Lippi next exhibits 'my covered bit of cloister-wall' to the 'faces' it mirrors; they in turn ratify the artefact with their approving praise. The terms of their praise add another element to the humanist paradigm:

> 'That's the very man!
> Look at the boy who stoops to pat the dog!
> That woman's like the Prior's niece who comes
> To care about his asthma: it's the life!'

> 168–71

Lippi has complemented the need to paint man with the need to paint him *accurately*, adding realism to individualism and becoming a 'man of fact', an essential characteristic of the Ruskinian Naturalist. This realism is a perfectly logical extension of humanist individualism, since, for a painter, individuals only become such through visual differentia. For ecclesiastical authority, however, as represented in the Prior of Lippi's monastery, naturalism represents the heresy of 'homage to the perishable clay' in one whose duty, as a monk, is to 'Make [men] forget there's such a thing as flesh'. Thus begins a battle which inverts Pictor's capitulation. Lippi struggles to argue that his naturalism is just as religious as the anonymous pieties of a Fra Angelico, and his self-defence rises to a mystical near-pantheism:

> you've seen the world
> – The beauty and the wonder and the power,
> The shapes of things, their colours, lights and shades,
> Changes, surprises, – and God made it all!
> – For what? Do you feel thankful, ay or no,
> For this fair town's face, yonder river's line,
> The mountain round it and the sky above,
> Much more the figures of man, woman, child,
> These are the frame to? What's it all about?
> To be passed over, despised? or dwelt upon,

Wondered at? oh, this last of course! - you say.
But why not do as well as say, - paint these
Just as they are, careless what comes of it?

282-94

The last phrase, however, reveals that the Prior was, in his own terms,
perfectly justified in his reaction to Lippi's art: Lippi rejects the didactic
and declares his naturalism aesthetic rather than moral. His celebration of
beauty takes place on the physical plane. From the premise that 'If you
get simple beauty and naught else, / You get about the best thing God
invents', he moves immediately to the sensual conclusion:

I always see the garden and God there
A-making man's wife: and, my lesson learned,
The value and significance of flesh,
I can't unlearn ten minutes afterwards.

266-9

It is at this point that Lippi's aesthetic theory reveals its affinity with the
'plot' of the poem. He speaks his monologue to explain to a law-officer
why he frequents brothels, arguing that just as 'You should not take a
fellow ten years old / And make him swear to never kiss the girls', so it was
wrong for the Church to compel him to repress his naturalism (the Prior
having made him erase his first painting's 'homage to the perishable clay')
and revert to the safety of sanctioned subjects and style in pursuit of a
hollow Purism. In consequence, he has become, as man, a 'beast' in need
of periodic bouts of promiscuity, and as artist, an ironic echoer of
liturgical orthodoxies and thus a traitor to his own ideal. He feels, in
consequence, a complex self-contempt. It is the Church's fault that he
turned out like this, but he has internalised its values and thus obsessively
characterises himself in animal terms, as a 'rat' or 'mouse', and reveals
that even without direct pressure from the priests (he is free under the
patronage of Cosimo de'Medici to 'paint now as I please') he still 'paint[s]
to please them'. His humanism can only appear in his art in the distorted
form of the irony which, as he explains at the end of his monologue, will
flicker across the painting he plans to give the nuns of 'Sant'Ambrogio'.
This painting, in a daring expression of his double problem, will both
contain the usual divine personnel, and introduce himself, as 'beast',

caught up with my monk's-things by mistake,
My old serge gown and rope that goes all round,
I in this presence, this pure company!
Where's a *hole*, where's a corner for escape?

                                366–9 (m.i.)

But humility becomes mockery. Imagining that one of his painted figures
intercedes to prevent his expulsion, he concludes

                    Thus I scuttle off
To some safe bench behind, not letting go
The palm of her, the little lily thing
That spoke the word for me in the nick,
Like the Prior's niece . . . Saint Lucy, I would say.

                                384–8

Lippi here grafts onto his static picture a life-episode it could not possibly
contain, with the motive, superficially, of reinforcing his 'beastliness' by
characterising as animal-like the human vitality it results from. But he
simultaneously inverts this self-abasement into a criticism of the timeless
and anonymous fixity of his heap of saints: 'God in the midst, Madonna
and her babe. . . . And then i' the front, of course a saint or two. . . . And
Job, I must have him there past mistake' (348, 353, 357). The outrageous
flippancy of his tone asserts his actual dominance over the 'pure
company' he paints – a dominance conceded in the 'little lily thing's'
defence of him:

        'He made you and devised you, after all,
    Though he's none of you! Could Saint John there draw –
    His camel-hair make up a painting-brush?
    We come to brother Lippi for all that,
    "*Iste perfecit opus!*" '

                                373–7

Through this passage, Lippi expresses his belief that art is inherently
substantive, and therefore that his own fleshly 'vices', which the Church
condemns, correlate with his genius, which it respects and exploits. Its
refusal to recognise this correlation has compelled him to forfeit

seriousness and generate his paintings out of the continuous incongruity between their divine subject-matter and his merely human execution of them. Such irony was unimaginable to Pictor, from whom Lippi therefore becomes a progression, for all that his personal ideal, like Pictor's, was unessayed after that first, censored attempt. Simultaneously, again unlike Pictor, Lippi welcomes the prospect of a more courageous art to follow:

> I'm a beast, I know.
> But see, now – why, I see as certainly
> As that the morning-star's about to shine,
> What will hap some day.
>
>   270–3

He anticipates that Masaccio, his pupil, will inaugurate a true Renaissance of which his own work will be seen as precursor: his final words, 'There's the grey beginning' catch up the 'morning-star' simile into a broader image of historical dawn.

*   *   *

Andrea del Sarto, the next poem in the sequence, again completes what was abortive in its predecessor. Lippi wished to paint things 'just as they are'; Andrea can do it, 'Do easily too – when I say, perfectly, / I do not boast, perhaps' (63–4) – so perfectly that he is, as he tells us Michelangelo has claimed, even Raphael's superior in that respect, and can correct the drawing in a Raphael he keeps in his studio. Michelangelo's praise emphasises that the 'faultlessness' of Andrea's painting – he is, the poem's subtitle informs us, 'called the faultless painter' – represents the ambition of his period as a whole, as indeed it perfects Lippi's naturalism, which in turn was a logical corollary of the Renaissance paradigm. Here again Browning's reading of High Renaissance art coincides with Ruskin's:

> Original thoughts belonging to this century are comparatively rare; even Raphael and Michael Angelo themselves borrowed all their principal ideas and plans of pictures from their predecessors; but they executed them with a precision up to that time unseen.
>
>   xii 109

To be 'the faultless painter', then, appeared to Victorian art-historians the characteristic ambition of Renaissance art.

But where is Lippi's *enthusiasm?* Andrea is 'much wearier than you think', his painting represents things 'all in a twilight' and he characterises 'alike my work and self' as '[a] twilight-piece'. Memories of Lippi's concluding anticipation of the 'morning-star' sharpen the actual eclipse underlying the apparent progression. The monologue affords a variety of explanations for Andrea's melancholia, many of them personal: he has married a whore, let his parents die in poverty, robbed a generous patron, and become in consequence a social pariah; the occasion of the monologue is a matrimonial quarrel; it concludes with his wife leaving for an assignation with a lover. As with Lippi, however, these existential elements relate to a complex *aesthetic* argument. In Sarto, Lippi's appreciation of 'the value and significance of flesh' has lost all contact with the 'soul' to which Lippi struggled to relate it, and become self-sufficient. He married his wife for her beauty, disregarding her stupidity and immorality. He robbed his patron to get money. And his art, with all its technical perfection, is produced for the same motive:

> I'll work then for your friend's friend, never fear,
> Treat his own subject after his own way,
> Fix his own time, accept too his own price,
> And shut the money into this small hand
> When next it takes mine.

> 5-9

The last two lines seem to alleviate his avarice by making it a reflex of his wife's, and she is indeed characterised as the typical gold-digger ('More gaming debts to pay? You smiled for that?' [222]). But his avarice is merely subtler than hers. By promising her money, he purchases her company for periods like the one the poem records. His monologue is the seal of a monetary bargain: 'If you would sit thus by me every night', he would, he tells her, 'work better', which he glosses as 'earn more, give you more' (205-7). Each picture is doubly sold, to his clients for money, and to his wife for 'smiles'.

Thus the horror inspired in Pictor by the commercial side of Renaissance art proves to have a real foundation. The conflict in his mind between the need to represent man to himself in art and the sordidness of the entailed financial transaction is realised by Sarto's single-minded concern with the transaction, to the exclusion of any sign of the enthusiasm, felt by both Pictor and Lippi, for their beholders' approbation. Sarto himself draws the contrast, as between himself and his greater contemporaries:

> The sudden blood of these men! at a word –
> Praise them, it boils, or blame them, it boils too.
> I, painting from myself and to myself,
> Know what I do, am unmoved by men's blame
> Or their praise either.
>
> 88–92

Working purely for money, he cares nothing for discriminating approval or disapproval, and by a subtle line of reasoning, this self-sufficiency is related to the character of his art:

> There burns a truer light of God in them,
> In their vexed beating stuffed and stopped-up brain,
> Heart, or whate'er else, than goes on to prompt
> This low-pulsed forthright craftsman's hand of mine.
>
> 79–82

The proposition is supported by the energy with which the unpunctuated second line surges through its impediments; Sarto's hesitation as to whether to use 'brain' or 'heart' to describe other painters' special endowment exposes his doubt as to whether he himself has anything to correspond. He means 'soul', but it is a word he never applies to himself, saving it for paintings, except at the point when he reproaches his wife by claiming, 'Had you . . . given me soul, / We might have risen to Raphael, I and you'. Here, the soul itself becomes something to be given or bought, and thus another of the transactions which have combined to stifle Andrea's artistic talent. It is *because* he has no soul that his work can be faultless and he care nothing about its reputation; the souls of his artistic superiors, Michelangelo and Raphael, become manifest precisely through the faults in their works and their trembling concern with their audience. They still work within the Renaissance paradigm; Sarto does not.

But there is a paradox here, in that as we have seen, Renaissance art began from the commitment to precisely the naturalism which Sarto's faultlessness enables him to achieve. It now appears that only the failure to achieve what they seek to achieve will allow Renaissance painters to achieve it. The comparison with Lippi helps to illuminate this point. The Church asked Lippi to 'paint the soul' but he preferred to 'fag on at flesh' hoping to 'add soul' later while deriding what he took to be the Church's demand that he 'paint soul, by painting body / So ill, the eye can't stop there, must go further / And can't fare worse!' (199–201). Andrea shares this contempt for incompetence, but with a troubled consciousness that nevertheless it is somehow through defect that soul is manifested in art, and therefore that his own art, by an excessive fidelity to Renaissance ambitions for painting, has betrayed those same ambitions and declined into materialism and cynicism. The ideal balance of spirit and flesh, anticipated by Pictor and Lippi, seems already to have gone by in Andrea, decadence following anticipation at disturbing speed.

*   *   *

Decadence is very obviously the subject of *The Bishop Orders his Tomb*, last in the explicitly Renaissance sequence in 2M&W. In this poem the spirit has shrunk to liturgical cliché, the *vanitas vanitatum* of a dying prelate whose final object in life – and death – is to force his heirs to build him a better sarcophagus than that of his hated rival, Gandolf. The aesthetic sensuality of Lippi and Sarto reappears in the Bishop's rhapsodies over 'peach-blossom marble', 'true peach, / Rosy and flawless', or

> Some lump, ah God, of *lapis lazuli*,
> Big as a Jew's head cut off at the nape,
> Blue as vein o'er the Madonna's breast . . .

> 42–4

and his craving for material beauty has, like Sarto's, turned him into a thief. But in him, the loss of soul is more complete, in that his conception of the afterlife itself – for a Christian, purely a spiritual idea – is of survival *in the body*, or rather, in and through the artefact of his projected tomb:

> For as I lie here, hours of the dead night,
> Dying in state and by such slow degrees,
> I fold my arms as if they clasped a crook,
> And stretch my feet forth straight as stone can point,

And let the bedclothes, for a mortcloth, drop
Into great laps and folds of sculptor's-work[.]

85–90

This passage explains the Bishop's obsession with his tomb. When, earlier in the poem, he cried, 'Old Gandolf with his paltry onion-stone, / Put me where I may look at him!' (31–2), he meant that the effigy on his tomb-top should be so placed, as the receptacle of his posthumous consciousness and the seal of his personal immorality. This of course fosters the poem's satirical anomaly, that there could be a Bishop who does not believe in the soul, who appears to have no conception, even, of the Christian idea of what the soul is; but there is a terrible intensity in his desire for metamorphosis which suggests that the Bishop regards stone not as a second-best copy of his living flesh but as a means of transcending it and therefore in principle itself a kind of soul. But not a stable one. In a parody of Dante's tripartite scheme, the Bishop distinguishes grades of 'afterlife' on the basis of grades of stone. The 'paltry onion-stone' of Gandolf's statue leaves its subject, in the Bishop's mind, convulsed with anguished disappointment at his inferior substance (Purgatory); his own likeness, if 'carved aright' from lapis lazuli or basalt, will ascend to the 'peace' and 'leisure' which his life of acquisitive intrigue has denied him, and from its inconceivably grand sarcophagus, survey its domain in a paradisial rapture of infinitely protracted final calm. But if, as he fears, he gets a stone inferior to Gandolf's, his fate will be even worse: 'Stone – / Gritstone, a-crumble! Clammy squares which sweat / As if the corpse they keep were oozing through[!]' (115–17). Such stone will be unable to assume the Bishop into itself, and he will be left not even in Hell, but as a mere corpse dissolving into slime. It is a macabre variant on the spirit-flesh dichotomy that in the Bishop's mind both sides can be represented materially, by different varieties of stone; it also marks the logical conclusion of the materialism which had played such a central part in the Renaissance paradigm of art.

*   *   *

The relation of life to art, figured in the Bishop's wish to fuse the two into immortal unity, is studied in all the Renaissance poems, and traces a pattern of hope and decline parallel to the one I have just outlined. Pictor, like the Bishop, confounds his own identity with that of his painting: 'going – *I, in each new picture,* forth. . . . Till *it* reached home, where learned age should greet / *My* face, and youth . . . lie learning at *my* feet!' (26, 33, 35[m.i.]). Lippi, as we have seen, will literally appear in his painting, and so will Sarto, whose evening argument with his wife turns into 'my painting ready-made . . . / All in a twilight, you and I alike'. The progression, or rather retrogression, adumbrated in this sequence is from an art striving to become life, to an art striving to turn life into art. Pictor's wish to immortalise the 'human faces' of his audience is presented in a rhetoric, not of appropriation but of moral edification. His paintings will *teach* their beholders, and his own imagined survival 'here on my earth' is thereby distinguished from the Bishop's selfish self-petrifaction by being characterised as the altruistic desire to maintain, through art, his living influence for good. Lippi feels the simpler need to furnish his living subjects with an equivalent life in art: 'Suppose I've made her eyes all right and blue, / Can't I take breath and try to add life's flash, / And then add soul and heighten them three-fold?' (212–14). The ambiguity of 'take breath' – meaning either that Lippi will pause to breathe or that he will seize the breath of life to give his sitter – shows how close painter and subject have grown; when, therefore, Lippi appears in his own painting it is hardly surprising that he presents himself in a language of action – 'up shall come', 'back I shrink' etc – which obliges the art to consecrate a temporal and circumstantial reality. His function of providing the beholder with a self-personification and point of moral entry into the 'pure company' of Saints and angels represents an altruism parallel to Pictor's. But Andrea, as we have seen, cares nothing for his beholder. *His* planned self-portrait, therefore, comes close to the Bishop's voluptuous narcissism:

> – You, at the point of your first pride in me
> (That's gone you know), – but I, at every point;
> My youth, my hope, my art, being all toned down
> To yonder sober pleasant Fiesole.

37–40

The fact that he is engaged in turning life into art emerges from the disparity between this agreeable image and the reality – a bitter quarrel – from which it is drawn. In fact, he seeks in life as well as in art to transform the promiscuous Lucretzia from her real self into an outrageously false ideality:

> So! keep looking so –
> My serpentining beauty, rounds on rounds! . . .
> Let my hands *frame* your face in your hair's gold,
> You beautiful Lucretzia *that are mine*!

25–6, 175–6 (m.i.)

The word 'frame' joins life to art and indicates how in both Andrea entraps his wife in fabrications; the final phrase reinforces this by offering a superficial paradox (she is not his if she is awaiting her lover) which actually fuses the two domains into a single falsehood. Framed, as she is in both portrait and monologue, Lucretzia is indeed his, and her silence, in life the sign of her combined indifference and stupidity, becomes a symbol of her actual bondage to the art which she treats as a commodity. Andrea's projected double portrait thus aptly prefaces the Bishop's more spectacular yearning to transmit his living spirit into the cold persistence and lifeless repose of statuary. No-one will, it seems, *see* his effigy: he imagines it always alone at the centre of his Church, in a solitude which cradles his narcissism and replicates his self-contemplating egotism.

IV

The next two poems, *Bishop Blougram's Apology* and *Cleon*, give an abbreviated exposition of the same pattern of hope and decline in the Victorian and the Hellenic cultures, but add to it an anticipation of spiritual renewal and cultural and artistic rejuvenation which, though bound in turn to suffer the same decline, affords the constantly receding prospect of perfection which keeps art imperfect and alive.

Blougram is a Catholic Cardinal who, like the Bishop of St Praxed's, has developed simple sensuality into the more refined pleasures of the connoisseur:

St Praxed's: And new-found agate urns as fresh as day,
                   And marble's language, Latin pure, discreet . . .

97–8

Blougram: my articles
                   On music, poetry, the fictile vase
                   Found at Albano, chess, Anacreon's Greek . . .

913–15

But there has been a progression in *self-consciousness*. Where the earlier Bishop remained comically unaware of the conflict in his language between the spiritual and the mundane, Blougram turns the same contrast to his advantage by casting it as a one-sided conflict between his own 'realism' and the arrogant 'idealism' of his interlocutor, 'Gigadibs the literary man'. Gigadibs has attacked what he considers the worldiness of Blougram, from the idealist standpoint; Blougram counters,

> You weigh and find, whatever more or less
> I boast of my ideal realised
> Is nothing in the balance when opposed
> To your ideal, your grand simple life,
> Of which you will not realise a jot.

79–83

The image of the 'balance' allows Blougram to enmesh Gigadibs in the paradox of believing that his, Blougram's, ideal, the 'ideal' of getting everything out of life one can, weighs 'nothing' despite its materiality, while Gigadibs's ideal, unrealised and therefore materially non-existent, could be considered as weighing more. The word 'realise' itself supports his point by its emphasis, in the whole poem, on the physical rather than the intellectual sense of the word; its reappearance in the course of Blougram's subsequent argument that connoisseurship is better than original art makes it a key to his voracious consumerism:

>   on points of taste
> Wherewith, to speak it humbly, [Shakespeare] and I
> Are dowered alike – I'll ask you, I or he,
> Which in our two lives *realises* most?
> Much, he imagined – somewhat, I possess.

502–7 (m.i.)

Blougram's insistence upon *reification* as a valid test for abstract ideas illustrates his commitment to a materialism which lies at the other end of the extreme represented by Gigadibs: thus between them they present as simultaneously available alternatives the polarities which in the Renaissance group are laid out as an evolving sequence. The relation between the two is strengthened by the passage in which Blougram rejects what he conceives to be Gigadibs' demand that because 'the aim, if reached or not, makes great the life' he, Blougram, should 'try to be Shakespeare'. The echo of Sarto's contention that 'a man's reach should exceed his grasp' is obvious; Blougram's argument that since he is Blougram there is no point trying to be Shakespeare, converts the difference between the *names* 'Blougram' and 'Shakespeare' into an absolute one, and thus reduces reification to an inertia deeper than Sarto's, since he at least could imagine its opposite.

Blougram does allow that Shakespeare, as Shakespeare, was right to create art; for Cleon, the speaker of the next poem in 2*M&W*, even art is discredited, in the absence of an afterlife – the 'heaven' which for Sarto gives aspiration its ultimate reward – since the time devoted to art steals so much immediate pleasure from life. Though (as a Greek of the Hellenistic period shortly after the death of Christ) Cleon lives historically earlier than any previous speaker, he is conceptually the most sophisticated, which accounts for his appearing here rather than near the beginning of the sequence: his being an artist ('all arts are mine') sharpens the point by casting him as an apostate to principles which he himself has actually embraced. Blougram and Cleon are alike, however, in admitting their decadence by perceiving themselves tragically dwarfed by earlier greatnesses. Cleon is 'not so great' as Homer, Terpander, Phidias; Blougram acknowledges that Luther led a life 'incomparably better than my own'. Blougram, however, manages to juggle away any possibility that he might follow Luther's example:

> If he succeeded, nothing's left to do:
> And if he did not altogether – well,
> Strauss is the next advance. All Strauss should be
> I might be also. But to what result?
> He looks upon no future: Luther did.

> 575–9

Here, Blougram effectively places himself at the conclusion of history, and this eschatological omen colours the language of all three decadents, the Bishop, Blougram and Cleon. Their common incapacity to transcend immediate pleasures signals the end of a historical progress and in principle the end of art, so their juxtaposition at the end of the Main Part concludes Browning's historical study in the common twilight of the Hellenic, Renaissance and modern eras, a twilight in which man's flesh has triumphed over the spirit, destroying the posited earlier balance. But the flesh is not triumphant in pleasure, but debilitated by the weight of

the substances to which it reduces everything, and the speakers are
depressed by the thought of a death which represents the extinction both
of themselves as individuals and of their cultures as producers of art:

> St Praxed's: Stone –
>   Gritstone, a crumble! Clammy squares which
>   sweat
>   As if the corpse they keep were oozing through –
>   And no more *lapis* to delight the world!
>
>   115–18

> Blougram: Just when we are safest, there's a sunset-touch,
>   A fancy from a flower-bell, some one's death . . .
>
>   182–3

> Cleon: every day my hairs fall more and more,
>   My hand shakes, and the heavy years increase –
>   The horror quickening still from year to year,
>   The consummation coming past escape
>   When . . . I, I, the feeling, thinking, acting man,
>   The man who loved his life so over-much,
>   Sleep in my urn.
>
>   313–16, 321–3

V

But the very paralleling of the three epochs suggests that a principle of
renewal is at work in human history, and *Cleon* vindicates the possibility
by the famous device of ending with a reference to Christianity, as a creed
which Cleon has heard of but can neither comprehend nor accept. The
Christian afterlife, repudiated by the Hellenist, offers precisely the
solution to the problem of death for which Cleon himself desperately
yearns:

> It is so horrible,
>   I dare at times imagine to my need
>   Some future state revealed to us by Zeus,

Unlimited in capability
For joy, as this is in desire for joy[.]

323-7

He even conceives the possibility that Zeus 'or other god descended here' only to dismiss it as 'a dream'. His reference to Christianity thus ironically answers his desire to find meaning in life and in art, and his personal rejection of it symbolically exiles him and his exhausted culture from a historical renewal which they can intellectually conceive but not literally credit. But though historicised at Christ's incarnation, such renewal is not limited to that historical moment. At the conclusion of *Bishop Blougram's Apology*, Blougram inwardly invites the defeated Gigadibs to 'sit with me this many a year'; but convinced not that Blougram is right but that he can only be proved wrong in (and by) practice, Gigadibs 'did not sit five minutes' before emigrating to Australia, where, Browning hopes, he will soon have 'tested his first plough, / And studied his last chapter of St John'. In which 'last chapter' Gigadibs would have found St John's forecast of Christ's *second* coming: 'Peter therefore seeing [John] saith to Jesus, Lord, and what shall this man do? Jesus saith unto him, If I will that he tarry till I come, what is that to thee?' (*John* xxi 21-2). In this metaphorical form, the Christian Incarnation becomes an omnipresent, trans-historical possibility of individual renewal. The whole collection revolves around this point. Karshish, an Arab physician supposedly writing in the years after Christ's death, encounters the Incarnation as a living rumour; the urgency of the poem arises from the speaker's partially successful effort to move from a historical to a moral understanding of its significance. The position of this poem at the opening of the Main Part of 2M&W extends and reinforces the cyclic implications of juxtaposing *Blougram* and *Cleon* at its close. The entire structure is made to revolve around the axis of the Incarnation, implying that the process of materialist decline which concludes all the historical forms of humanism will invariably be reversed by a renewed assertion of incarnate spirit as the ideal balance between 'purism' and 'sensuality'.

I want now to consider the means by which Browning introduces the idea of the Incarnation into the poems which, flanked by *Karshish* and *Cleon*, make up the centre of the collection's Main Part.

The climax of *Karshish*, when the speaker suddenly reveals that he does acknowledge the potentially supreme importance of Christ's claim to be Son of God characterises the Incarnation as the moral centre of history.

Simultaneously, it introduces as the material representation of Incarnation the 'Face' which corresponds to man's and instructs man that God by that act and in that person manifested a 'heart' like his own. It is at this moment, also, that Christian art is born, out of the need to recapture, in the material substantiality of paint, Christ's face as a token of his self-renewing Incarnation in time; it is that face, therefore, which, in both presence and absence, dominates the art of the following poems and reinforces their patterns of decline and recuperation by presenting these in terms of an approximation to or deviation from the originating 'Face'.

Each of the three Renaissance painters, Pictor, Lippi and Andrea del Sarto, is automatically involved in the production of religious art, and all mention or describe paintings which in effect represent the Incarnation. Pictor paints 'Virgin, Babe and Saint'. Lippi paints 'Madonna and her Babe'. Andrea's 'Virgin is his wife'. In each case, however, the representation amounts to a distortion or evasion of the meaning grasped by Karshish and issued as a demand upon subsequent religious art. For Pictor, 'Virgin, Babe and Saint' become the formulaic ensemble with whose mechanical reiteration he evades the 'human faces' to which he really feels allegiance. Lippi's equivalently codified religious art includes Christ as one item in a long list of religious props, in which – suggestively – he figures as Madonna's babe rather than God's. Andrea del Sarto makes no reference at all to the Christ-child, being solely concerned with the physical beauty of the Virgin, or rather, of his wife masquerading as the Virgin.

This progressive disappearance of the divine 'Face' from religious art is intensified in the next two poems of the sequence. On the Bishop's tomb, Christ first becomes a mere item in the crazy jumble of pagan and Christian motifs and is eventually garbled into 'St Praxed at his Sermon on the Mount'. Blougram avoids *any* direct reference to Christ, using his name only formulaically – 'a Corpus Christi day', 'What think you of Christ, friend?' – and elsewhere substituting periphrases such as 'The Way, the Truth, the Life', 'Peter's creed' etc etc. He mentions only secular paintings, whose only 'face' proves to be 'a Pan's', and when discussing Strauss's objections to the historicity and divinity of Christ, replaces Christ's name with his own. Cleon's speculation that Christ might be the same man as St Paul concludes the process of eliminating the explicit image of Christ, in counterpoint to the pattern of moral and artistic decline from the Incarnational paradigm.

There is one passage, however, in which Christ's face appears to take on something of the significance it had for Karshish. Lippi's description

of his first painting mentions the son of a murdered man, who, having
pursued the murderer to the sanctuary of the Church, stands

> Shaking a fist at him with one fierce arm,
> Signing himself with the other because of Christ
> (Whose sad face on the cross sees only this
> After the passion of a thousand years)[.]

154–7

Christ's 'sad face' arises parenthetically in the text in token of human
neglect of its significance, brooding over a scene which simultaneously
conceals him admidst the paraphernalia of the Church and concedes the
centre to the ferocities of human passion. It is appropriate that Lippi
chooses the Passion rather than the nativity for his image of the
Incarnation: the Passion, as the representation of Christ's sacrifice of
himself for man's sin, is a suitable complement to the carnival of
wrongdoing his image confronts. Lippi's phrasing contrives to add the
further suggestion that in enduring 'the passion of a thousand years' on
the cross, Christ acknowledges, as it were, that human sin was *not*
redeemed by his Passion, and further, that Christ was in effect and as a
result *not resurrected*, but left eternally suspended over an inveterately
bestial humankind.

If we compare this passage with Lippi's description of 'The
Coronation of the Virgin' at the end of the poem, we can see that
Browning has differentiated two phases of the Incarnation, the Nativity
and the Passion, assigning to the first a purely formulaic significance, to
the second a full moral seriousness; and has gestured towards the
Resurrection, third cardinal element of the Incarnation, as having
meaning *in absentia*. This configuration is systematic. Lippi's two
paintings polarise the first two phases of the Incarnation by
distinguishing the *fact* of Incarnation as represented in the Nativity from
the moral *action* of Incarnation in the Passion. This is a falling-away from
Karshish's grasp of their essential unity. In Christ's 'Face' Karshish
captures the mystical moment of Incarnation, but he proceeds without
hiatus to envisage Christ's death as having completed the moral logic of
the Incarnation in God's claim thereby to 'have died for man'. Karshish
has, however, no knowledge of the Resurrection. Believing that 'the
learned leech / Perished in a tumult long ago', he (involuntarily) curtails
the full span of the Incarnation, and Browning alerts the reader to the
omission by counterpoising it to the centrality, in the poem, of Lazarus'

resurrection from the dead. Karshish, as a physician, fully appreciates the significance of resurrection as a medical idea, and develops a powerful diagnosis of Lazarus's allegedly deranged condition on the basis of the difficulty any man would experience in adjusting to temporal life after a temporary experience of eternity. But Karshish is unable to complete the standard typological identification of Lazarus with Christ, and the reader in this instance corrects the speaker's otherwise impressive intuition of the meaning of the Christian Incarnation.

In *Cleon* this incomprehension of Christian Resurrection becomes the centre of Browning's characterisation of the moral despair of Hellenism. What fills Cleon's soul with a terror which the measured cadences of his monologue only make more haunting, is the thought of his own death as confirming man's innate materiality and characterising human aspiration as self-deceit. And the 'doctrine' which, in his view, 'could be held by no sane man' is ironically not merely the Incarnation as such, but the promise, underwritten by Christ's individual resurrection, of future resurrection for all men, – in short, that 'future state revealed to us by Zeus' whose denial within Greek theology is the source of Cleon's despair. Resurrection, which Cleon dismisses as an absurdity, is in fact precisely the doctrine which St Paul, the 'Paulus' of whom Cleon has heard, preaches in the chapter from which Browning took the epigraph to the poem ('as certain also of your own poets have said'):

But now [God] commandeth men that they should all everywhere repent: inasmuch as he hath appointed a day, in the which he will judge the world in righteousness by the man whom he hath ordained; whereof he hath given assurance unto all men, in that he hath raised him from the dead.

Acts xvii 30–1

Resurrection is thus what the Incarnation *adds* to man, in token of the divine element amalgamated with his flesh; the moment when an epoch, ending, projects from itself a future renewal to proclaim the reality and persistence of man's divinity. The span of Christ's life from Incarnation through Passion to Resurrection corresponds to the historical development of an epoch from inception through decline to re-incarnation in the next and models the cyclically repeated narrative of history. Framing the Main Part of 2*M&W*, *Cleon* and *Karshish* position the Resurrection as an absent centre which represents the renewal which no speaker can adequately imagine because it can only emanate from divine fiat. Without such a concept of renewal, the cyclic order of the

Main Part would be tragically meaningless. With it, the cycle is dynamic.
The failure of human protagonists quite to grasp this fact, or ever to
encompass the complete meaning of the Incarnation in one uninhibited
intuition, exemplifies the rationale of the cycle as a combined falling-
away from and return to a paradigm which is at once necessary to man and
beyond his understanding.

VI

The symbolic act of the Incarnation of Christ offered Browning an
analogy of his own experience as a creative artist . . . As God clothed
himself in human flesh, so the poet speaks in words the vision he has
seen. If the artist manages to convey in language the truth of his vision,
he will have unfolded something of the Divine Word in his human words.
        Beryl Stone, *Browning and Incarnation*, (unpublished MA thesis),
                quoted W. Whitla, *The Central Truth: the Incarnation in
                            Browning's Poetry* (Toronto, 1963) 5

In support of his view that the Incarnation provided Browning with a
model concept of creativity, William Whitla, from whose book, *The
Central Truth*, the above quotation comes, cites *Paracelsus*:

> God is the perfect poet
> Who in creation acts his own conceptions.
> Shall man refuse to be aught less than God?
> Man's weakness is his glory – for the strength
> Which raises him to heaven and near God's self
> Came spite of it. God's strength his glory is,
> For thence came with our weakness sympathy
> Which brought God down to earth, a man like us.

                                        (1849 edn)

It is easy to understand why Browning should have been attracted by this
idea. His problem, as described in the early poems, is that the analogy of
poetry to divine creation, Coleridge's 'repetition in the finite mind of the
infinite I AM', necessarily makes the physical medium, words or paint,
appear inadequate to its communication except by and as irony. This
problem is represented in *Men and Women* by the story of Lazarus, who in
Karshish is described as having experienced 'heaven opened to a soul

while yet on earth' (141) yet as being unable to give any verbal shape to his experience. Likewise Andrea del Sarto's rivals:

> Their works drop groundwards, but themselves, I know,
> Reach many a time a heaven that's shut to me,
> Enter and take their place there sure enough,
> Though they come back and cannot tell the world.

83–6

The use of the Incarnation as the analogy for human creation solves this problem. As 'the perfect poet', God embodies 'his own conceptions' in the 'creation' of a manlike self able to 'walk the earth'; refusing 'to be aught less than God', the human poet reaches upwards towards 'heaven' and 'God's self' through that same manlike self, which corresponds to the words in which his own poetic conception finds embodiment. The idea of Christ gives Karshish the courage and the words to describe God – a God who, speaking, matches and ratifies human words. Coleridge arrived at the same conclusion:

> [T]he redeemed & sanctified become finally themselves Words of the *Word* – even as articulate sounds are made by the Reason to represent Forms, in the Mind, and Forms are a language of the Notions – Verba significant phaenomena, phaenomena sunt quasi verba poematum* (TON NOUMENON). As he in the Father, even so we in him!
> [* 'Words signify things, things are like the words of a poem'.]
>
> *Notebooks*, ed. K. Coburn (1957) i 17.21

Like Browning, Coleridge here distinguishes between the poem (defined by the bracketed *ton noumenon* as 'that which is conceived') and its words (verba). And like Browning he compares this disjunction to that between God the Father and Christ the Son, using to the full the Johannine characterisation of Christ as God's *Word* to reinforce the analogy. Another hint of this idea appears in the Preface to Shelley's *Cenci*: 'Imagination is as the immortal God which should assume flesh for the redemption of mortal passion'.

Whitla fails to note that the passage from *Paracelsus* on which he rests his concept of the Incarnational analogy rests was added in 1849, and therefore that it was not in 1835 but during the period leading up to the 1855 *Men and Women* that Browning was evolving his use of it. Further evidence for this is to be found in *Saul*, which Browning completed at this time and included in *Men and Women*. DeVane points out that in 1845, when he began *Saul*, Browning was unable to give it a satisfactory conclusion; it was in 1855 that it acquired its present ending, and this arose out of a new consciousness of the significance of the divine Incarnation. Yearning to help Saul to overcome his depression, David suddenly realises that this very yearning, and the very weakness that renders it impotent, represent a moral rectitude in man which demands an equivalent gesture from God. That gesture, God's lowering of himself towards the mankind rising towards him, is prophesied in the famous climax of the poem when David 'see[s] the Christ stand!' (312). The resemblance to the 1849 addition to *Paracelsus* is obvious, and reinforced by the hovering analogy to poetic creation which prompts both the insistence upon David's status as poet, and the glance at the Johannine 'Word' in a line describing 'that act where my soul was thy servant, thy word was my word'. Here Browning unites the Old Testament 'suffering servant' with the New Testament 'Word' in order to combine the moral and aesthetic strands of his Incarnational theory: David, the Psalmist who later becomes King (his recital of Saul's political virtues proleptically describes his own) represents the human counterpart to Christ, the ideal blend of spirit and flesh which produces both moral integrity and poetic creativity in man. The analogy is completed by his status, in the Synoptic genealogies, as Christ's literal ancestor.

But in 1863, Browning omitted *Saul* from 2*M&W*, and removed from *Paracelsus* the passage he had added in 1849.

The effect of omitting *Saul* was not, of course, to eliminate the Incarnation from 2*M&W*, since *Karshish* and *Cleon* remain; no trace survives, however, at least on the explicit level, of the analogy between the Incarnation and human creativity, and its simultaneous disappearance from *Paracelsus* confirms that Browning had become shy of stating it. He did not, however, abandon it altogether. In the first book of *The Ring and the Book*, written at the same time as 2*M&W*, he simply took the step of replacing the analogy between human creativity and the Incarnation with a more limited – and limiting – analogy with the Resurrection. I have already discussed the appearance of the Resurrection as a motif in the Prologue to 2*M&W*, where it occupies a similar structural position to that of the same motif in *Ring*. The latter context establishes clearly that Browning was using the idea of Resurrection to avoid Romantic hubris, a blasphemous usurpation of the divine role:

> "In the beginning God made heaven and earth;"
> From which, no matter with what lisp, I spell

And speak you out a consequence – that man,
Man, – as befits the made, the inferior thing, –
Purposed, since made, to grow, not make in turn,
Yet forced to try and make, else fail to grow, –
Forced to rise, reach at, if not grasp and gain
The good beyond him, – which attempt is growth, –
Repeats God's process in man's due degree,
Attaining man's proportionate result, –
Creates, no, but resuscitates, perhaps.

i 709–19

The contrast here between the majesty of Biblical language and the 'lisp' involved in Browning's obsessive repetitions and coiling parentheses reinforces the central point that the divine fiat is not to be emulated by the human poet, who must instead content himself with 'resuscitating' men and women who have already lived and died. Though the analogy is transparently with Christ's resurrection, Browning avoids mentioning the latter, thereby doubling the distance that separates this principle from the earlier Incarnational analogy and suggesting that his retreat was motivated by a sense that that anology had been blasphemous – as indeed the line in the 1849 *Paracelsus*, 'Shall man refuse to be aught less than God?' does have the Faustian air which Browning disavows in *Ring*.

Browning here rejects, once again, the Romatic preoccupation with a poetics of unmediated vision, and defines his aesthetic as being in and for the world. And as before, it is an aesthetic of love, a love like that manifested through Christ towards man, that replaces Romantic vision and motivates poetic utterance. The argument which explains this position emerges in the last three poems in *2M&W*, *Cleon*, *Rudel*, and *One Word More*. These poems are spoken *by poets*; they thus echo and amplify the aesthetic arguments of the Prologue; and the progression between them culminates on Browning's own position as composer of the collection.

Being, like Rudel and Browning himself, a poet, Cleon (chrono)-logically takes his place in front of them, but shows a total lack of love not merely in his failure to grasp, like Karshish, the Incarnation as an expression of divine love for man, but in his selfish refusal to allow anyone else's identity to stand in front of his own ('thy' in the following passage applies to Protus, Cleon's correspondent, who has sent him gifts including a female slave and an ornate cup):

'But', sayest thou . . . 'what
Thou writest, paintest stays; that does not die:
Sappho survives, because we sing her songs,
And Aeschylus, because we read his plays!'
Why, if they live still, let them come and take
Thy slave in my despite, drink from thy cup,
Speak in my place.

301, 302-8

Obsession with his own mortality both produces and expresses Cleon's ravenous egotism: because his own self, and its transience, is so immediate and so urgent, no-one can be suffered, by 'speak[ing] in [his] place' to rob him of a passing minute or two of personal delight. No love is involved, or even possible, here.

Rudel to the Lady of Tripoli, as the bridge-poem between *Cleon* and *One Word More*, contains a movement away from Cleon's self-absorption, though not a complete one. Rudel is capable of love; indeed, his historical prototype reputedly died of love for the Lady of Tripoli. And his sense of the magnitude and inexpressibility of love leads him to reject his own professional skill, poetry, for its expression. In this he contrasts with Cleon, who repudiated poetry only on the grounds that it exacted too high a price from its practitioner. Recognising that love transcends mere human skill, Rudel sends a 'speech' rather than 'a poem' with the emblem he entrusts to the poem's addressee:

Go! – saying ever as thou dost proceed
That I, French Rudel, choose for my device
A sunflower outspread like a sacrifice
Before its idol. See! These inexpert
And hurried fingers could not fail to hurt
The woven picture; 'tis a woman's skill
Indeed; but nothing baffled me, so ill
Or well, the work is finished.

23-30

The significance of this change of medium is elucidated in *One Word More*, where Browning argues that every artist who 'lives and loves' (both words are important, and in effect interchangeable) wishes to express his love by:

> Using nature that's an art to others,
> Not, this one time, art that's turned his nature. . . .
> Does he paint? he fain would write a poem, –
> Does he write? he fain would paint a picture.
>
>   63–4, 67–8

In order to become visible as a 'man', the artist must separate himself from his art, which involves, as Rudel perceives, abandoning the skills he has acquired, and turning to an art in which he is – necessarily – 'inexpert'. The meaning of such art will be ironic, its failure in expertise indicating the writer's abandonment of a poetics of skilful expression. But Browning himself seems to be exempted from this requirement, since it is in a poem that his desire to escape from the art of poetry is expressed. Alone amongst his speakers, his change of medium involves passing between two varieties of the same medium. The reason for this privilege is that, unlike Rudel, he has used poetry as a means of resurrecting and transfiguring other people. Though more admirable than Cleon's self-absorption, Rudel's love was selfish to the extent that it sought self-portrayal, and limited, like that of the objective poet, by its exclusive devotion to one object. Browning's personal appearance in *One Word More* follows a collection from which his own identity was uniformly effaced. Cleon refused to allow anyone to 'speak in my place'; but we hear Cleon's voice because Browning has allowed Cleon to speak in *his* place. Because of his own awareness of the promise of the Resurrection, Browning can efface his own identity and dedicate himself, like Christ during his life, to the resuscitation of others' without threat to his own existence, secure in the confidence of an afterlife – Andrea's 'heaven' – to replace the lost moments. And not merely that: he has also turned Cleon's epistle and Rudel's 'speech' back into the 'poem' which Cleon repudiated and Rudel temporarily abjured, as Lippi, for instance, was allowed to turn static paintings into narrative poems in response to his willingness to supply their subjects with 'breath' from his own living body. Browning appears, therefore, after having established his credentials as a lover of his kind – and appears, moreover, to express the particular love he feels for his wife, as both complement and contrast to his general love of mankind. It complements his love for mankind by characterising his capacity for love not merely as philanthropic exertion, but genuine warmth of heart; it contrasts with his general love by appearing as a privileged and inexpressible extreme of love. Like Rudel, he cannot expound his feelings; but the act of dedication performed in *One Word More* shelters him from irony by allowing the love of 'my fifty men and women' to seem the natural outcome and even the indirect expression of the domestic love which, like the dark side of the moon, can never become externally visible. He thereby gains for himself the resurrection for which Cleon so desperately and self-defeatingly longed, and which only Karshish and Lippi of previous speakers came anywhere near envisaging. Within the collection as a whole, the speakers of 2*M&W* are put through an examination of their love or otherwise for their artistic subjects, as part of a larger examination of the nature of love as a divine and human attribute, which concludes when Browning turns himself into one of his own speakers and – perhaps not surprisingly – passes his own examination.

6

The Unity of *Dramatis Personae*

I DOUBT AND LOSS

Dramatis Personae deals with two distinct though related themes: death or loss in love-relations, and religious doubt. Browning's wife had died three years before the collection appeared, so his choice of the first of these topics is hardly a surprise. Death, whether of a woman (*Gold Hair, Too Late, Euridice to Orpheus, Prospice*), a man or men (*May and Death, A Death in the Desert, Apparent Failure*) is all-pervasive, and even poems which appear not involve it invoke its counterpart, the death-in-life to which existential failure consigns lovers who have failed to grasp their opportunity (*Dis Aliter Visum, Youth and Art, A Likeness*). Equally, it is unsurprising that *Dramatis Personae* should centre on religious doubt. Biblical criticism, widely interpreted as a deliberate attack on the foundations of the Christian faith, had concerned Browning at least since the publication, in 1846, of George Eliot's translation of David Strauss's *Das Leben Jesu*. And Ernest Renan's *Vie de Jésus*, published in 1863, evidently rekindled or heightened that interest. Browning expressed to Isa Blagden (*DI* 180) his objections to Renan's thesis that 'miracles were a cheat' and that the St John of history was not the author of the books ascribed to him in the Biblical canon, objections which he then creatively utilised in *Dramatis Personae* with his exploration of the psychology of Mr Sludge 'the Medium', faker of miracles, and in his revival of a St John who claims authorship of the whole Johannine corpus in *A Death in the Desert*. Renan himself figures as the second of three speakers in the *Epilogue* to *Dramatis Personae*, which is also the poem in which Browning most fully explores the nature and consequences of Renan's proclamation that man has progressively lost his perception of God, and thence his faith in God. The first speaker, speaking as the Old Testament David, stands too near the historical source of faith to have experienced such loss, and therefore finds God's identity unproblematically housed in the actual fabric of his 'Temple':

133

> For the presence of the Lord,
> In the glory of His cloud,
> Had filled the House of the Lord.
>
>   19–21

For the 'second speaker: as Renan', no such access to God remains possible, and he begins with a direct comment on 'David's' privilege:

> Gone now! All gone across the dark so far,
>   Sharpening fast, shuddering ever, shutting still,
> Dwindling into the distance, dies that star
> Which came, stood, opened once! We gazed our fill
> With upturned faces on as real a Face . . .
>
>   22–6

The third speaker (unnamed) reviews both his predecessors' arguments ('Friends, I have seen through your eyes: now use mine!'), only to substitute his own:

> Why, where's the need of Temple, when the walls
> O' the world are that? What use of swells and falls
> From Levites' choir, Priests' cries, and trumpet-calls?
>
> That one Face, far from vanish, rather grows,
> Or decomposes but to recompose,
> Become my universe that feels and knows.
>
>   96–101

Again, as in 2*M&W* we meet the image of the 'Face'. But in *Dramatis Personae* the image is not confined to the religious dimension of the collection, but also features in the parallel topic of erotic loss initiated in the first poem of *Dramatis Personae*, *James Lee's Wife*.

James Lee's Wife is a monodrama, a series of lyrics in which the eponymous speaker traces the course of her marriage from honeymoon rapture to despair and separation as a result of her husband's literal or metaphorical adultery. His infidelity is set against the 'face' which, in an ideal union, would have merged their separate identities into unity, as she bitterly tells him at the moment of her departure in the final lyric in the sequence, 'On Deck':

> Strange, if a face, when you thought of me,
> Rose like your own face present now,
> With eyes as dear in their due degree,
> Much such a mouth, and as bright a brow,
> Till you saw yourself, while you cried, "Tis She!'
>
>   25-9

Such an event would be 'strange' because by his conduct he has made it impossible, and committed himself to a mutability which is opposite to the eternity in which their ideal unity would have placed them. As in the *Epilogue* it is God's 'Face' which symbolises his unified essence as perceived by man, so in *James Lee's Wife* the speaker figures erotic unity as the lovers' evolving a single face; and this image extends through the rest of *Dramatis Personae* as a synecdoche for the entire identity, in a context in which that identity, human or divine, has been lost or become fragmented. The speaker in *Too Late* longs passionately for a face which exists only in his memory. St John's face can no longer be seen in the world. Euridice desires to actualise her memory of Orpheus' face in present-time, though such a repossession will forfeit it forever. The speaker of *A Likeness* cherishes a print which enshrines a face for which, perhaps, no actual original exists. These situations are analogues both for each other and for that in the *Epilogue*, where, however, the Face is God's. Though the image of the face was also important, as I have shown, in 2*M&W*, in *Dramatis Personae* its use is both more extensive and much more troubled in tone.

As well as stating the cardinal themes of the collection, these two poems – *James Lee's Wife* and *Epilogue* – also exemplify its general structure. It will already be evident from my discussion that both are 'compound works', and thus scale models of the structured collection principle. But they are different models. In the *Epilogue* the utterances of three different speakers form a dialectical sequence of thesis, antithesis and successful synthesis; in *James Lee's Wife*, although the lyrics are unified as the utterance of a single speaker, their organisation is episodic, leaving its issues unresolved and constantly threatening to fall apart. Browning remarked of *James Lee's Wife*: 'I have expressed it all insufficiently, and will break the chain up, one day, and leave so many separate little round rings to roll each its way, if it can' (To Julia Wedgwood 31 Dec. 1864: *LJW* 123). The form of the poem presents the complex of unity and multeity inherent in the structured collection form, where again separate poems, capable of being cut out for anthologies, establish a trembling sequential unity between themselves. The *Epilogue*, by contrast, implies that a dialectical order can protect unity, and keep the structured collection structured. Both statements are true, since a structure which has recessed its central government to the provinces is necessarily in an ambiguous condition. It is unified. But is its 'unity' imminent, actual, or departing? Does it even exist? These questions, as they are raised by the collection's form, reappear in its content as a pervasive doubt about the reality of God or lover, the lost guarantors of coherence.

II THE DIALECTIC: EARTH VS. HEAVEN

The poems of the first half of *Dramatis Personae* fall into two sharply distinguished groups:

A	B
1. James Lee's Wife	6. Abt Vogler
2. Gold Hair	7. Rabbi ben Ezra
3. The Worst of It	8. A Death in the Desert
4. Dis Aliter Visum	9. Caliban upon Setebos
5. Too Late	

Group A, beginning with *James Lee's Wife*, deals with the effect upon human beings of death and loss; Group B, beginning with *Abt Vogler* and ending with *Caliban upon Setebos*, analyses the possibility of a religious answer to death and loss. In *James Lee's Wife*, the woman loses her husband's love, as a result of which he loses her. In *The Worst of It* the speaker laments the loss of, again, an unfaithful spouse. In *Dis Aliter Visum* a woman reproaches the man who, ten years before, refused to make her his mistress. In *Too Late* the speaker rages against the woman he lost to another man. The obvious similarity between these stories is enhanced by the echoing of situational details: in *Dis Aliter Visum* and *Too Late* characters have 'married a dancer', three of the five poems are set in Pornic. The sequential relation between *James Lee's Wife* and *Gold Hair* is emphasised by continuity of versification: the stanza-form is identical and the a-rhyme of the final stanza of 'On Deck' ('me . . . tree . . . Lee') reappears as the b-rhyme of *Gold Hair's* first stanza ('sea . . . Brittany').

It is *Gold Hair*, the only poem not explicitly concerned with sexual ethics, which provides the most direct statement of the theme unifying the group. A young girl dies. In obedience to her deathbed plea that they should 'let my poor hair alone', her parents have her buried with her gold hair untouched; then 'All kissed her face, like a silver wedge / Mid the yellow wealth', mourning her as a saint. But Browning enmeshes the in a double irony. When her corpse is later unearthed, her hair, far from being as the girl claimed 'poor', provides 'wealth' in the quite literal form of the 'Louis-d'or, some six times five' which, it transpires, she had concealed in it during life. Her face, meanwhile, in contrast to the 'silver' to which it was compared, has rotted to a 'skull'. The juxtaposition emphasizes the absurdity of her childish wish to transport solid gold into the next life; but that wish, with its imputed absurdity, applies also to the general human addiction to material things. A similar debate between worldly and spiritual values pervades the other poems in this group. Each speaker, conscious of some failure or shortcoming in his or her search for happiness in the material world, invokes an idea of the spiritual world to counteract or qualify it. James Lee's wife contrasts the changeable 'earth' with an immortal stability 'above':

> If you loved only what were worth your love,
> Love were clear gain, and wholly well for you:
>   Make the low nature better by your throes!
>   Give earth yourself, go up for gain above!

240–3

The woman speaker of *Dis Aliter Visum*, by contrast, believes that a successful love-affair might have proved the reverse of the conventionally sinful, in its expression of an energy by comparison to which conventional values shrink to luxurious inertia:

> Was there nought better than to enjoy?
>   No feat which, done, would make time break,
> And let us pent-up creatures through
>   Into eternity, our due?

116–19

She thereby denies the claim of James Lee's wife that sexual experience represents 'mere earth'. In the event however no such fusion as she envisages took place, and in the following poem, *Too Late*, the rapport between the spiritual and the material is parodied by the speaker's perversion, at the end of the poem, of Holy Communion into sexual cannibalism:

> There you stand,
> Warm too, and white too: would this wine
> Had washed all over that body of yours,
> Ere I drank it, and you down with it, thus!

141–4

It is noteworthy that the synecdoche by which the face is made to stand for a person's total identity has been here replaced by an image of the whole body. The same holds for *Dis Aliter Visum*. Whereas the 'hero' of the latter poem had focussed his desire on the heroine's face – 'two *cheeks* freshened by youth and sea' – she, reviewing their failure ten years later, comments 'You loved, with *body* worn and weak', and concludes with an image which relates physical to spiritual wholeness:

> Let the mere star-fish in his vault
> Crawl in a wash of weed, indeed,
> Rose-jacynth to the finger-tips:
> He, *whole in body and soul*, outstrips
> Man, found with either in default.

136–40 (m.i.)

At the moment of imagined erotic union, the image of the face is replaced by that of the total from which it had been subtracted. But if that is the ideal, it is an ideal *in absentia*, for none of these liaisons actually happened. The secular approach to reunification fails in each of these poems.

The second group of speakers jointly propose the religious antithesis to the secular thesis. Rabbi ben Ezra and St John both repudiate the pursuit of pleasure: Ezra claims,

> Poor vaunt of life indeed,
> Were man but formed to feed
> On joy, to solely seek and find and feast[!]

19–21

St John argues that 'the soul learns diversely from the flesh' in that while the soul constantly progresses, the body remains fixed to its original enjoyments, and can therefore yield no more than 'basement for the soul's emprise.' The speakers of the first group, though capable of perceiving this distinction – 'An instinct had bidden the girl's hand grope / For gold, the true sort' – had all been reluctant to utilise it: ' "Gold in heaven, if you will; / But I keep earth's too, I hope" '. The solution is not, however, as these quotations might suggest, the 'asceticism' that E.B.B. reprimanded Browning for appearing to advocate in *Easter-Day*. Rather, Browning arranges the sequence of poems in group B in turn dialectically, to present religious experience itself as a complex negotiation between the human and the divine, the spiritual and the material spheres.

Through 'the musical instrument of his invention', Abt Vogler feels 'the finger of God, a flash of the will that can' and in that transcendent moment builds 'my rampired walls of gold as transparent as glass'. The moment passes. Yet, accepting its transience, Vogler invests the meaning of his life in such mystical epiphanies. By contrast, the speaker of the next poem, *Rabbi ben Ezra*, emphasises the *continuity* of physical existence and the importance of the *conduct* of life:

> Grow old along with me!
> The best is yet to be,
> The last of life, for which the first was made:
> Our times are in His hand
> Who saith 'A whole I planned,
> Youth shows but half; trust God: see all nor be afraid!'

1–6

In a letter to Julia Wedgwood of the year of *Dramatis Personae*'s publication Browning amplified this idea:

> You should *live*, step by step, *up* to the proper place where the pin-point of light is visible: nothing is to be overleaped, the joy no more than the sorrow, and then, your part done, God's may follow, and will, I trust.

to Julia Wedgwood 27 June 1864: *LJW* 36

Life progresses towards a conclusion – death – which is in turn an opening to further life. Pain and loss, therefore, bane of the group A speakers, invert from threats to blessings, we must

> *welcome* each rebuff
> That turns earth's smoothness rough,
> Each sting that bids nor sit nor stand but go!

31–3 (m.i.)

From the vantage-point of this ethical self-assurance, Ezra in effect
reviews and rejects the typical imagery, and with it the philosophy also, of
the group A speakers: the gold which signified 'original sin' in *Gold Hair*
becomes again a token of value:

> Youth ended, I shall try
> My gain or loss thereby;
> Leave the fire ashes, what survives is *gold* . . .

                                                              85–7

– and the communion wine which the speaker of *Too Late* blasphemously
imagined pouring over his mistress's body is restored to its religious
context:

> Look thou not down but up!
> To uses of a cup,
> The festal board, lamp's flash and trumpet's peal,
> The new wine's foaming flow,
> The Master's lips a-glow!
> Thou, heaven's consummate cup, what need'st thou with earth's
>   wheel?

                                                              175–80

– compare the ending of *Too Late* (quoted p. 000). The hard, bright
imagery and high-pitched tone in themselves contrast with the more
elegiac cadences in which previous speakers lamented their failures.

In *A Death in the Desert*, Browning's conflation of the three New
Testament figures called John enables him to synthesise the philosophies
of Vogler and Ezra. As St John the Gospeller, John has actually witnessed
the God in Christ, and this empirical certainty underwrites his Vogler-
like mystical experience as St John the Divine, author of *Revelation*. But
the *writing* of his Gospel and his Epistles derives from his competing
sense that, as Ezra contends, life must thereafter be lived through as
having its own separate value in interpreting revelation:

> '[I p]atient stated much of the Lord's life
> Forgotten or misdelivered, and let it work . . .
> Since much that at the first, in deed and word
> Lay simply and sufficiently exposed,

Had grown (or else my soul was grown to match . . .)
Of new significance and fresh result;
What first were guessed as points, I now knew stars,
And named them in the Gospel I have writ.[']

166-7, 168-70, 173-5

In the process, his life takes on the evolutionary character of Rabbi ben Ezra's, and John even adopts the latter's image of old age, echoing Ezra's 'Leave the fire ashes, what survives is gold' (*Ezra* 87) in his description of himself as 'A stick, once fire from end to end; / Now, ashes save the tip that holds a spark!' (*Death* 105–6).

At the same time, John extends this idea to cover history as well as the individual life. By a bold device, Browning has him imagine how a Strauss or a Renan will eventually doubt his, John's, very existence: ' "Was John at all, and did he say he saw?" ' In response, John argues that moral progress is only possible if the Incarnation of God in Christ becomes historically remote, leaving man to reincarnate it from his own nature. As a result, the apparent spiritual exhaustion of a century which questions Christ's very existence becomes, like John' own 'decrepitude', a means of enhancing spiritual insight by basing it upon deduction rather than revelation. The entropy time imposes upon revelation, whether locally in the personal life or globally in history, is thereby made redemptive in itself, and time becomes the axis which connects spiritual to worldly life and thus reconciles their dialectical opposition. Browning reinforces the point through the double chronology by which the three poems' philosophical advance from vision (Vogler) through existence (Ezra) to illuminated death (John), is historically reversed in the simultaneous retrogression from a seventeenth-century composer through a tenth-century Jewish teacher to an Apostle of Christ. Movement along the axis of individual life is countered by movement towards the historical source of revelation, abolishing the linearity of the group by suggesting a continuous access to its spiritual centre.

Caliban too, in *Caliban upon Setebos*, seeks a religious explanation of existence, and the reference to 'natural theology' in the poem's subtitle (*Natural Theology in the Islands*) informs the reader that he will do this by proposing an analogy between God's nature and his own – the ultimate effort, in one direction, to unite the secular and the eternal. But Caliban's is not the Christian analogy. For, reasons Caliban, since Caliban is capriciously cruel, so must God be. Since Caliban is capriciously benign, so must God be. Caliban's 'Setebos', a vindictive and irrational tyrant utterly bankrupt of moral authority, is a mocking antitype of the Christ whom Strauss, as paraphrased by St John in the preceding poem, saw as the mirror of man's nature:

> . . . we acknowledge Christ –
> A proof we comprehend His love, a proof
> We had such love already in ourselves[. . . .]
> 'Tis mere projection from man's inmost mind[.]

379–81, 383

A God thus projected must logically mirror *all* of man's 'inmost mind', and Setebos mirrors the evil and ferocious impulses laundered out of Strauss's 'Myth of Christ'. Browning's purpose is not merely parody, however, and his St John explains the moral obligation to empathise with even the savage mind:

> 'if a babe were born inside this grot,
> Grew to a boy here, heard us praise the sun,
> Yet had but yon sole glimmer in light's place –
> One loving him and wishful he should learn,
> Would much rejoice himself was blinded first
> Month by month here, so made to understand
> How eyes, born darkling, apprehend amiss[.']

340–6

Caliban in turn has

> a sea-beast, lumpish, which he snared,
> *Blinded* the eyes of, and brought somewhat tame,
> And split its toe-webs, and now pens the drudge
> In a *hole* o' the rock and calls him Caliban[.]

163–6 (m.i.)

But whereas John believes he 'could explain to such a child / There was more glow outside than the gleams he caught', Caliban's sea-beast remains 'a bitter heart that bides his time and bites' (though even such negative empathy has its moral significance in relation to the enslaved state in which, after all, Prospero keeps Caliban).

Caliban upon Setebos stands to the preceding trio of speakers as the concluding satyr-play to the trilogy of Greek tragedy. This analogy is encouraged by St. John's reference to the lost satyr-play which concluded Aeschylus' *Prometheia*, whose satyrs, confronted with the fire which Prometheus gave mankind, 'touched it in gay wonder at the thing' (286). But though parodic, Caliban's gargoyle theology contains within it all the elements with which a more sophisticated theology such as John's or Ezra's or Vogler's must come to terms, and within Browning's mythology of history Caliban presages man's passage from mere animal performance to moral existence. Again, St John establishes the point in what is clearly an anticipation of *Caliban*: ' "Before the point was mooted 'What is God?' / No savage man inquired 'What am myself?' " ' (549–50). Caliban's tendency to refer to himself in the third person, and without a personal pronoun ("Thinketh . . .') illustrates his primitive inability to inquire 'What am myself?', countered by the need, grammatical as much as ontological, to differentiate himself from Setebos's 'He' by the use of 'I', a pronoun which in effect *comes into existence* in the course of the poem as the nativity of that self-consciousness which, for Browning, as for earlier Romantic philosophers, distinguishes man from the animal creation. An idea of God, even of a gargoyle God, again represents the incentive and medium of human development: in that sense, *Caliban* confirms as much as it parodies the theologies it succeeds.

III THE SYNTHESIS: HEAVEN ON EARTH

The second half of *Dramatis Personae* represents the synthesis, so far as one is practicable, of the preceding material–spiritual dialectic. It consists of the following poems:

C
1. Confessions
2. May and Death
3. Deaf and Dumb*
4. Prospice
5. Euridice to Orpheus*
6. Youth and Art
7. A Face
8. A Likeness
9. Mr Sludge 'the Medium'

10. Apparent Failure
11. Epilogue
[* = poem added in second edition]

In this section, the loss, pain and failure which beset the Group A speakers reappear, but no longer to be faced by an austere injunction to live a better life. The tone has changed.

> What is he buzzing in my ears?
>   'Now that I come to die,
> Do I view this world as a vale of tears?'
>   Ah, reverend sir, not I!

Confessions 1–4

Like St John in *A Death in the Desert*, this speaker is on his death-bed; like the speakers of group A he mourns a past relationship, in his case a love-affair with a housemaid who

> stood by the rose-wreathed gate. Alas,
>   We loved, sir – used to meet:
> How sad and mad and bad it was –
>   But then, how it was sweet!

33–6

Into the word 'alas' he compresses both the poignant brevity of his idyll and a mock-penitence over its conventional disreputability in the eyes of the priest, his interlocutor. But the priest is wrong, and his question about death-bed repentance is delicately satirised by the playfulness with which the speaker translates the décor of his bedroom into the scenery of his amour:

> That lane sloped, much as the bottles do,
>   From a house you could descry
> O'er the garden-wall: is the curtain blue
>   Or green to a healthy eye?
>
> To mine, it serves for the old June weather
>   Blue above lane and wall;
> And that farthest bottle labelled 'Ether'
>   Is the house o'er-topping all.

9–16

Throughout this group of poems, a strange jauntiness of tone tinges the recital of the heavy losses of life. *Youth and Art*, for instance, in describing a situation – two people's failure to have a love-affair – almost identical to that which for the speaker of *Dis Aliter Visum* warranted pain and rage and bitterness, reduces it to affectionate banter:

> Your trade was with sticks and clay,
> You thumbed, thrust, patted and polished,
> Then laughed 'They will see some day
> Smith made, and Gibson demolished.'
>
> My business was song, song, song;
> I chirped, cheeped, trilled and twittered,
> 'Kate Brown's on the boards ere long,
> And Grisi's existence embittered!'

> 5–12

The subversive Bohemianism of the couple's life is endorsed by the running metaphor of sparrows, lusty and joyful; yet their failure to respond by 'pairing' is reprimanded only gently:

> Each life unfulfilled, you see;
> It hangs still, patchy and scrappy:
> We have not sighed deep, laughed free,
> Starved, feasted, despaired, – been happy.

> 61–4

There is a delicate syntactic doubling in the last phrase, whereby 'been happy' is both the expected antonym of 'despaired', completing the sequence of antithetical pairs, and a synthesis of all the antitheses. This reflects the value their love-affair would have held through all its environment of social/religious disapproval, and crystallises the effort, in this group of poems, to squeeze secular bliss out of the rigid dialectic of the first half of the collection. Such an attempt cannot afford to be harsh even upon the failure to bring about the love-affair it requires, and the poem expresses none of the hysteria of *Dis Aliter Visum* or *Too Late*. Similarly, the death of the speaker's friend 'Charles', in *May and Death*, is not allowed to interrupt others' pleasures:

There must be many a pair of friends
Who, arm in arm, deserve the warm
Moon-births and the long evening-ends.

So, for their sake, be May still May!
Let their new time, as mine of old,
Do all it did for me: I bid
Sweet sights and sounds throng manifold.

6–12

And in *A Likeness*, an incongruous vivacity contradicts the painfulness of the speaker's longing for a 'face' which he has lost, or never known, and possesses only in the form of a print to show visitors:

After we've turned over twenty,
And the debt of wonder my crony owes
Is paid to my Marc Antonios,
He stops me – '*Festina lente!*
What's that sweet thing there, the etching?'
How my waistcoat-strings want stretching,
How my cheeks grow red as tomatoes,
How my heart leaps! But hearts, after leaps, ache.

52–9

The note of loss, poignantly captured in precisely the most ludicrous rhyme in the poem ('leaps, ache' / 'keepsake'), coexists with the speaker's hunger to renew his passion by this kind of clandestine disclosure of its 'sweet face' and thus acquires, perversely, some sort of positive value. Similarly the speaker of *Mr Sludge 'the Medium'*, having been caught cheating and thrashed, treats the situation with rollicking bravado:

Fol-lol-the-rido-liddle-iddle-ol . . .
So, off we push, illy-oh-ho, trim the boat,
On we sweep with a cataract ahead,
We're midway to the Horseshoe: stop, who can,
The dance of bubbles gap about our prow!

83, 284–7

This gaity, perverse as it seems, reflects a situation in which the dialectic of the first half has been *reduced*: time and eternity are no longer antithetical, and in *Prospice* they even merge into one at the imagined moment of death:

> For sudden the worst turns the best to the brave,
>   The black minute's at end,
> And the elements' rage, the fiend-voices that rave,
>   Shall dwindle, shall blend,
> Shall change, shall become first a peace out of pain,
>   Then a light, then thy breast,
> O thou soul of my soul! I shall clasp thee again,
>   And with God be the rest!

                                                            21–8

Futurity – here the after-life – doubles back to comprise life-moments whose very transience originally enhanced their value: a context in which Euridice's loss of Orpheus ceases to be tragic:

> Hold me but safe again within the bond
>   Of one immortal look! All woe that was,
> Forgotten, and all terror that may be,
> Defied, – no past is mine, no future: look at me!

                                                            5–8

Here the 'midst' of life, characterised as passion and sheared away from the destructively antithetical 'past' and 'future' of diurnal time, becomes 'immortal' precisely through its courage to defy time by voluntarily reducing itself to the single moment in which the lovers' 'look' will be permitted to endure.

The relation of life to eternity receives its lengthiest and most complex treatment in *Mr Sludge 'the Medium'*. Sludge realises the destructive power of yet another antithesis, that between youth and age, to reduce life to meaninglessness:

>   Young, you've force
> Wasted like well-streams: old, – oh, then indeed,
> Behold a labyrinth of hydraulic pipes
> Through which you'd play off wondrous waterwork;

Only, no water's left to feed their play.
Young, – you've a hope, an aim, a love: it's tossed
And crossed and lost: you struggle on, some spark
Shut in your heart against the puffs around,
Through cold and pain; these in due time subside,
Now then for age's triumph, the hoarded light
You mean to loose on the altered face of things, –
Up with it on the tripod! It's extinct.

							1367–78

The vision here is so reductive as to contradict St John's belief that at
death a 'spark' survives, and Prospice's insistence that 'pain, darkness
and cold' could give way to a renewal of youth's joy. But Sludge's
profession, as a 'medium', allows him to transform this drab 'world':

I cheat, and what's the happy consequence? . . .
You're supplemented, made a whole at last,
Bacon advises, Shakespeare writes you songs,
And Mary Queen of Scots embraces you. . . .
Why, here's the Golden Age, old Paradise
Or new Eutopia! Here's true life indeed,
And the world well won now, mine for the first time!

						1398, 1407–9, 1431–3

Sludge reports to his clients that the next world is identical in content to
this one, thus erasing the antithesis between time and eternity, along with
subsidiary antitheses between spirit and flesh, and conventional right and
wrong (sex, for example, seems to be freely available in Sludge's heaven).
The *Epilogue* confirms that such an effort cannot be dismissed as merely
specious. Here, eternity, in a complementary gesture, is interpolated into
the time it sponsors and redeems:

That one Face, far from vanish, rather grows,
Or decomposes but to recompose,
Become my universe that sees and knows.

							99–101

As in *Karshish,* but now with more radical explicitness, God becomes part of – or simply becomes – the material universe, making himself subject, by a remarkable paradox, to the time which he himself created, and to the *mutability* which in Platonic/Christian theologies is the logical obverse of his eternal substance. This formulation represents the climax of a constant erosion of the conventional theological conception of mutability. In *Dramatis Personae* change itself, traditionally the enemy of man and the thief of his mortal substance, becomes a constitutive feature of being and a ground of redemption.

IV MUTABILITY AND ETERNITY

For Shelley, as for Plato, 'time and space and number', the domain of 'Life' (and death) were a nightmare from which man is trying to wake up, and for him as much as for Plato it was in a transcendent world beyond the corruptions of matter, 'the Infinite, the Eternal, and the One', that redemption was to be found. Such a position is not unusual. The antithesis between mutablity and eternity, the ideal and the real, especially in its Christian form, has been fundamental to Western thought since Plato. But Shelley's contemporaries, in particular Wordsworth, Byron and Keats, made less absolute distinctions, and in the process eroded the antithetical habits of thought fostered by the terms themselves. For Byron, mutability, symbolised by sexual infidelity, could take on positive value:

> that which
> Men call inconstancy is nothing more
> Than admiration due where nature's rich
> Profusion with young beauty covers o'er
> Some favour'd object[.]

Don Juan ii 1681–5

Such a statement, ratified as it is by the fluency of Don Juan's changes of partner, amounts to a glorification of the very transience which was traditionally lamented – in, for example, Shakespeare's sonnets – as the enemy of mortal 'beauty'. Behind Byron's position lies Goethe's version of Faust's pact with the devil. Faust undertook to surrender his soul to Mephistophiles when and only when he was heard asking to *stand still*, and cease to move continually onwards through fresh encounters with experience. Like Byron, Goethe illustrates the consequences of such a philosophy in the form of sexual promiscuity: so does Browning, in his

own Don Juan in *Fifine at the Fair*, and in the unspeaking James Lee in
James Lee's Wife. Promiscuity, Browning's Juan argues, is not a moral
evil; rather, it represents *experiential receptivity*, essential to life and true
knowledge. In section vi of *James Lee's Wife*, the woman, in response to
her husband's pragmatic adoption of the same philosophy, attempts a
similar recognition:

> Then, when the wind begins among the vines,
>   So low, so low, what shall it say but this?
> 'Here is the change beginning, here the lines
>   Circumscribe beauty, set to bliss
> The limit time assigns.'
>
> Why this is the old woe o' the world;
>   Tune, to whose rise and fall we live and die.
> Rise with it, then! Rejoice that man is hurled
>   From change to change unceasingly,
>   His soul's wing never furled!
>
>   207–11, 217–21

With unexpected daring, she theologises change itself – here change as
mutability in time – as a potential value. Her rejection of this gesture later
in the poem is a consequence of her location in the group A sequence
rather than a criticism of the idea itself.

Other poems, mainly those in group C, similarly set out to transvalue
change in *space*. The most obvious example is *Deaf and Dumb*, which uses
Browning's favourite image of multitudinousness;

> Only the prism's obstruction shows aright
> The secret of a sunbeam, breaks its light
> Into the jewelled bow from blankest white,
>   So may a glory from defect arise . . .
>
>   1–4

The Simplon Pass episode from Wordsworth's *Prelude* provides a
Romantic prototype of this argument:

>   The immeasurable height
> Of woods decaying, never to be decayed,

The stationary blasts of waterfalls,
And in the narrow rent, at every turn
5   Winds thwarting winds bewildered and forlorn,
The torrents shooting from the clear blue sky,
The rocks that muttered close upon our ears,
Black drizzling crags that spake by the wayside
As if a voice were in them, the sick sight
10   And giddy prospect of the raving stream,
The unfettered clouds and region of the heavens,
Tumult and peace, the darkness and the light –
Were all like workings of one mind, the features
Of the same face, blossoms upon one tree,
15   Characters of the great Apocalypse,
The types and symbols of Eternity,
Of first, and last, and midst, and without end.

'The Simplon Pass' 4–20; also *The Prelude* vi 623–40

In each case, the diversity of life, a diversity comprising all that is
conventionally 'defective' or 'sick' as well as the beautiful and delightful,
is said to be precisely the manifestation – possibly the only proper
manifestation – of a unitary God whose 'face' both is and underlies
material variety. The marked similarity between Wordsworth's image of
God's 'face', and Browning's in the *Epilogue* to *Dramatis Personae*,
suggests a direct debt. A similar proposition is advanced by Hopkins's
shift, in *Pied Beauty*, from 'Glory be to God for *dappled* things' to 'He
fathers-forth whose beauty is *past change*' (m.i.). And in *Spelt from Sybil's
Leaves* Hopkins directly admonishes the power of antithesis to slur the
delicate gradations of 'skeined stained veined variety':

Let life, waned, ah let life wind
Off her once skeined stained veined variety upon, all on two
spools; part, pen, pack
Now her all in two flocks, two folds – black, white; right,
wrong; reckon but, reck but, mind
But these two; ware of a world where but these two tell, each
off the other; of a rack
Where, selfwrung, selfstrung, sheathe- and shelterless,
thoughts against thoughts in groans grind.

10–14

The fact that 'ware' can mean 'aware' as well as 'beware' and 'commodity' indicates, however, Hopkins's necessary ambivalence, as a Jesuit, towards the proposition that the infinite variety of life and of the world could have a value independent of and superior to its stony division into 'right' and 'wrong' – an ambivalence less apparent in the more purely Romantic Wordsworth and Browning. Yet even for them there is ambivalence. It is hardly necessary to emphasise the dread and terror which accompany the ecstasy of the Simplon Pass, yet the systematic disruption of the discourse – note the increasing impossibility of composing a coherent perspective out of the visual snapshots – works to subvert the final proposition of unity in a way which takes terror beyond the conventional frisson of the Sublime, or of religious awe. The experience is that of a *scattering* which is reversed by an asserted – but at the same time an unconvincing – integration. The assertion is unconvincing because it is introduced as a *simile* – 'were all *like* workings of one mind' – when the proposition made – that God is immanent in all things – is such as to require the authority of an unequivocal statement. Indeed metaphor itself is an inappropriate mode to the extent that it involves a contrast between the material dissimilarity of the things compared, and their conceptual kinship; the real-ideal antithesis reappears in the moment of its denial. The shift from natural 'blossoms' to a language of language – 'characters . . . types and symbols' confirms that the asserted unity is purely linguistic, altogether less ontologically assured than rhetorically vehement: the very need to affirm unity becomes an anxiety in the presence of such recalcitrant material. Similarly, while James Lee's wife may 'rejoice that man is hurled / From change to change', it remains nevertheless 'bitter', in her mind, that he cannot 'grave / On his soul's hands' palms one fair good wise thing / Just as he grasped it'. And the portrait of God in he *Epilogue* almost collapses – inevitably and polemically *does* collapse – under the ontological paradox it evokes. For *how* can 'that one face' – the unitary (and unseen) 'face' of an eternal God – so enter time as to 'grow' and 'decompose' like a mutable being, yet remain the unmoved mover, the original cause of a creation which simultaneously creates *him*?

The commitment to mutability undermines both the origin of experience, epitomised in God, and stability within experience, epitomised in the perpetuation of love, and is thus antithetical to the two major yearnings represented in *Dramatis Personae*. In poem 7 of group C, *A Face*, these yearnings confront mutability in a context which involves also the question of the status of art itself generally, and the art of *Dramatis Personae* in particular, within a theology of mutability.

Browning imagines how the beauty of a young woman might find representation in Corregio's heaven:

> I know, Correggio loves to mass, in rifts
> Of heaven, his angel faces, orb on orb
> Breaking its outline, burning shapes absorb:
> But these are only massed there, I should think,
>   Waiting to see some wonder momently
>   Grow out, stand full, fade slow against the sky
>   (That's the pale ground you'd see this sweet face by),
>   All heaven, meanwhile, condensed into one eye
> Which fears to lose the wonder, should it wink.

14–22

The stasis of eternity becomes the anticipation of an event which is in effect the introduction of time into it. The young woman's face does not passively take up its niche in heaven, but 'grows' and 'fades' there, in token of the mutability which is inseparable from its beauty; simultaneously, she displaces God from the centre of the picture both spatially (she is what the angels will look at) and in time (her appearance is what they await: the very idea of waiting redefines eternity as diuturnity). Her beauty even takes responsibility for the divine unity, and 'condenses' heaven 'into one eye'; yet the final line re-emphasises the transience of that beauty, and the helplessness of God himself to detain it. Time thus controls God in the double sense that he admires its products but cannot arrest its course, and the metaphor that reduces him to a sentimental bachelor expresses both the triumph of mutability and the exorbitant cost of that triumph in the loss of an idea of God as origin and manager of the course of time. Simultaneously, the idea of art as having an immortality equivalent to God's is discredited. Corregio's art is both anachronistic to its putative subject, and unable to represent its mobility. Art, in its claim to manufacture an eternal image, is put in question by the same gesture which on the theological level challenges the authority of the concept of eternity.

The two gestures – glorification of mutability and deprecation of art – are also linked in Byron's work. In Canto xvi of *Don Juan*, Juan inspects a picture-gallery:

> And the pale smile of Beauties in the grave,
>   The charms of other days, in starlight
>   gleams

> Glimmer on high: their buried locks still wave
>   Along the canvas; their eyes glance like dreams
> 5   On ours, on spars within some dusky cave,
>   But death is imaged in their shadowy beams.
>   A picture is the past; even ere its frame
>   Be gilt, who sate hath ceased to be the same.

Don Juan xvi 145–52

The first five lines outline the standard conception that art makes a monument which keeps life alive for future ages. In 1.6, however, this process is reinterpreted: inasmuch as we know that the subject of a portrait is dead, the portrait is a *memento mori*, and its evocation of life a mocking and substanceless delusion, as words like 'pale', 'glimmer', 'dreams' had previously hinted. The final couplet takes the revaluation further. A picture is not merely a *memento mori*, but itself a death-in-life or premature burial for its living subject. Its immobility fossilises a moment of time from which that subject has already departed; the phrase 'buried locks' in 1.3 compares this process to one of burial, the picture itself to a tomb, and the Horatian monument to an epitaph, shockingly composed *during life* and thus in effect a death-sentence. Hence the representational puzzle of *A Face*: because she is living in time, its subject has to be absent from the picture.

Of course, painting is not the same as poetry, and Browning, like Byron, frequently contrasts the two in terms of the rigidity of one versus the mobility of the other. But such contrasts are finally unreal. In the central section of *James Lee's Wife* – perhaps the one which gave rise to the composition of the whole poem – the speaker reads one of Browning's own early poems, *Still Ailing, Wind?*, and condemns it on the grounds that its writer evokes various instances of 'failure and mistake, / Relinquishment, disgrace' only to make them, as James Lee's wife puts it, 'examples for his sake', callously separating himself from their living substance:

> Oh, he know what defeat means, and the rest!
>   Himself the undefeated that shall be:
>   Failure, disgrace, he flings them you to test, –
>   His triumph, in eternity
>   Too plainly manifest!

192–6

Again 'eternity' is linked with the idea of art in joint antithesis to the actual pains of life, and the point is repeated when James Lee's wife imagines herself in turn a poetic subject:

> And 'tis all an old story, and my despair
> Fit subject for some new song:
> 'How the light, light love he has wings to fly
> At suspicion of a bond:
> My wisdom has bidden your pleasure good-bye,
> Which will turn up next in a laughing eye,
> And why should you look beyond?'

177–21

Of course, her 'despair' is indeed Browning's 'subject', and the resulting sense that the text is a trap or web is enhanced by the fact that this 'new song' is actually a close paraphrase of a Pope couplet ('Love, free as air, at sight of human ties, / Spreads his light wings, and in a moment flies' [*Eloisa to Abelard* 75–6]). This double movement of her living 'despair' forward into the text of *James Lee's Wife* and backwards into its predecessor texts marks the literary, and perhaps writing itself, as an autonomous mode, self-generated and insensitive to actual life. This point is repeated in two other poems in group A, *Dis Aliter Visum* and *Too Late*, both of which include a poet among their protagonists. In the first, the woman's timid poet-lover is tempted by the attractions of simple life in the form of 'love, found, gained and kept', only to turn them down:

> ' "What? All I am, was, and might be,
> All books taught, art brought, life's whole strife,
> Painful results since precious, just
>
> Were fitly exchanged, in wise disgust,
> For two cheeks freshened by youth and sea?
>
> ' "All for a nosegay!" '

91–6

For the woman, such Arnoldian asceticism represents a thin-blooded indifference to the delights of life, as is even more radically argued in *Too Late* by the speaker's contrast between his own way of mourning his dead mistress and that of her poet/husband: 'See, I bleed these tears in the dark / Till comfort come and the last be bled: / He? He is tagging your epitaph' (94–6). Art for these speakers is the enemy of life, an epitaph or memorial masquerading as a monument. Others, however, are tempted by its permanence into including it in, and as, the ritual of mourning in which they are engaged. The speaker of *A Face*, as I have shown, does wish, however improbably, 'to have that little head of hers / Painted'; the speaker of *A Likeness* keeps his print 'Because it has more than a hint / Of a certain face'. *Deaf and Dumb* and *Euridice to Orpheus*, actually composed as epigraphs for a sculpture and a painting respectively, represent the monumental urge in another form. Yet both the latter poems contain, as we have seen, a glorification of mutability. They thus, in a sense, contradict the stationary artefacts they 'describe', renounce their own immortality as text, and require of Browning's art in *Dramatis Personae* that it evolve a mutable form.

But if it is the physical permanence of art which gives it its memorial character, how can art become a celebration of mutability in any principled sense? *Abt Vogler* gives a visionary answer to this question. In the most literal way possible, this poem is concerned with the equation between art, monumentation, and eternity: Vogler's music becomes an actual portrait of heaven, figured as the construction of the 'rampired walls of gold as transparent as glass' of 'the beautiful building of mine' – the New Jerusalem of *Revelation*, no less. And Vogler is tempted to wish that 'it might tarry', like Solomon's temple, only to allow his nostalgia for permanence to be absorbed into the energy of his vision, in which 'emulous heaven yearned down, made effort to reach the earth, / As the earth had done her best, in my passion, to scale the sky' (27–8).But this fusion of earth and heaven, temporality and eternity is accomplished, not by an art which monumentalises, but by an art – musical improvisation – which embraces transience:

> All through my keys that gave their sounds to a wish of my
>   soul,
> All through my soul that praised as its wish flowed visibly
>   forth,
> All through music and me! For think, had I painted the whole,
>   Why, there it had stood, to see, nor the process so wonder-
>   worth;
> Had I written the same, made verse – still, effect proceeds
>   from cause,
> Ye know why the forms are fair, ye hear how the tale is
>   told;

It is all triumphant art, but art in obedience to laws,
  Painter and poet are proud in the artist-list enrolled: –
But here is the finger of God, a flash of the will that can,
  Existent behind all laws, that made them and, lo, they are!

                                                    43–50

The arts of painter and poet are arts in the conventional sense, seeking a
permanence which enables them to stand to be seen; Vogler's musical
improvisation, as the momentary confluence of 'music and me' will never
like them form a separate or recoverable structure. But that is its saving
virtue. Mutability, conventionally that which art strives to overcome, is
incorporated into art as the condition of its perfection. In extempore
composition, conception and execution are blended and inseparable,
bringing it as close as humanly possible to the simultaneity of divine
creation, in contrast to artefacts whose very immobility invites an analysis
which divides product from producer and process, separating the
monument from its origin in experience.

But it embraces transience in order to apprehend eternity. Browning's
art, in *Dramatis Personae*, is an attempt to combine the antithetical
positions of Byron and Shelley. He rejects Shelley's claim that poetry
both reflects and is itself an eternal substance, and commits his poetry to
the world of mutability; but even as he does so, he refocusses eternity –
momentarily – in the flawed lens. To do this, he has to reconsider the
status of both 'reality' as that which the poem represents, and the
materials of poetry itself, language and structure. The result is a continual
questioning of the nature of representation. The poem as memorial is
discovered to have nothing concrete to memorialise, but simultaneously
no transcendent ideal to represent.

V MEANING VS. MEANINGLESSNESS: FORMLESSNESS
VS. FORM

Dramatis Personae develops a whole series of stylistic devices to
emphasise the motif of impenetrability, whether of things by ideas or of
words by meanings. The connections which normally join together a
written or spoken discourse are dissolved, and the resulting blocks of
unclassified information swollen and multiplied by unnecessary
repetition or paraphrase. In the passage from *A Likeness* quoted above,
the clusters of synonyms ('a print, an etching, a mezzotint . . . a study, a

fancy, a fiction') gesture towards a precision which their redundancy simultaneously obscures. There is a pervasive sense of omitted connection, or connection incorrectly specified:

> 'What a shade beneath her nose!
> Snuff-taking, I suppose, – '
> Adds the cousin, while John's corn ail.

8–10

Here the grammatical connective 'while' provides a purely temporal ordering of events which cry out for a causal linkage: even if its function is that of an adversative conjunction (Boycott bats, while Trueman bowls), still no explanation of the opposition is forthcoming. The effect is one of combined superfluity in spatio-temporal description – 'and' would be sufficient, 'while' gives too much information – and of poverty at the level of explanation – 'so' would at least hint at the real connection, 'while' gives too little information. The fact that the reader's inference of the link – John is hurt and upset by the abuse of his picture – leads to reinterpretation of the meaning of 'his corns' (his wife has 'trodden on his corns', as we say), and adds another sense in which the physical metonymically replaces and trivialises the spiritual or psychic.

Browning's style had always tended towards the abrupt and jerky, but in *Dramatis Personae* this characteristic reaches an extreme:

> But the priest bethought him: 'Milk that's spilt!
> You know the adage! Watch and pray!
> Saints tumble to earth with so slight a tilt!
> It would buld a new altar; that we may!

Gold Hair 131–4

> You judged the porch
> We left by, Norman; took our look
> At sea and sky; wondered so few
> Find out the place for air and view;
> Remarked the sun began to scorch . . .

Dis Aliter Visum 101–5

In the first example, the priest means that the money concealed in the dead girl's hair can be appropriated and put to use by the church. But he carefully conceals this slightly macabre proposal behind a profusion of apparently random clichés whose effect is to render the crucial 'It' (i.e. the money) superficially uninterpretable. The example from *Dis Aliter Visum* involves the equally extreme device of omitting the pronoun before 'took our look' to reinforce the sense of absent connections (the previous subject being 'You', a first-person pronoun is technically obligatory).

The effect of these techniques is to turn poems into *lists* by substituting enumeration for progression. Browning had occasionally included lists in poems before – *The Englishman in Italy* (1846), for example, is in effect a versified catalogue – but in *Dramatis Personae* this device gains at once an extraordinary prominence and a new aggressive baldness:

> the portrait's queen of the place,
> Alone 'mid the other spoils
> Of youth, – masks, gloves and foils,
> And pipe-sticks, rose, cherry-tree, jasmine,
>   And the long whip, the tandem-lasher,
> And the cast from a fist ('not, alas! mine,
>   But my master's, the Tipton Slasher'),
> And the cards where pistol-balls mark ace,
>   And a satin shoe used for a cigar-case,
> And the chamois-horns ('shot in the Chablais')
>   And prints – Rarey drumming on Cruiser,
>   And Sayers, our champion, the bruiser,
> And the little edition of Rabelais:
> Where a friend, with both hands in his pockets,
> May saunter up close to examine it . . .

A Likeness 12–26

The paradox that the portait is '*alone* mid the *other* spoils' is aggravated by its disappearance into the subsequent list and consummated by the locative '*where* a friend . . .', which provokes the response that we have been denied any chance of determining where – and in a sense, what – the portrait is. The insistent polysyndeton ('And . . . And . . . And') generates a nightmare sense of oppression by its refusal to specify any relation beyond a perspectiveless co-presence for the objects it links and divides.

Similarly, Mr Sludge vitiates his proposed defence of a juvenile thief by a self-defeating plenitude of excuses:

'He picked it up,
His cousin died and left it him by will,
The President flung it to him, riding by,
An actress trucked it for a curl of his hair,
He dreamed of luck and found his shoe enriched,
He dug up clay and out of clay made gold' –

109–14

and later, dissipates his vision of human heroism into increasingly farcical
particulars:

Are all men born to play Bach's fiddle-fugues,
'Time' with the foil in carte, jump their own height,
Cut the mutton with the broadsword, skate a five,
Make the red hazard with the cue, clip nails
While swimming, in five minutes row a mile,
Pull themselves up three feet by the left arm,
Do sums of fifty figures in their head,
And so on, by the score of instances?

1224–31

In their larger structures, the poems of *Dramatis Personae* present a
similar fragmentedness. The speaker of *A Likeness* begins by positing two
distinct scenes involving 'portraits', and on arrival at his own case,
distinguishes it from both by insisting that it is a print rather than a
portrait that *he* owns ('*Some* people hang *portraits* up. . . . All that *I* own is
a *print*'). Caliban's argument is constructed as a disparate series of
analogies separated by the formulaic 'So He', St John's as a series of
answers to progressssively more sceptical interlocutors: the matching
discontinuity of his model of existence as insular phases of revelation and
doubt enhances the disruption. Similarly, Mr Sludge, in *Mr Sludge 'the
Medium'* puts not one but three cases in defending himself from the
charge of fraud: (a) that he did cheat, but was forced into it by poverty, (b)
that he didn't cheat, because 'there was something in it, after all', and (c)
that 'I cheat in self-defence, / And that's my answer to a world of cheats!'
The sense of fragmentation necessarily becomes extreme in a case where
the separate elements actually contradict each other, frustrating our
attempt to derive a cumulative logic.

Browning backs up these discontinuities of sense by other kinds of structural disruption. Both *A Death in the Desert* and *Caliban upon Setebos*, for instance, open and conclude with passages wrapped up in square brackets, and *A Death* interpolates another square-bracketed passage near the start of St John's monologue. Browning had never used square brackets before *Dramatis Personae*. In both poems, the effect is, obviously enough, to slice the discourse into pieces; it also emphasises the status of the poems as physical documents, since square brackets, unlike round ones, which represent a particular parenthetical intonation, are purely typographical signs interpolating editorial glosses. The effect is made odder, in *Caliban*, by the fact that the introductory and concluding passages are spoken in Caliban's characteristic idiom; here, editorial intervention fragments the internally unbroken utterance of a speaker into ranked 'levels'.

On the level of versification, the collection is dominated by the use of what I will call Byronic rhyme, in which I include both the kind of grotesque end-rhyming which Browning inherited from Byron and used throughout his career, and *internal* rhyme, rare in his previous work but absolutely pervasive in *Dramatis Personae*. As Jakobson and others have pointed out, the function of rhyme is traditionally to join either similar or opposite things. In *Dramatis Personae*, it is frequently used to join elements which are simply unrelated, simultaneously drawing attention to their unrelatedness by its own apparently meaningless prominence. I have already cited a typical example of grotesque end-rhyme in 'leaps, ache . . . keepsake' (*A Likeness*); its effect, here and elsewhere, is, by intruding a kind of redundant virtuosity, to trivialise feeling. This tendency cooperates with violent incongruities of tone to produce an atmosphere of cynicism and banality. 'But hearts, after leaps, ache' is a bitterly serious epigram; 'By the way, you must take, for a keepsake' is, in its banality, so violently discontinuous on the emotional level that the rhyme which seems to link the two lines actually stresses, by contrast, their separateness and thus enhances the fragmentary effect. Internal rhyme is not of course inherently a fragmenting or trivialising device, but it again foregrounds the mechanisms of poetry in such a way as to make heavy demands on the semantic harmony of the elements it phonetically joins. In *The Worst of It, May and Death* and *Dis Aliter Visum*, internal rhyme becomes a structural feature; elsewhere, it appears intermittently, for particular effects. The most striking examples are those which appear in dramatic monologues, where the convention that the blank verse idiom represents speech throws the passages of 'poetry' (actually doggerel) into peculiarly sharp relief:

'What I *hate*, be consecr*ate*
To celebr*ate* Thee and Thy *state*, no *mate*
For *Thee*; what *see* for envy in poor *me*?'

Caliban upon Setebos 276–8

Young, you've a hope, an aim, a love: it's *tossed*
And *crossed* and *lost* . . .

Fine, draw the *line*
Somewhere, but, sir, your somewhere is not *mine*!

Mr Sludge 'The Medium' 1372–3, 1182–3

'And this young beauty, *round and sound*
As a mountain-apple, *youth and truth*
With *loves and doves*, at all events
With money in the Three per Cents;
Whose choice of me would seem profound . . .'

Dis Aliter Visum 61–5

In the last example the effect is not merely grotesque; its tone, in alliance
with the sentiments expressed, is openly cynical; the fact that its speaker
is described, in the poem's subtitle, as 'Le Byron de nos jours' encourages
us to recall similar devices in the satirical poetry of Byron, especially –
again – *Don Juan*. Byron's commitment to mutability in *Don Juan*
involves him in an attack upon Art and The Poet which logically includes
his poem and himself; self-ridicule, therefore, became his principal
strategy, and grotesque rhymes a prominent tool in the attempt to point
up the artificiality of art and inversely imply a living reality beyond it. In
Dramatis Personae poets come off no less badly. The poet of *Dis Aliter
Visum* is a coward masquerading as a cynic, that of *Too Late* an insensitive
hack whose idea of mourning his wife is to set about 'tagging [her]
epitaph'. Internal rhyme is pointedly associated with this insensitivity:
'He rhymed you his rubbish nobody read, / *Loved* you and *doved* you –
did not I laugh!' (*Too Late* 89–90). Similarly, Mr Sludge's reaction to his
own outbursts of doggerel is a transparently ironic claim of poetic afflatus
('Bless us, I'm turning poet!' [1184]).

But if life accuses poetry of insensitivity, poetry accuses life of
incoherence. The highlighting of poetic artifice draws attention to the
failure of reality to supply materials for the hierarchies of poetic form.

The paratactic anarchy of the collection's syntax, the redundancy that tries and fails to introduce definition into a chaos of objects are the poetry's ironic reflection of a crazy materialism incapable of an idea of order. With the withdrawal of a divine order, the poetic world becomes a trivial verbal game while the real world subsides into a heap of what Coleridge described as 'essentially fixed and dead' objects.

VI THE IDEAL, THE REAL, AND THE POEM

In many poems, the problem of the relation between the ideal, the real and art appears as a question about the site and provenance of the poetic subject: it is real or imagined, in or out of the world? *A Death in the Desert* deals with this question directly:

> The statuary ere he mould a shape
> Boasts a like gift, the shape's idea, and next
> The aspiration to produce the same;
> So, taking clay, he calls his shape thereout,
> Cries ever 'Now I have the thing I see':
> Yet all the while goes changing what is wrought,
> From falsehood like the truth, to truth itself.
> How were it had he cried 'I see no face,
> No breast, no feet i' the ineffectual clay?'
> Rather commend him that he clapped his hands,
> And laughed 'It is my shape and lives again!'
> Enjoyed the falsehood, touched it on to truth,
> Until yourselves applaud the flesh indeed
> In what is still flesh-imitating clay.

> 608–21

The artist's conception of an ideal form, 'the shape's idea', leads him to attempt to produce it actually in and for the world. This procedure involves him in the delusion that his inhospitable medium can, as he proceeds, really embody his conception, and adds to this delusion the irony that his audience, on receipt of the final product, mistakes it for a mere imitation of the real world. But this mutual misunderstanding can reverse into truth if the audience, by recognising that the art produces 'flesh-*imitating* clay', can next correctly grasp that the act of representation denotes, not the infidelity of art to reality, but its primary duty to the artist's ideal. The 'trick' or 'cheat' of art, its pretence really to duplicate reality, is there precisely to be unmasked in order that the audience may sense, in the inconguity between medium and subject, clay and flesh, the missing presence of something which is neither clay nor flesh. Both the illusion of reality and the departure of that illusion are essential to the process.

But the argument here is by no means straightforwardly Platonic, for the ideal, conspicuous by its absence from the material art-work, is all the time a piece of reality – here, a human figure – returning us to the world from which we had just withdrawn, and maintaining at a philosophical level the ambiguity which I have noted in *A Face* concerning the identity and locale of the object in art. A similar equivocation reshapes the ideal/real antithesis in 'By the Drawing-Board' from *James Lee's Wife*. The speaker compares the 'poor coarse hand' of a living peasant-woman to a clay cast supposedly made by Leonardo of a woman's hand. She calls the cast 'the perfect thing', and suggests that Leonardo made it in despair of being able to reproduce its subject's hand's beauty in a drawing. By contrast, the peasant-woman's misshapen hand seems to her the token of a world from which beauty has departed; she concludes that in consequence 'Art is null and study void'. Reality and art are jointly criticised by a 'Hand live once, dead long ago', or more abstractly, a 'beauty' which 'lived long ago or was never born'. Yet the latter phrasing generates a curious, apparently superfluous ambivalence as to the *site* of the original, whether in the real world or a world of Forms. We have been clearly told that Leonardo made the cast from a *real* hand; in what sense, then, does it constitute an ideal ('never born')? The fact that what it represents is a fragment of a complete human being contributes a further query to its claim of ideal status. Browning seems to play off against each other the three ideas, reality, art and the ideal. Art is inferior to reality; reality in turn is inferior to an ideal which is conveyed by art yet composed again of a reality.

The consummation of these paradoxical aesthetics is to be found in what is to my mind the collection's finest lyric, *A Likeness*.

A Likeness repeats the critique of art as memorial. In the poem's first two paragraphs, someone asks an owner of a 'portrait' who it's a portrait *of* ('Who was the lady, I wonder?'; 'Jane Lamb, that we danced with at Vichy'), on the casual assumption that it must memorialise some actual relationship or acquaintance. In each case, the owner reacts as though with pain, the first suffering in silence under his wife's furious claim that ''Tis a daub John bought at a sale', the second contradicting, perhaps petulantly, his friend's suggestion that 'Jane Lamb' might have been his portrait's subject. These reactions are ambiguous, in that they could signify either that the portrait really is of a former lover (in which case the wife's claim about the first portrait is a lie, while the second represents, say, Joan Lumb, not Jane Lamb), or that it represents no *person* at all, but an ideal, which the owners are outraged to see reduced to a mere reality. The third situation, that of the poem's speaker, is no less ambiguous. In the passage I cited above (p. 157-8), the sense in which this 'print' is a 'fact' remains unclear, for though in a secondary relation to 'a certain face', it was clearly not (being in itself 'a fancy, a fiction') devised to represent that face, and the face in turn could either belong to a real woman whose features the speaker has never seen reproduced in any other, or an ideal which he has never physically encountered anywhere outside this print (and even that only 'hints' at it). His interlocutor, unlike the earlier ones, opts for the second alternative, but this purely aesthetic reaction seems to be as inadequate as theirs, for the speaker scornfully diverts his interlocutor's attention to 'That other [print] you praised, of Volpato's', while thinking,

> The fool! would he try a flight further and say –
> He never saw, never before today,
> What was able to take his breath away,
> A face to lose youth for, to occupy age
> With the dream of, meet death with, – why, I'll not engage
> But that, half in a rapture and half in a rage,
> I should toss him the thing's self – ''Tis only a duplicate,
> A thing of no value! Take it, I supplicate!'

>   62-9

He is, it seems, as affronted by the purely aesthetic view of the print as his predecessors were at the biographical reading of their 'portraits', yet it is still not clear – becomes, as the poem proceeds, less and less clear – what its reality *is*. The problem is summarised in his assertion that the print is a 'duplicate'. Is it a duplicate of a real person, copied by art? or of something – a Platonic Form, in effect – which does not exist in the world? For the 'fool', of course, it is merely the duplicate of the original painting from which the print was taken.

In *A Death in the Desert* the problem of representation is considered in relation to the written text, and the problematic 'face' of *A Likeness* becomes the no less problematic *voice* of St John, as represented or otherwise in the poem's array of linguistic signs. Unlike most of Browning's earlier monologues, *A Death in the Desert* is the imitation of a

document rather than an utterance, and it centres upon the question of
the authority of any document's claim to represent a real voice. The poem
purports to be a record of the last words of St John, uttered in the secrecy
of a desert cave to which a group of faithful disciples have carried him to
hide him from unspecified persecutors. This record is in the form of a
document, which its owner keeps concealed in 'the surnamed Golden
Chest'. He even conceals his own name, presumably from fear of similar
persecution. His preamble takes the form of an introductory written
gloss, explaining that the document is 'Supposed of Pamphylax the
Antiochene'. What follows is the narrative of an again unnamed witness
of St John's death, whom we presume, on the authority of the
introductory gloss, to be this 'Pamphylax'. But he proves not to be. After
the long monologue of St John himself, the narrator records his death,
and concludes:

> By this, the cave's mouth must be filled with sand.
> Valens is lost, I know not of his trace;
> The Bactrian was but a wild childish man,
> Who could not write nor speak, but only loved:
> So, lest the memory of this go quite,
> Seeing that I tomorrow fight the beasts,
> I tell the same to Phoebas, whom believe!
> For many look again to find that face,
> Beloved John's to whom I ministered,
> Somewhere in life about the world; they err[.]

647–56

Here the voice of John, transferred to the 'cave's *mouth*', falls silent, to be
disseminated, or rather, dissipated, by lost or mute witnesses. For the
document is not, clearly, written by the witness of St John's death-
speech, but reported by him to one 'Phoebas'. But if, as simultaneously
becomes probable, the name 'Pamphylax' applies to the scribe who has
written the document rather than the witness of St John's final words, we
are obliged to posit an indefinite number of intermediate oral reports,
making St John's speech a product of that notorious liar, the oral
tradition. This recession of reporters, and John's own equivalent status as
the reporter of a further recessed origin, Christ himself, confirms that the
'voice of John' constitutes an origin beyond secure recovery, whose loss
therefore threatens the claim of authority for the text. The consequences
of such decay for language itself are made evident in the introductory
gloss:

[Supposed of Pamphylax the Antiochine;
It is a parchment, of my rolls the fifth,
Hath three skins glued together, is all Greek,
And goeth from *Epsilon* down to *Mu*:
Lies second in the surnamed Golden Chest,
Stained and conserved with juice of terebinth,
Covered with cloth of hair, and lettered *Xi*,
From Xanthus, my wife's uncle, now at peace:
Mu and *Epsilon* stand for my own name.
I may not write it, but I make a cross
To show I wait His coming, with the rest . . .]

1–11

As an introduction, nothing could be less helpful. Instead of telling us anything useful about his document, the writer sedulously *conceals* it. As it lies hidden in 'the surnamed Golden Chest' amidst a mêlée of equivalents amongst which it comes 'second' (or 'fifth'?) rather than first or last, so the 'information' which the writer gives about it conceals its significance behind a baffling proliferation of merely physical characteristics. The letter-coding '*Xi* . . . *Mu* and *Epsilon*' transfers this deliberate occultation not merely to the name of the writer ('I may not write it'), but to linguistic signification itself: words turn into arbitrary alphabetic signs when the meaning they represent – here, the identity of the writer – becomes irrecoverable. Like the document that contains them, and like the 'print' at the end of *A Likeness*, the text of the poem has become a physical object populated by impenetrable symbols. The voiceless anonymity of the writer of the text registers the entailed presumption that it can contain neither himself, epitomised in the name he witholds, nor by extension any real voice whatever.

VII THE RETURN OF ORDER AND OF GOD

Yet this situation is always on the point of being reversed by the return of meaning to the fragments. Compare two passages from *Dis Aliter Visum*:

1.   You judged the porch
    We left by, Norman; took our look
    At sea and sky; wondered so few

> Find out the place for air and view;
> Remarked the sun began to scorch . . .
>
>   101–5

> 2. The devil laughed at you in his sleeve!
>   You knew not? That I well believe;
>   Or you had saved two souls: nay, four.

> For Stephanie sprained last night her wrist,
>   Ankle, or something. 'Pooh', cry you?
> At any rate she danced, all say,
>   Vilely; her vogue has had its day.
> Here comes my husband from his whist.
>
>   143–50

The first passage, as we have seen, presents the collapse of the possible relationship into banal social chatter, and its discontinuities reflect the actual emptiness of the recollected conversation. The second, by contrast, imparts an intense and coherent meaning to similar discontinuities, a meaning foreshadowed by the logical connective 'For' (compare '*while* John's corns ail'), though not explained by it, since it is not logically applicable to the situations it links. The speaker means that as a result of their failure to consummate their relationship, she and her 'lover' have frustrated both themselves and those with whom they have alternatively coupled, he by reducing love-relationships to the status of cynical liaisons, she by a mundane marriage. She renders this meaning metonymically, by the evocation of the bald circumstances of these unions, with no attempt at direct comment; but metonymy becomes metaphor as the mistress and husband crystallise both their own and their partners' futility in the second-rate, disappointing actions in which they are photographed.

In other examples, a reinterpretation is involved. The fact that the portrait in the second paragraph of *A Likeness*, first item in the catalogue of the contents of the room, is 'alone mid the *other* spoils', suggests that despite the surface randomness *some* kind of continuity nevertheless holds between the listed items. This is the case. As 'spoils of youth' they mutually gesture towards bachelor prowess and masculine strength: foils, pipe-sticks, whip, the cast from a fist all suggest male aggression even if we ignore the phallic quality of the first three, and if we don't, the 'satin shoe used for cigar-case' in conjunction with 'the little edition of

Rabelais' could suggest the sexual fate of that 'other spoil', the girl depicted in the 'portrait'. At the same time, a more delicate shading is introduced by the implication that these trophies lack the confidence they aspire to represent: the qualification 'Not, alas! mine, but my master's . . .' set up a double distance between the object and the man who seeks symbolic virility through it (it is a *cast* which represents *someone else's* fist). Similarly, his denial that the portrait is of 'Jane Lamb, that we danced with at Vichy' withdraws the merely sexual innuendo into the sense of a wistfully inaccessible essence.

But if this speaker too is involved in the game of occulting meaning, his predicament must be *the same as* his narrator's, not contrary to it. To read the poem's key line with different stress-placements – '*All* that I *own* is a print' – is to confirm this possibility. Read in this way, this line loses the contrastive force of its other realisation ('All that *I* own . . .) and parallels itself to 'alone mid the other spoils' by suggesting the pathos of a true value struggling for recognition in midst of the disorderly imbroglio of mere objects. And 'John's corns ail' for the same reason as the narrator's 'waistcoat-strings want stretching': another person has singled out his 'likeness' for attention or praise and thereby robbed him of it. These characters all *own* their likeness in the sense that its value is uniquely perceived by them: the crisis arrives when another person invades that emotional privacy by compelling them to *own* it, admit its value publicly and thereby offer it as a substantive reality to the world. It was deliberately concealed, amongst the clatter of tea-cups, the 'spoils of youth' or the 'portfolio' of prints, but only as a test of the perceiver's capacity to intuit value by singling it out from other objects in confirmation of the owner's valuation. At the moment when this occurs he communes, though in a perverse sense, with his 'crony', while at the same time the reader perceives the congruity of all three situations in the poem, and is thus drawn into restoring the lost symbolic level at which unity exists.

The option of considering things either in isolation or ensemble connects with the collection's critique of the relation between part and whole. The cases I have been examining, like Wordsworth's *Simplon Pass*, all involve the arraying of elements in such a way as to raise the question, are they parts of a unified whole? or is each an independent whole, incapable of concatenation? This question can be considered in various ways. On the theological plane, it reflects the relation between God and the visible universe, whose traditional form is summed up by Pope's 'All are but parts of one stupendous whole, / Whose body Nature is, and God the soul'. In rhetorical terms, this becomes the question, is such and such a particular thing a case of *synecdoche* (part for whole)? The

use of synecdoche as a figure presupposes that the elements of which it is
composed contribute to a whole of which they form parts. In *Dis Aliter
Visum* for instance, the physical details of the remembered scene are first
given casually: 'the church . . . Where a few graveyard crosses are, / And
garlands for the swallows' perch', but later recapitulated as capable of a
synecdochic representation of the combined horror ('Crosses and
graves') and sublimity ('the sea . . . swallows' call') of mutability, and an
exhortation to effort:

> Who made all things plain in vain?
> What was the sea for? What, the grey
> Sad church, that solitary day,
> Crosses and graves and swallows' call?

112–15

Similarly, the fragmented text with which *A Death in the Desert* looks
forward to being repossessed by the divine order, withdrawn as explicit
presence by the death of Christ and its symbolic echo, the death of John,
but due to reappear with 'His coming', the return of Christ (or John) to
the world.

Frequently in *Dramatis Personae*, knowledge or wholeness is
anticipated as a future event: 'on earth the broken arcs; in heaven the
perfect round' (*Abt Vogler*), suggesting that the part-whole relationship
requires *time* within which to unfold. This formulation connects with the
moral argument with whose help St John explains the necessity of a loss
of God's presence and his own. Wholeness is to be repossessed after an
interlude of suspension, in order that man's moral energy can be
exercised against the epistemological adversity which makes it sublime.
In the meantime, wholeness is a thing to distrust:

> Let the mere star-fish in his vault
> Crawl in a wash of weed, indeed,
> Rose-jacinth to the finger-tips:
> He, whole in body and soul, outstrips
> Man, found with either in default.
>
> But what's whole, can increase no more,
> Is dwarfed and dies, since here's its sphere.

Dis Aliter Visum 136–42

Here, the starfish represents a whole whose parts symmetrically radiate from its centre, but is disparaged by comparison to that which, as part, struggles to repossess a whole beyond its immediate grasp. The mistake of the man in this poem is to have made

> No wise beginning, here and now,
>   What cannot grow complete (earth's feat)
> And heaven must finish, there and then?
>   No tasting earth's true food for men,
> Its sweet in sad, its sad in sweet?

> 121–5

Significantly, this is the only stanza in the poem in which the jingling second line with its internal rhyme finds an external rhyme (abccb instead of abcca); appropriately, it rhymes with a line which itself expresses the perfectness of imperfection and the imperfection of perfectness by a symmetrical mirror-inversion of terms. The poetic system can, it seems, be coupled to a transcendent order.

It is left to the nameless reporter of *A Death in the Desert* to complete the conversion of the collection's moral argument into its theory of textuality. In the passage I have quoted from *A Death in the Desert* (647–56), the speaker dramatises a 'recovery' of the sanctioned voice which is really founded upon its loss: telling it to 'Phoebas' as an oral record, he bases its future survival as a written text upon the absolute loss of its origin, John. The very *need* for a text is a product of the uncertainty which the ebbing of God from the visible world inevitably entails. Textuality is born of uncertainty, but at the same time validated by it, as St John's words are simultaneously 'stained and conserved' by the physical palpability of the document which contains them.

The Epilogue to *Dramatis Personae* recapitulates the collection's study of the part-whole relation in both its metaphysical and poetic contexts. In the first two poems, as we have seen, God is first present and celebrated, then absent and lamented; the third speaker dialectically resolves the conflict. He first posits that each man 'differs from his fellows utterly' because produced within a world which 'Divide[s] us, each from other, me from you'. The sense in which the contents of such a world can become a series is inevitably a paradox:

> watch when nature by degrees
> Grows live around him, as in Arctic seas
> (They said of old) the instinctive water flees

Towards some elected point of central rock
As though for its sake only roamed the flock
Of waves about the waste: awhile they mock . . .

The mimic monarch of the whirlpool, king
O' the current for a minute: then they wring
Up by the roots and oversweep the thing,

And hasten off, to play again elsewhere
The same part, choose another peak as bare,
They find and flatter, feast and finish there.

                            72–8, 82–7

The double movement by which the water 'flees / *Towards*' the rock
articulates the paradox of a connectedness which is in fact an assertion of
distinctness, just as each dramatic monologue orientates the world to a
speaker's vision only to replace him with another of equal privilege,
equally to be superceded, within the scheme of an entire structured
collection. But unity, in the sense of a continuously articulated structure,
is something that the structured collection has already refused to accept.
The option of reading it as a discrete series is always encouraged as the
antithesis which the thesis of unity must not disparage.

Dramatis Personae is the extremest of Browning's structured
collections, in that the aesthetics of the form infiltrate the theological and
passional issues which it presents, by positing a unity which, because
unstated, is constantly 'decomposing' into fragments in the reader's mind
only to 'recompose' again, making the collection, as Browning's
aesthetics demand, mutable – not as text, since text is inveterately
monumental, but in the dynamics of reading.

7

The Unity of *The Ring and the Book*

I

> Well, the sum of my ideas is: If you took up some one great subject, and tasked all your powers upon it for a long while, vowing to Heaven that you would be plain to mean capacities, then – ! –
>
> Carlyle to Browning 25 Apr. 1856; *CH* 200

> It's a wonderful book, one of the most wonderful poems ever written. I re-read it all through—all made out of an Old Bailey story that might have been told in ten lines, and only wants forgetting!
>
> Garnett, *Life of Carlyle* (1887) 146

> There is a profound and moving irony in the structure of the poem. Any other human transaction that ever was, tragic or comic or plain prosaic, may be looked at in a like spirit.
>
> *Fortnightly Review* xi (1869) 331–43; 337

From the time of its first publication, the form of *The Ring and the Book* has been its most widely discussed feature. This is hardly surprising, since there was no obvious precedent for its use of multiple narration of the same sequence of events by a variety of speakers. Opinion as to the effectiveness of the method has always varied: aesthetic critics such as Henry James and George Santayana deprecated the sacrifice, as they saw it, of the classical shaping of poetic form to a principle of repetition and accumulation; Robert Langbaum is typical of those on the other side who, finding in Browning's method an expression of what Pater called 'the relative spirit' have gone on to claim the poem as a prototype 'modernist' text.[1]

A number of structural studies have demonstrated the skill with which the story is divided up between the various monologues; one in particular, B. R. McElderry's 'The Narrative Structure of Browning's *The Ring and the Book*', provides an extremely useful account of the interweaving of

173

the strands.[2] I do not intend, therefore, to repeat the practice of my previous two chapters, and analyse the form of the poem. I will concentrate instead on the relation of the technique of multiple narration to the structured collection principle, and its implications as a method, before discussing the reception of the poem.

Browning began work on *The Ring and the Book* in October 1864, immediately after the publication of *Dramatis Personae*. It was four years since he had bought the poem's source-material, the 'Old Yellow Book', on a Florentine bookstall. He describes that discovery in book i of the poem, making it clear that though immediately aware of the creative possibilities of the story, he did not at once set about making a poem of it: indeed, he is known to have offered it to at least two novelists, and, by one account, also to Tennyson, before deciding to use it himself.[3] These facts suggest strongly that it took him some time to arrive at a conception of the form his poem might take, a suggestion corroborated by W. M. Rossetti's recollection of Browning's account of the matter in conversation:

> He began it in October '64. Was staying at Bayonne, and walked out to a mountain-gorge traditionally said to have been cut or kicked out by Roland, and there laid out the full plan of his twelve cantos, accurately carried out in the execution.
>
> *Rossetti Papers* (1903) 302

A number of references in letters of late 1864 to the Pas de Roland suggest that Rossetti's date is correct, and therefore that the period when Browning began writing the poem was also the time when its plan came to him.[4] The plan dates, then, from the period of the revised *Men and Women* and *Dramatis Personae*, and is a variation on their structured collection method.

In a structured collection, disparate poems are brought together in such a way as to suggest the possibility of a common thematic 'ground', or even a developing 'story', though this level remains subordinate to the experience of the poems as independent wholes. The separate monologues of *The Ring and the Book* – ten in all, or twelve including Browning's own opening and concluding discourses – mutually refer to a story which, being historical, stands outside all of them, yet which, being the story all narrate, is simultaneously the centre of all. Thus, in the terms Browning uses in the first book of the poem, each monologue is a 'ring' through whose centre passes a 'djereed' (javelin) which binds and unites them all, like the historical and conceptual dialectics of 2*M&W* and *Dramatis Personae*.

In one sense, this procedure reverses that of the structured collection. Browning's account of the poem's inception makes it clear that the story came first, and that the individual monologues cannot be considered independent of it, or of each other. The structured collection 'centre', hitherto an occulted level of meaning, becomes public as the 'Roman Murder-Story' on which the poem is based. But the effect of such a method, despite the publicity given to the concept of a centre, is, no less than with the structured collection, to render that centre implicit. No two tellings of the story perfectly agree. Speakers stress different aspects or phases, diverge in their interpretation of particular events or in their belief in the reality of particular events, most of all they tirelessly argue over the motives, attitudes and characters of the protagonists (note however that the word 'argue' must be used metaphorically, since none of the monologues is spoken in the presence of, or substantially reported to the speaker of any other). Each, including Browning as speaker of the first and last monologues, claims to have the only valid version of the story, yet their multiplicity mutually subordinates them to the 'true' version, which, as the Pope says, is 'nowhere' yet 'everywhere in these – / Not absolutely in a portion, yet / Evolvible from the whole' (x 228–30). In other words, the centre of *The Ring and the Book* is in real terms no less implicit than the consolidating theme of a structured collection, which means that history, source of the story of the poem, like the 'Face' of God in the structured collections is encountered as dubiety rather than certitude. This is a necessary entailment of the form, since the outright privileging of any one account would cause the whole structure to collapse beneath its discovered redundancy. Multiple narration can only function, is only reasonable if its centre is absent from the visible parts.

Nevertheless, the *avowal* of unity in *The Ring and the Book* modifies structured collection form by making it publicly answerable for the novelty of its departure from traditional means. *The Ring and the Book* is a 20,000 word poem; such dimensions, and the poem's twelve-book form, inevitably invokes the precedent of classical epic. Yet both the method of narration and the story told are the reverse of epic. Epic narrative is in principle monolinear; epic action traditionally bears a significance which is either national (*Iliad, Aeneid*) or metaphysical (*Divina Commedia, Paradise Lost*). Carlyle's conclusion that the story of *The Ring and the Book* 'only wants forgetting', and his description of the poem as 'the absurdest of things',[5] highlights the extraordinary combination of a trivial subject and a monumentally laborious narration of it; he thereby questions – as subsequent commentators have also questioned – the relation between the poem's form and its content.

II

Here it is, this I take and toss again;
Small-quarto size, part print part manuscript:
A book in shape but, really, pure crude fact
Secreted from man's life when hearts beat hard,
And brains, high-blooded, ticked two centuries since.

i 84-8

It is the second symbol in the poem's title, the 'Book', that explains Browning's choice of a subject which his wife, for one, found merely repulsive.[6] The Old Yellow Book, being a document from the actual era of its events, represented in his eyes 'pure crude fact', – and that, for a Victorian, might be enough to make it equivalent to the epic action. Langbaum puts it that 'his truth had to be taken seriously, which meant in a positivistic age that it had to have the facts behind it, had to emerge from the facts',[7] and when his friend Julia Wedgwood pressed him on the subject, it was more or less in these terms that Browning justified himself:

> the business has been, as I specify, to explain *fact* – and the fact is what you see [.] . . . Before I die, I hope to purely invent something, – here my pride was concerned to invent nothing: the minutest circumstance that denotes character is *true*: the black is so much – the white, no more.
>
> to Julia Wedgwood 19 Nov. 1868: *LJW* 158–9

Compare Carlyle's comment, in his essay on Biography, on a trivial incident recorded there:

> Strange power of *Reality*! Not even this poorest of occurrences, but now, after seventy years are come and gone, has a meaning for us. Do but consider that it is *true*; that it did in very deed occur!
>
> 'Biography' (1832), *Misc* iii p. 56

It is highly probable that Browning's decision to base his poem on a historical fact, even upon the 'poorest of occurrences', derived from Carlyle's exhortations, tirelessly repeated through and after the 1830s, to authors in general and poets in particular to abandon fiction for 'pure crude fact':

History, after all, is the true Poetry; . . . Reality, if rightly interpreted, is grander than Fiction, nay . . . even in the right interpretation of Reality and History does genuine Poetry consist.

Misc iii p. 79

Fiction, while the feigner of it knows that he is feigning, partakes, more than we suspect, of the nature of *lying*; and has ever an, in some degree, unsatisfactory character.

49

[T]he Epic Poems of old time, so long as they continued *epic*, and had any complete impressiveness, were Histories, and understood to be narratives of *facts*.

49–50

One could cite a dozen parallel statements from Carlyle's essays of the 1830s, and on receipt of a copy of *Sordello* in 1840 he promptly made the point to Browning directly:

One must first make a *true* intellectual representation of a thing before any poetic interest that is true will supervene.

21 June 1841: *New Letters of Carlyle* ed. A. Carlyle (1904)
i p. 234

– insistently repeating it throughout their long subsequent correspondence. It is significant that the first poem of Browning's to which he gave unequivocal praise was *How It Strikes a Contemporary*, and that his more general praise of Browning in the same letter was clearly influenced by the poem:

I shall look far, I believe, to find such a pair of *eyes* as I see busy there inspecting human life this long while. The keenest just insight into *men and things*.

25 Apr. 1856: *Letters to Mill, Sterling and Browning* p. 298
(m.i.)

(He took such cognisance of *men and things*,
If any beat a horse you felt he *saw*[.])
How It Strikes a Contemporary 30–1 (m.i.)

His conclusion was:

If you took up some one *great* subject, and tasked all your powers upon it for a long while, vowing to heaven you *would* be plain to mean capacities, then – ! –

loc. cit. p. 300

The promotion of *How It Strikes* to the Prologue of the revised *Men and Women* marks, I think, Browning's response to this praise; the equivalence between that poem and Browning's presentation of himself as a historical researcher in book i of *The Ring and the Book* points to the direct descent of that poem from Carlyle's theories; the scale of *The Ring and the Book* encourages the speculation that it was intended to be the 'one great subject' Carlyle required. Browning even imagines a Carlylean objection to the fanciful version of this story which he used to tell before he became a researcher:

> 'Do you tell the story, now, in off-hand style,
> Straight from the book? Or simply here and there,
> (The while you vault it through the loose and large)
> Hang to a hint? Or is there book at all,
> And don't you deal in poetry, make-believe,
> And the white lies it sounds like?'

i 451–6

The echo of Carlyle's 'fiction . . . partakes of the nature of lying' is clear enough to suggest that Browning's decision to centre this structured collection on a historical fact places him in the wake of Carlyle's strenuous polemic against poetry.

This would seem perverse in a poet, had Carlyle not been prepared – grudgingly – to tolerate poetry when it subordinated itself to 'fact', and even to prefer it to the more orthodox historiography to which he gave the title 'Dryasdust'. For Carlyle's definition of 'fact' is unusual in its total repudiation of what he calls 'exterior occurrences' and 'enactments of quite superficial phenomena':

> The thing I want to see is not Redbook Lists and ad Court Calendars, and Parliamentary Registers, but the LIFE OF MAN in England: . . . the form, especially the spirit, of their terrestrial existence, its outward environment, its inward principle: *how* and *what* it was.

'Boswell's *Life of Johnson*' *Misc* iii p. 81

For Carlyle, as a Romantic historian, 'fact' includes – if it does not entirely consist in – the inwardnesses of personal existence, and the excavation of the inner life of the dead is, as he recognised at least at the outset of his career, essentially a poetic activity:

> For the great characters there dimly shadowed forth, [the poet] becomes a kind of new creator. The faint traces they have left remain uninterpreted and barren in the eyes of the chronicler: to the poet's eye they are like the fragments of an antediluvian animal, as contemplated by the mind of a Cuvier – dark to others and void of meaning, but discovering to his experienced sagacity, the form and habits of a species long extinct.
>
> 'Joanna Baillie', *New Edinburgh Review* i (Oct. 1821) 393–414: 399

In response to the charge that his work consists of 'white lies' Browning in book i of *The Ring and the Book* argues that the poet 'creates, no – but resuscitates, perhaps', and supports this claim with an image that may owe something to Carlyle's picture of Cuvier, the 'Mage' who 'May chance upon some fragment of a whole, / Rag of flesh, scrap of bone in dim disuse', which he promptly appropriates and vivifies. The role of poetry, in relation to the fact with which it should properly concern itself, is to rediscover its inner principle, the 'life' which has been overlain and obscured by historical remoteness, and reconstitute this as a belated echo for modern ears.

III

A novel country: I might make it mine
By choosing which one aspect of the year
Suited mood best, and putting solely that
On panel somewhere in the House of Fame,
Landscaping what I saved, not what I saw . . .
Thus were abolished Spring and Autumn both,
The land dwarfed to one likeness of the land,
Life cramped corpse-fashion. Rather learn and love
Each facet-flash of the revolving year! –
Red, green and blue that whirl into a white,
The variance now, the eventual unity

> Which make the miracle. See it for yourselves,
> This man's act, changeable because alive!

i 1348–52, 1358–65[8]

— —

But how is the poet to set about reconstituting the 'LIFE OF MAN'? *The Ring and the Book* takes two approaches to this problem, one negative, the other positive. On the negative side, Browning reinforces Carlyle's polemic against fiction by casting fiction as the invariable enemy of the life which he, as historian, is trying to resuscitate; on the positive side, he claims that the very form of his poem, with its kaleidoscopic multiplicity of fictional accounts, makes the past, because 'changeable', 'alive' once more.

The hostility of the poem's 'evil' characters to life is constantly figured as a tendency to rely on literary precedents to explain human behaviour. To prove that Pompilia and Caponsacchi committed adultery, Guido cries,

> Why, I appeal to . . . sun and moon? Not I!
> Rather to Plautus, Terence, Boccaccio's Book,
> My townsman, frank Ser Franco's merry Tales[.]

v 558–60

The play on 'frank Ser Franco' illustrates the ease with which, once the fictional has been given primacy, language subordinates reality, and in Guido Browning represents the case of a man in whom the aesthetic has become at once a whole way of life and a pure instrument of evil. It is appropriate, therefore, that in describing the failure of his plot against Pompilia, Guido should use a language of artistery:

> Why fell things out not so nor otherwise?
> Ask that particular devil whose task it is
> To trip the all-but-at-perfection, – slur
> The line of the painter just where paint leaves off
> And life begins, – put ice into the ode
> O' the poet while he cries 'Next stanza – fire!'
> Inscribe all human effort with one word,
> Artistry's haunting curse, the Incomplete!

xi 1555–61

What emerges from this passage is, first, that Guido sees his plot as a work of art, and second that he believes art to be simultaneously hostile and inferior to life. '[L]ife begins' just where 'paint leaves off'; the 'perfection' of art can only be accomplished by the denial of life.

The difference between art and life, and the reason for their mutual antipathy, is that art is determinate, life indeterminate; art seeks a representational perfection which life triumphantly eludes. I have touched upon this distinction in chapter 6; *The Ring and the Book* was Browning's most systematic attempt to translate the mobility of life into an equivalently mobile artistic form. The structured collection is indeterminate to the extent that its 'form' is provided by the reader's hypothesisation of links between successive poems; the centring of *The Ring and the Book* round a single story allow this indeterminacy to challenge the possibility of a fixed event or character. Browning's descriptions of the characters, and the characteristics revealed by their monologues, make it clear that his concept of character is essentially fluid: Caponsacchi is

> Man and priest – could you comprehend the coil! –
> . . . Now heaven, now earth, now heaven and earth at once,
> Had plucked at and perplexed their puppet here . . .

> i 1017, 1020–1

Pompilia lives the paradox of being 'the one Christian *mother, wife* and *girl*' (x 1946), and Guido attracts the very word 'ambiguous' (x 486) from the Pope, who in turn separates his own pontifical identity as 'Innocent X11' from his wordly self 'Antonio Pignatelli': *no* character, good or bad, is left altogether 'classed and done with' by Browning's description because all are viewed dialectically. And these conflicts are carried through into their monologues. Caponsacchi's double nature as 'man and priest' is responsible for the rapid and extreme alternations of feeling in his monologue, as typically at its end. The Pope experiences a similar conflict when self-compelled, at the close of *his* monologue, to listen to the arguments of 'the educated man' which as priest he will have to repudiate. More surprisingly. Guido's second monologue discloses a conflict between the hatred which as man he felt for Pompilia, and a repressed 'religious' consciousness of her true value which his final appeal to her acknowledges.

Even the minor characters, necessarily 'flatter' than the main protagonists, illustrate indeterminacy, evinced, in the case of the two

Half-Romes, in the sheer arbitrariness of their chosen narrative
standpoints. If their view of the case were to be presented as properly
worked out, it would occupy a secure place in their characters, become
fixed and fix *them*; Browning presents them, however, as almost
whimsical in their choice of position:

> With this Half-Rome, – the source of swerving, call
> Over-belief in Guido's right and wrong
> Rather than in Pompilia's wrong and right:
> Who shall say how, who shall say why? 'Tis there –
> The instinctive theorising whence a fact
> Looks to the eye as the eye likes the look.

i 859–64

Here the outburst of chiming echoes and casual inversions ('right and
wrong . . . wrong and right', 'Looks . . . eye . . . eye . . . look') juggles
away linguistic determinacy in a way which corresponds to the casualness
with which 'Half-Rome' has chosen his side. Likewise 'the Other Half-
Rome', whose preference is explained by this image:

> One wears drab, one pink;
> Who wears pink, ask him 'Which shall win the race,
> Of coupled runners like as egg and egg?'
> 'Why, if I must choose, he with the pink scarf.'

i 888–91

Tertium Quid, a third to follow these first two, is also offered to us in a
language of paradox. 'One and one breed the inevitable three', we are
told; but one and one *add up to* two, or can breed *one*: the momentary
semantic confusion reinforces the speaker's intangibility as 'neither this
nor that . . . something bred of both', in anticipation of the irresolvible
dialectic of his account. A similar language of contrast characterises
Pompilia's lawyer Bottinius: 'composite, he, . . . Odds of age joined in
him with ends of youth' (i 1174–6); his rival Arcangelis, with a mind
incessantly shifting between the drafting of his case and the great feast
planned for his son's birthday, illustrates 'Paternity at smiling strife with
law' (i 1146).

It is Bottinius and the Pope who directly introduce the relation
between the motif of indeterminacy in character and the poem's structure

and process. Bottinius, Pompilia's lawyer, begins his monologue by describing how a painter, commissioned to paint the Holy Family, will naturally begin with a series of preliminary studies of the different elements, Mary, Joseph, the ass and so on. But how absurd it would be, argues Bottinius, if when asked for his picture he were to offer this portfolio of studies! No, he sorts, refines, defines, selects and fuses them into a single, composite image, as he, Bottinius, will set aside the low traffic in evidence in order to 'soar the height prescribed / And, bowing low, proffer my picture's self!' (ix 158-9) – the portrait of Pompilia as a 'faultless nature in a flawless form'. Which seems fair enough until, reading on, we discover that by this argument Bottinius has licensed himself to manufacture a totally fictional version of Pompilia's character. Belonging as she does to 'the weaker sex' she will naturally exhibit 'desire' and practice 'melting wiles, deliciousest deceits'; Bottinius accordingly equips her with a wholly imaginary pre-marital sex-life and describes her behaviour, in marriage, in terms perfectly compatible with sexual infidelity. Such a procedure specifies Bottinius as committed, like Guido, to the fixities of stereotype; his 'portrait' of Pompilia 'cramps' her true fluidity in symmetrical inversion of the way in which Browning's art seeks to make her, like Guido, 'changeable because alive'. In rejecting Bottinius' portrait, then, we also reject the very idea of fixed portraiture, and therefore invert his seductive pictorial analogy: that painter who submitted 'his fifty studies one by one' comes, after all, rather closer to Browning's procedure in *Men and Women* and its successors, and it is a procedure whose necessary *plurality* corresponds to the *indeterminacy* which is vital to Browning's method of representation as described in the first book.

Each monologue may be read as a study of the case, and the whole poem as a portfolio of studies in which the principles of variation and redundancy force life into the textual material. Even the statements of allies exhibit variation. The 'Other Half-Rome', staunch supporter of Caponsacchi and Pompilia, describes their first meeting thus:

> Pompilia and Caponsacchi met, in fine,
> She at her window, he i' the street beneath,
> And understood each other at first look.
> All was determined and performed at once.

> iii 1061-4

Caponsacchi and Pompilia confirm the bald circumstance, but dispute the 'at once', noting that Caponsacchi delayed a day in returning with a worked-out plan for the elopement. While Pompilia makes little of this, calling his procrastination only 'a cloud' and adding confidently, 'The second night, he came', Caponsacchi describes in morbid detail what he sees as the cowardly scruples that held him back. This difference conditions their divergent accounts of their dialogue. Caponsacchi describes Pompilia as reproaching him upon his belated reappearance: 'Why is it you have suffered me to stay / Breaking my heart two days more than was need?' (v 1065–6). Pompilia mentions no words of her own at all, but reports Caponsacchi, not (as he recalls) apologising for delay, but expressing concern for the risk to her life and reputation entailed by the proposed elopement. Their reports of their initial meeting differ likewise. Pompilia reports Caponsacchi's first words as

> an eternity
> Of speech, to match the immeasurable depth
> O' the soul that then broke silence – 'I am yours'.
>
>   vii 1445–7

In Caponsacchi's version, he is simply businesslike: 'It shall be when it can be. / I will go hence and do your pleasure' (vi 881–2). It is easy enough to give these differences a psychological rationale. Pompilia has cut out a chivalric pattern for Caponsacchi, and re-shaped the story to fit it. The ideas of sexual passion in a priest, or worldly cowardice in a man of honour seem alike laughable to her, and she can therefore record words which look like one, or omit words which betray the other, with equal lack of self-consciousness or difficulty. Caponsacchi by contrast is pre-occupied with her role in his conversion from worldliness to sanctity, and accordingly emphasises his own fallibility at that stage, while simultaneously skating over passages which might support the charge – upheld even by his supporter, 'Other Half-Rome' – that his motivation in helping Pompilia was love or lust. In that way, the principle of variation services the poem's psychological analyses, but its more important function is precisely, in awaking such speculation, to ensure that the reader is involved, and involved, moreover, in puzzling over what words were actually, historically, spoken by the two.

The Pope is directly concerned with the historical dimension of indeterminacy; his vision includes and transcends that of the other characters by enveloping all judgements, including his own, and all individuals, including himself, in historical dubiety. He begins his monologue by recounting how Pope Stephen convicted his predecessor Formosus of uncanonic behaviour, initiating a dialectic of Papal judgement and counter-judgement stretching over four Popes' reigns and never satisfactorily resolved. The Pope himself uses this case to illustrate why he need not shy away from pronouncing judgement on Guido merely because some later analyst may reverse his verdict. Browning's comments in book i (quoted at the head of this section) suggest the relation of this ecclesiastical squabble to the priority of indeterminacy: as Guido's 'man's act' forms and re-forms in speakers' contending accounts, so we will realise what no single account could render, the penumbra of life-giving dubiety fringing *every* action in the kinesis of its performance. And Browning boldly considers what would conventionally be regarded as the penalty of such a scheme, its moral incertitude, to be an associated asset:

> Action now shrouds, nor shows the informing thought;
> Man, like a glass ball with a spark a-top,
> Out of the magic fire that lurks inside,
> Shows one tint at a time to take the eye:
> Which, let a finger touch the silent sleep,
> Shifted a hair's breath shoots you dark for bright,
> Suffuses bright with dark, and baffles so
> Your sentence absolute for shine or shade.

> i 1366–74

He concludes,

> Once set such orbs, – white styled, black stigmatised, –
> A-rolling, see them once on the other side
> Your good men and your bad men every one
> From Guido Franceschini to Guy Faux,
> Oft would you rub your eyes and change your names.

> i 1374–8

The Pope participates, as he perceives, in a historical process in which judgments suffer periodic reversal, but such reversals are what set 'the orbs . . . A-rolling' and render historical events 'changeable because alive'. The form of *The Ring and the Book* creates a system of contemporary refractions of its events which anticipates their larger historical dubiety, but recasts dubiety as the essential condition of their resuscitation. It is, in a sense, the logical conclusion of 'organic form', in which the principles of life and death become interdependent contributors towards a saving mutability, like the mutability which proved so central to the organisation of *Dramatis Personae*.

IV

In a real sense, therefore, the form of *The Ring and the Book*, to which Carlyle implicitly objected, was a direct outcome of Carlyle's own historiographical emphasis on 'the LIFE OF MAN'. But Carlyle was never really prepared to countenance epistemological indeterminacy, lamenting, in his essay 'On History',

> Nay, even with regard to those occurrences which do stand recorded, . . . is not our understanding of them altogether incomplete; is it even possible to represent them as they were?
>
> 'On History' *Misc* ii 87

It is multiplicity of witness, Carlyle makes clear, that is responsible for this difficulty:

> Consider how it is that historical documents and records originate. . . . At first, among the various witnesses, who are also parties interested, there is only vague wonder, and fear or hope, and the noise of Rumour's thousand tongues[.]
>
> 87

The similarity of this situation to that in *The Ring and the Book* is enhanced by Carlyle's clinching analogy:

> The old story of Sir Walter Raleigh's looking from his prison-window, on some street-tumult, which afterwards three witnesses reported in three different ways, himself differing from them all, is still a true lesson for us.
>
> 87

Carlyle's pupil Froude later put the point in gloomier language:

It appears as if men could not relate facts precisely as they saw or as they heard them. The different parts of a story strike different imaginations unequally; and the mind, as the circumstances pass through it, alters their proportions unconsciously, or shifts the perspective.

'A Plea for the Free Discussion of Theological Difficulties', *Short Studies on Great Subjects* (1867) i 212–13

Froude's pessimism perhaps results from his position in the wake of what became known as 'critical historiography', pioneered by Niebuhr and consummated by Ranke, whose object was to reinvestigate the supposedly solid facts of history in the light of the actual indeterminacy resulting from the unreliability of a transmission through unsteady oral traditions or biassed scribes. The belief that the single, plenary historical event really survives in a recoverable form came under attack, an attack which then rapidly spread to other disciplines. Froude obliquely reveals a parallel development in the case of literature, ironically during an attempt to console himself for the loss of historical certitude:

The 'Iliad' is from two to three thousand years older than 'Macbeth', and yet it is as fresh as if it had been written yesterday . . . [Homer] represents to us faithfully the men and women among whom he lived . . . although no Agamemnon, king of men, ever led a Grecian fleet to Ilium . . . though Ulysses and Diomed and Nestor were but names, and Helen but a dream, . . . those old Greeks will still stand out from amidst the darkness. . . . For the mere hard purposes of history, the 'Iliad' and 'Odyssey' are the most effective books which were ever written.

'The Science of History', *Short Studies* 30

Despite his final claim, Froude cannot expel an elegiac note from such phrases as 'were but names . . . but a dream', or a revealing emphasis on his inability to call the Homeric epics 'the most true' rather than 'the most effective books which were ever written'. He was only too well aware that the historicity of the 'Siege of Troy' had seemingly disintegrated as early as 1792 in the hands of Bryant's *War of Troy*:

the account of the Trojan War, as delivered to us by Homer and other Grecian writers, is attended with so many instances of inconsistency, and so many contradictions, that it is an insult to reason. . . . I do not believe that Helen of Sparta was ever carried away by Paris; and, consequently, that no such armament ever took place, as we find described by the poet; and that Troy in Phrygia was never besieged. Indeed I am confident it never existed.

						Bryant, *War of Troy* (1792) 2

Froude's point, of course, is that we can nevertheless read the Homeric epics as *social* history of 'the men and women among whom [Homer] lived'; however, even the consolation of identifying the author of the Homeric texts had disintegrated under the criticism, in this case, of Friedrich August Wolf, whose *Prolegomena* to Homer, almost contemporary with Bryant's attack, had buried the supposed 'Homer' beneath a heap of nameless revisers and interpolators. As Wolf's English populariser Wilkins later put it:

> [t]he putting together of the Homeric poems, like the proverbial building of Rome, was not the work of a single day, nor of a single man, nor even of a single age.
>
> 			Wilkins *The Growth of the Homeric Poems* (1885) 30

Even these blows, however, were only preliminaries to the ultimate effort of critical historiography, which was the dismantling of the Bible, or at least of its credibility as a historical record of the events it describes.

The classic work of what became known as the 'Higher Criticism' of the Bible was David Strauss's *Life of Jesus*, in which Strauss, a trainee of the Wolf school of scholarship, applied to the four Gospels similar techniques of textual collation to those which had previously dismembered 'Homer'. His procedure consisted of an exhaustive compilation of the numerous instances of contradiction between the Gospels, on the assumption that such contradiction invariably threatens their claim to be considered reliable eye-witness accounts:

> In the first place, when two narratives mutually exclude one another, one only is thereby proved to be unhistorical. . . . But upon a more particular consideration it will appear that, since one account is false, it is possible that the other may be so likewise.
>
> 			*Strauss's Life of Jesus* trans. George Eliot (1846) i 92

The result of Strauss's massive compilation and exegesis is a radical scepticism towards the truth of *any* of the Gospel narratives, especially in their miraculous aspect, and Strauss himself anticipates the popular reaction to his work as to an iconoclastic outrage:

The boundless store of truth and life which for eighteen centuries has been the aliment of humanity, seems irretrievably dissipated; the most sublime levelled with the dust, God divested of his grace, man of his dignity, and the tie between heaven and earth broken.

iii 396

But this is only the most extreme example of the general effect of critical historiography, which was to attack myths of single origin, untroubled authorship and historical certitude wherever they were predicated of written records or literary works.

Browning's familiarity with every aspect of the critical attack is easy to establish. In 'Historiography and *The Ring and the Book*',[9] Morse Peckham has noted a debt to Ranke, foremost of the contemporary critical historians, and Browning himself, in the late poem *Development* (1889), annotated his interest in Wolf and Strauss:

> Had you asked
> The all-accomplished scholar, twelve years old,
> 'Who was it wrote the Iliad?' – what a laugh!
> 'Why, Homer, all the world knows[.']
> . . . Thus did youth spend a comfortable time;
> Until – 'What's this the Germans say is fact
> That Wolf found out first?
> . . . So, I bent brow o'er *Prolegomena*.
> And, after Wolf, a dozen of his like
> Proved there was never any Troy at all,
> Neither Besiegers nor Besieged, – nay, worse, –
> No actual Homer, no authentic text,
> No warrant for the fiction I, as fact,
> Had treasured in my heart and soul so long[.]

50–3, 62–4, 67–73

Thus in *Development* (1889) Browning describes his attitude to the criticism of the Homeric texts, and his initial reaction to Strauss, judging by *Christmas-Eve and Easter Day*, was equally alarmed:

> But the Critic leaves no air to poison;
> Pumps out with ruthless ingenuity
> Atom by atom, and leaves you – vacuity.

Christmas-Eve 911–13

Eleanor Shaffer has shown, however, that Browning's view of Strauss
had become far more hospitable by the time he wrote *A Death in the Desert*
in 1864.[10] In that poem, Browning doubled the problems of textual
provenance by positing a complex machinery of oral/scribal transmission
liable, like the Gospel narratives, to a Straussian reduction. The 'claim' of
'St John' to have been the single author of all the Johannine texts (a claim
disputed by the Higher Criticism) is hardly reinforced by its imputed
lineage as a shadowy product of oral tradition (as Strauss argued the
Gospels were), or by its amazing inclusion of Strauss himself amongst the
visionary company John sees; in fact, Browning seems deliberately to
have loaded his poem with all the elements which would damn a historical
text in the eyes of a conscientious critical historian. Browning's object is
not, however, simply to 'concede' Strauss's case; rather, he concedes its
necessity in the formation of an adequate moral basis for the religion it
superficially questions; in broader terms, the necessity of epistemological indeterminacy in relation to all claims of ontological stability for
writing.

St John's response to Strauss's objections to his, St John's, record of
Christ's life is that such objections are essential to the formation of a
morally mature understanding of the Incarnation:

> 'I say, that as the babe, you feed awhile,
> Becomes a boy and fit to feed himself,
> So, minds at first must be spoon-fed with truth:
> When they can eat, babe's-nurture is withdrawn.
> . . . Therefore, I say, to test man, the proofs shift.
> Nor may he grasp that fact like other fact[.']

                                                    433–6, 295–6

Belief must become a progressively stiffer obstacle-race, and in
consequence its secure tenure becomes lost during its retreat into remoter
history, until, under the pressure of a Strauss's objections to its merely
historical validity, its moral significance can re-emerge as, after all, the
better claim to truth. The latter point is more clearly formulated by the
Pope in *The Ring and the Book*, whom Browning likewise endows with a
prophetic knowledge of the kind of objection Strauss was to make:

> Nor do I much perplex me with aught hard,
> Dubious in the transmitting of the tale, –
> No, nor with certain riddles set to solve.

> This life is training and a passage[;]
> ... The moral sense grows but by exercise.

x 1408–11, 1415

He even welcomes the iconoclasm which he foresees in the 18th century after him:

> As we broke up that old faith of the world,
> Have we, next age, to break up this the new –
> Faith, in the thing, grown faith in the report
> Whence need to bravely disbelieve report
> Through increased faith i' the things reports belie?

x 1864–8

To recognise, as Strauss did, irresolvable contradictions in the Gospel accounts is to do Christianity a *service* by forcing the faithful to appreciate that the reality, the truth of their religion is not located in such accounts. This is a position parallel to that adopted by John Stuart Mill, who in the *Essay on Liberty* was similarly prepared to subordinate ontology to epistemology:

> However unwillingly a person who has a strong opinion may admit the possibility that his opinion may be false, he ought to be moved by the consideration that, however true it may be, if it is not fully, frequently, and fearlessly discussed, it will be held as a dead dogma, not a living truth.
> *On Liberty* ed. G. Himmelfarb (Harmondsworth, Middx, 1974) 96–7

Of those who know 'truth' – already such an application of the word seems paradoxical – only as 'dead dogma', Mill remarks,

> [T]heir conclusion may be true, but it might be false for anything they knew: they have never thrown themselves into the mental position of those who think differently from them, and considered what such people might have to say; and, consequently, they do not, in any proper sense of the word, know the doctrine which they themselves profess.
> 99

Mill even significantly anticipates the very sense in which *The Ring and*

the Book restores 'living truth' by forcing readers to 'throw themselves
into the mental position of people who think differently':

> I confess I should like to see the teachers of mankind endeavouring to
> provide ... some contrivance for making the difficulties of the
> question as present to the learner's consciousness as if they were
> pressed upon him by a dissentient champion, eager for his
> conversion.

106

But the Pope goes further than either Mill or St John, by recovering
ontological certainty – Mill's 'truth' – from the very centre of this
epistemological dubiety. Because the 'difficulties of the question' are so
inveterately obtrusive, the truth of the Incarnation, he argues, cannot be
predicated of it in any scientific sense, but rather subsists in its prior
congruence with man's ethical constitution. The process is dialectical:

> There is, beside the works, a tale of Thee
> In the world's mouth, which I find credible:
> I love it with my heart: unsatisfied,
> I try it with my reason, nor discept
> From any point I probe and pronouce sound.

x 1348–52

The primary impulse here is moral – the 'tale' is lovable – followed by the
apparently antithetical appeal to 'reason' for corroboration or refutation.
But the Pope's description of the rational process unfixes the antithesis.
He claims that the appropriate 'test' of the truth of the 'tale' will emerge
from a contemplation of the make-up of God's universe:

> Is there strength there? – enough: intelligence?
> Ample: but goodness in a like degree?
> Not to the human eye in the present state,
> An isoscele deficient in the base.
> What lacks, then, of perfection fit for God
> But just the instance which this tale supplies
> Of love without a limit? So is strength,
> So is intelligence; let love be so,
> Unlimited in its self-sacrifice:
> Then is the tale true and God shows complete.

x 1363–72

God's 'power' and 'intelligence' may be known inductively, from the visible substance and structure of things, but his 'love' can only emerge deductively, from man's awareness that he himself possesses such a quality. For if it is in man, love must also belong to God, the author of all things; and the Incarnation, explicable only as God's revelation of such a quality in himself, therefore becomes the 'evidence' for something – that God loves – which because it must be the case, becomes in turn our 'evidence' for the Incarnation. Because it fills a moral gap in the universe, in other words, the Incarnation must be presumed to have taken place as a physical event, and the difficulties which surround its transmission are mere background noise designed to make the would-be believer sharpen his moral sensibilities. Mill's refusal to countenance the 'intuitionist' principle upon which this argument ultimately rests prevented him from embracing its complete span;[11] thinkers, like Froude and even Carlyle himself were scared off by the epistemological dubiety which Mill and Browning welcome; only Browning seems to have been able to combine a sense of the baffling multiplicity and dubiety of truth with a certainty that truth exists in a determinate form, finding at the end of *Development*, for instance, that the events of the Trojan War, despite – or perhaps because of – all the dubiety with which Wolf and his successors hedged it round, remained a hard fact because, again, of their consonance with the moral order available to introspection.

V

The Pope knows the truth about the 'Roman Murder-Story' in the same way he knows the truth about the Incarnation; indeed, the two events are, for him, made perfectly equivalent by Caponsacchi's self-sacrifice:

> How can man love but what he yearns to help?
> And that which men think weakness within strength,
> But angels know for strength and stronger yet –
> What were it else but the first things made new,
> But repetition of the miracle,
> The divine instance of self-sacrifice
> That never ends and aye begins for man?

x 1652–8

The truth of *any* event, it seems, may be established on a moral basis which proleptically estabishes its actual occurrence.

But the analogy between the events of *The Ring and the Book* and the
Incarnation is not merely casual, as an inspection of the monologues
reveals. There is no speaker and no protagonist who does not parallel
some element of the story to the Christian pattern, Guido, for instance,
identifying his judicial torture with Christ's Passion at the very beginning
of his first monologue:

> Fortified by the sip of . . . why, 'tis wine,
> Velletri, – and not vinegar and gall,
> So changed and good the times grow!
>
> v 4–6

and again in the second, when he exclaims, 'Abate, gird your loins and
wash my feet!' (xi 616). Caponsacchi, however, prefers to see him as
Judas, Bottinius as Herod. Similarly, Tertium Quid describes Violante's
'finding' of Pompilia by comic identification with the Virgin Mary's
Annunciation, only for Pompilia to take over the same identity in
comparing herself to

> the poor Virgin that I used to know
> At our street-corner in a lonely niche, –
> The babe, that sat upon her knees, broke off[.]
>
> vii 77–9

The image is apt, since prior to Guido's attack she has been separated
from her child, and will, in the course of her monologue, deny Guido any
share in its paternity. Other speakers nevertheless elect to compare her to
Mary Magdalen. There is nothing strained or self-conscious about this
typological preoccupation in a Catholic culture; Browning had Shelley's
warrant for the view that '[r]eligion . . . in the mind of an Italian Catholic
. . . is interwoven with the whole fabric of life';[12] but his aim was more
than simple sociological veracity, for the most important formal
precedent for *The Ring and the Book* is the four Christian Gospels.

The New Testament, or rather, that part of it on which the Christian
faith is primarily based, consists of three 'eye-witness accounts' of the
same story, Christ's life (the Synoptic Gospels), followed by a fourth (*St
John*) which takes a more distanced and philosophic approach to the same
subject. *The Ring and the Book* is based on three eye-witness accounts of
the main story, Guido's, Caponsacchi's and Pompilia's, followed by a

fourth, the Pope's, which like St John's Gospel constitutes a more abstract philosophic meditation (the close resemblance between the Pope's theories, not to mention his personality and situation, and those of Browning's St John in *A Death in the Desert* reinforces the analogy). The Pope's suggestion that in this story could be renewed 'that divine instance of self-sacrifice / That aye never ends and begins for men' is carried through onto the further level at which the poem's form replicates the form in which that divine instance was transmitted.

It should by now be clear why I believe Browning did this. It allowed him to preserve the essential propriety of the structured collection form, the absence of the linking motif, in a double sense: as history, the 'Roman Murder-Story' is both constantly absent and continually invoked; its typological re-enactment of the Gospel story opens the further recession at which exists its *significance* for Browning, and the justification of its adoption for epic. This significance is, at the directly thematic level, the Christian belief that the Incarnation is a moveable event, continuously renewed through history – Hopkins's belief that it 'rides time like riding a river'. On the implicit formal level, it is the epic of reader-dependence. Browning sets up a hermeneutic ring of accounts to replicate the hermeneutic ring around the Christian narrative, and in doing so, makes them mutually supportive: the Incarnation lends the Roman Murder-Story importance, as the Roman Murder-Story lends the Incarnation historical credibility. For what we are never invited to doubt, amidst the multiplied doubts that multiple narrative inflicts upon his story, is the real existence of that story as a presumed though inaccessible guarantor of the poem's historical basis. But this is exactly what Strauss had denied in the case of the Gospels. His 'Mythic explanation' allowed, in principle, the entire Christian story to have been manufactured out of man's psychological need to have such a story to tell and believe, dissolving its historical reality, as Wolf did Homer's. By associating the Gospel narrative, formally as well as typologically with 'the poorest of occurrences', Browning affirmed his belief that behind the gossip of Gospel voices a similar real occurrence lay concealed, as substantively unknowable as its successor yet as ontologically solid as well. In that sense, Carlyle's objection that 'the woman and the handsome young priest were lovers', in its unquestioning acceptance of the essential historicity of the 'Roman Murder-Story', fulfils the poem's real aim, which is to activate the reader as exegete of an event whose reality the mere act of exegesis confirms. Browning's greatest structured collection was built round the development of critical historiography, to which Browning reacted by adopting its procedures as a means of making readers assert their own free-will – in that sense, Strauss is a brother-liberator – against certainties which threatened to harden into tyranny over the mind.

VI

There can be little doubt either that *The Ring and the Book* was Browning's greatest popular triumph,[13] or that it was a rather unexpected one. The 1860s had seen a steady improvement in his reputation, (see my essay *Periodicals and the Practice of Literary Criticism 1855-1864* in *The Victorian Periodical Press* ed. Shattock and Wolff [Leicester 1982]) but nothing that could have led him to expect notices like R. W. Buchanan's:

> At last, the *opus magnum* of our generation lies before the world – the 'ring is rounded'; and we are left in doubt which to admire most, the supremely precious gold of the material or the wondrous beauty of the workmanship. The fascination of the work is still so strong upon us . . . that . . . we must record at once our conviction, not merely that *The Ring and the Book* is beyond all parallel the supremest poetical achievement of our time, but that it is the most precious and profound spiritual treasure that England has produced since the days of Shakespeare.
>
> R. W. Buchanan in *The Athenaeum* 2160 (20 Mar. 1869) 399–400: 399 *CH* 317

The less ecstatic but perhaps more acute reviewer in the *Westminster Review* noted the relation between the new poem and Browning's previous difficulties with his critics and public:

> Mr Browning's new poem promises to be the greatest of all his works. But before we proceed to criticise it, we have a word or two to say on a personal matter. Twice in the poem Mr Browning breaks away from his subject to sneer at the
>
> > "British Public, ye who like me not,
> >   God love you."
>
> Now, the real truth is, that the British Public do not know Mr Browning. There is no question of liking or disliking in the matter. Ten years ago he was quite unknown except to a select few. We distinctly remember hearing in the winter of 1860 a well-known author, and

editor of one of the most influential reviews of the day, declare that he had never read a word of Mr Browning's poetry. And the declaration struck nobody present as at all surprising. The exception, then, was to have read him. Such a declaration, however, in the year 1869 would be a confession of ignorance. But the British public at large still know no more about Mr Browning than they did about Mill before he became member for Westminster. *The Ring and the Book* will, however, we venture to say, introduce Mr Browning to the British public. Hitherto Mr Browning's admirers have been few though fit. His present poem will do much to make him popular, no bad test, even remembering Mr Martin Tupper's position, of the real worth of any poet.

The Westminster Review xci (n.s. xxxv) (1 Jan. 1869) 298-300:299:*CH*310

This is a perfectly reasonable summary, and it indicates that with *The Ring and the Book* Browning's long search for popularity was at last officially over. Though many reviewers cavilled at aspects of the poem, none felt able to deal out the kind of rollicking denunciation that *Men and Women* had enjoyed, and most spoke of it with considerable respect. Though this change of tone was no doubt prompted in part by Browning's installation, during the sixties, as a kind of semi-official sub-Laureate to Tennyson, a process in part stimulated by his adoption of the structured collection principle, there can be no question but that *The Ring and the Book* satisfied his contemporaries as no previous work of his had done.

Nor was this result accidental. If my reading of Browning's middle period is correct, *The Ring and the Book* was the climax of a series of experiments in reconciling himself, as far as he was able, to the taste of the time. I will conclude this chapter by noting the features which, in alliance with the structured collection principle, helped the poem to achieve this result.

Reviewers were not unnaturally most forcibly struck by the feature of the poem which was developed directly from the structured collection, its technique of multiple narration; the *Cornhill* put it, 'Everybody has heard by this time what the plan is of this wonderful story, and knows how original and how daring was the attempt'.[14] Most commended the scheme, not only for its originality but for its clarity - 'the result is attained that the reader does in the end understand the plot'[15] - confirming the opinion of Julia Wedgwood, whom Browning had given a preview of the poem, that the 'stereoscopic view' given by multiple narration makes both 'the design' and 'the details' 'perfectly clear' (*LJW* 152). In remarking that 'fertility of psychological explanation is the *raison d'être* of

The Ring and the Book', Walter Bagehot linked this characteristic to what he called 'the recurrent "or"' in Browning's mind.[16] There can be little doubt that these features both in structure and in style were dictated in part by the desire for clarity. Browning even complained to Carlyle that his execution of this task in the poem 'was like shouting in the ear of a deaf man'[17] – referring, presumably to his use of multiple narration, but the expression applies equally well to the local style, which, especially in the expository first book, proceeds to extraordinary lengths of parenthetical self-paraphrase (see p. 128–9).

It was however as much the bulk produced by the poem's method as the method itself which impressed critics: 'we confess to something like awe at the prodigality of the force which is lavished on these pages'.[18] Some went on, not surprisingly, to find in the poem precisely the modern epic for which they had been clamouring for so many years:

> We saw the other day, in a paper set at one of our public schools, this question asked – 'Why are epic poems not written nowadays' The questioner, if he had seen Mr Browning's poem, would surely have thought his inquiry somewhat premature.
>
> *The Saturday Review* xxvi (1868) 832–4833; *CH* 297

This assertion is prompted by the perception that in spite of, or perhaps in a sense because of its use of multiple narration, the poem 'has a natural unity in itself', a unity superior, thought one critic, to that of any Romantic long poem.[19] Yet there is some hesitation as to whether the poem can legitimately be described as an epic, and a certain amount of good-natured perplexity as to what genre it does belong to. Different reviewers compare it to Balzac, Shakespeare and Carlyle, and the net effect is a widespread though unhostile uncertainty as to whether, if not an epic, it is to be classed as novel, drama or history, or some combination of the three. This too seems to have been intentional on Browning's part. *The Ring and the Book* is eclectic in genre, and in being so was able to gather in a larger audience than would have been available for a work more narrowly circumscribed to one or other of its genres.

The twelve-book form necessarily recalls epic, but Buxton Forman, in calling it an 'Epic of Psychology', points, as Bagehot also does, to the fact that 'the action, and passion, and incidents coming before you are psychical, not physical'.[20] Another reviewer directly asserts, 'nothing could be more unlike the incidents which Homer delights in than this story', adding, 'the story is of no account, except as it serves the poet's purpose of showing a few characters in a great variety of relations, and of illustrating his thesis'.[21] The analogy with drama is similarly both invoked and revoked. The *Edinburgh Review* calls the poem 'a drama', but the *Athenaeum* put it: 'in exchange for the drama we get the monologue', and John Addington Symons in *Macmillan's* explains that this feature reflects the fact that 'ours is not a dramatic age. We want to get behind the scenes, to trace the inmost working of motives'.[22]

Both these lines of reasoning find their echo in the poem. Comparisons between characters and their epic prototypes are common – Guido as Vulcan, Pompilia and Caponsacchi as Venus and Mars; Guido as Menelaus, Pompilia and Caponsacchi as Helen and Paris, and so on – but they are mostly cited by bookish characters like the lawyers and Guido, and are invariably introduced with a contrast, implicit or explicit, between the grandeur of the epic figures and the diminished status of their modern 'equivalents'.[23] This is so even with the most apparently serious example, Guido's claim, in his second monologue, to a Pagan morality which equates him with Virgil, or with Odysseus. A trivial mistake about what book of the *Aeneid* he is quoting brings out the mere bookishness of his self-aggrandisement, as the Circe with whom he wishes he had coupled has no existence outside his book-fed imagination (see xi 1919–30, 2207–13).

Similarly, Browning in Book i of the poem invokes the analogy with drama only to reject or qualify it:

> Let this old woe step on the stage again!
> Act itself o'er anew for men to judge,
> Not by the very sense and sight indeed –
> (Which take at best imperfect cognisance . . .)
>
> i 824–7

Here, the inwardness that makes *The Ring and the Book* a drama as well as an epic of psychology is seen, consistently with Browning's belief as expressed in and after the Prologue to *Paracelsus*, as an advantage over genres which rely upon 'the gross machinery of external events'. In this feature, the poem moves towards the novel, and many critics make this comparison, though as often on the grounds of the poem's realism as for its emphasis on psychology. Comparisons with Balzac are frequent; Dickens and George Eliot are mentioned; Moncure Conway however is the only reviewer roundly to assert that 'this extraordinary work is a novel'. Conway goes on to include among the features which make it a novel its use, remarked by many critics, of police-court sensationalism:

There is nothing new in making the interest of a story turn up on a crime and a trial, though novelists, rather than poets, have inclined to use that well-worn machinery.

Atlantic Monthly xxiii (1869) 256–9; 256

The *North American Review* notes the market calculation behind such a choice:

No incident in private life excites such general and prolonged interest as a murder. The first reports of the affair are eagerly read.

North American Review cix (1869) 279–83; 281

The North British Review remarked that 'Mr Browning's poem is cousin-german to a series of newspaper articles', *The British Quarterly Review* called it 'the newspaper in blank verse'.[24] Such comparisons point equally to an element of documentary journalism, and Conway himself remarks that though a novel, *The Ring and the Book* is 'not a fiction', exposing the purely historical dimension which takes Browning's realism beyond even that of Balzac. Balzac had argued, in the *Avant-Propos* to the *Comédie Humaine*, that while fiction should be accurate in its details, it remained free, in its larger organisation, to 'tendre vers le beau idéal'.[25] As he explained to Julia Wedgwood, Browning altogether repudiated such a distinction, at least for *The Ring and the Book*:

the business has been . . . to explain *fact*[.] . . . The question with me has never been, 'Could not one, by changing the factors, work out the sum to a better result?' but declare and prove the actual result[.]

19 Nov. 1868: *LJW* 158

Nevertheless, as critics appreciated, the poem draws substantially upon novel-technique, and in particular upon the practice of serialising novels. *Bells and Pomegranates* had been issued serially, but as a series of separate works; *The Ring and the Book* was issued, originally, in four chronologically separated sections of three books apiece, involving a far more thoroughgoing analogy with the serial novel.[26] Most reviewers who noted this feature approved it, *The Fortnightly Review* because 'it ensures that slow and prolonged absorption of the story which is essential to the success of the method in which it is composed', *The Spectator* because each part would 'form a whole in itself, organically complete'.[27] There is certainly nothing haphazard about the quadripartite division. Each 'part' begins with a monologue having some claim to objectivity, next presents Guido's viewpoint, and ends with one which is in some sense a partisan statement on Pompilia's behalf. Browning, the speaker of the first monologue, is necessarily in principle the objective voice of the poem; Half-Rome supports Guido, Other Half-Rome Pompilia. Tertium Quid, who opens part two, claims an objective view; Guido is naturally on his own side, Caponsacchi as naturally on Pompilia's. Pompilia, at the beginning of part three, is inspired by the proximity of death to an objectivity that lifts her above partisanship; she is followed by, respectively, Guido's lawyer and her own. The Pope opens the last part with an authoritative *ex cathedra* judgment; Guido again speaks for himself; and the last book, 'The Book and the Ring' is once more dominated by a pro-Pompilia statement, this time by the Augustinian monk who heard her dying confession.

This plan had many advantages. It ensured that at least one popular favourite was present in each part, after the first: Caponsacchi, Pompilia and the Pope were much the most popular speakers, though a maverick minority admired Guido. Julia Wedgwood's response to reading part three – 'Pray make haste to send me the old Pope to take the taste of the lawyers out of my mouth!' (*LJW* 171) – illustrates the effectiveness of this aspect of the strategy, as well as its contribution to a certain kind of 'suspense', as the audience, left suspended by the partisan reading, awaits the synthesis which will open the next part. More importantly, the gradual exposure of the stories through successive packages of monologues projects into the experience of reading the indeterminacy which is so crucial to the 'life' of the poem.

VII

Not only the publication of *The Ring and the Book* in parts, but the arrangement of material within the parts, was designed to facilitate the reader's participation in the poem. The first part has a largely expository function. Its monologues tell the story in a relatively straightforward fashion, supplying readers with a simple map of the essential course of events, in preparation for the more complex kinds of presentation which follow. In later parts, Browning's method can become progressively more allusive and elliptical, without danger of his being accused of the hopeless obscurity which readers had experienced in *Sordello*. In fact, the leading monologues of parts ii, iii and iv are, in narrative terms, hardly less complex than *Sordello*, but the preliminary experience of the exposition of part i furnishes the reader with so powerful an orientation that he or she is not thrown off-balance, but encounters the difficulties almost without recognising that they *are* difficulties.

A case in point is book vii, Pompilia's monologue. Being at the point of death, and having already told her story for judicial and confessional purposes, Pompilia feels free to reflect upon rather than narrate it;

indeed, her monologue hardly involves narrative at all. Instead, she proceeds associatively, throwing selective highlights on the parts of the story which interest her. The fact that her interlocutors, the women attendants of the hospital in which she is staying, already know the raw sequence of events, enables her to do this without losing contact with them; the fact that readers of the poem are by now in a similar position makes her allusive method accessible to them in turn.

At first sight, her monologue looks like an associative ramble, like the murmurings of the dying bishop in *The Bishop Orders his Tomb*. But this is not the case. She wishes to express her love for her child and her love for Caponsacchi, while exonerating the latter from the charge of having loved her – implicitly, the charge that he is father of her child. Her interlocutors' knowledge leaves them sceptical, as the reader may also be, of the claim that she and Caponsacchi were sexually innocent; she must, then, with her dying words, at once exonerate Caponsacchi from the charge of loving her, and send her child pure into the world. She presents this double aim dramatically, when she imagines her child, grown to adulthood, questioning her conduct:

> Why did you venture out of the safe street?
> Why go so far from help to that lone house?
> Why open at the whisper and the knock?

vii 217–19

The subtext of this question, never directly mentioned by her but familiar to the reader from earlier accounts, is the fact that Guido, in order to gain access to the house in which she and her parents had hidden themselves, used Caponsacchi's name; its implication, therefore, is that she and Caponsacchi shared a love, whether guilty or pure, which contradicts the case that there was nothing between them – an implication sharpened by the fact that in *his* monologue, immediately preceding hers, Caponsacchi had come dangerously close to confessing something like love on his side.

The crucial function of the knock at the door in Pompilia's own view of the case appears in her constant recurrence to it. Indeed, she never bothers to describe the superficially more spectacular succeeding event, the murder of her parents and the fatal wounding of herself. Little of what earlier speakers had perceived as central to the story is even mentioned in her monologue. Instead, she begins with a rhapsody over her child (1–129), and couples it with a meditation on the parallel of her own birth and childhood. Underneath her account of her adoptive parents' declaration that she is not their child but a prostitute's (130–49) lurks the danger that posterity, in the shape of *her* child, will trace the same pattern in her case: the fact that she has been, since before the murder, separated from him, as she was from her mother, sharpens the threatened equation. It is by natural association of ideas that she next mentions her husband (150-8) and Caponsacchi (159-80); her son's imagined question, with its invocation of the fateful knock in which husband and Caponsacchi are grotesquely blended, naturally follows.

Her response to the question is, in the first instance, to repeat it. Her initial description of the knock describes the cosy domestic scene between herself and her adoptive parents; then, 'at the door, / A tap: we started up: you know the rest' (266-7). 'The rest' is the murder, but she ignores it, and instead passes immediately to the issue of her supposed mother's guilt in contriving to pass off her (Pompilia) as her daughter. This meditation leads her closer to conventional narrative, as she details the events of the marriage contrived by Violante. But this narrative has no story-function – we have already had the details – rather, it is designed to show that the marriage was a result of Violante's conscience, and her desire to secure for Pompilia a position more socially stable than illegitimacy could allow the child or unmarried girl. Hence, urged to detail the more spectacular aftermath of the marriage, her sadistic persecution by Guido and his household, she refuses to do so, in a gesture complementing her failure to describe the murder. Instead, after a casual mention of her elopement with Caponsacchi (860) she moves, again associatively, to her natural mother and her own child, and thence to Caponsacchi, as needing exculpation from the charge of being too deeply involved with her, and to another stretch of more straightforward narrative of the elopement, which she presents as the biological outcome of her pregnancy. This movement occupies lines 1200-1693, and concludes by weaving Caponsacchi and the child together, with him in the role of its saviour, the man whose self-sacrificial action enabled the child to be born. When, again, the fatal 'tap' recurs (1695), it now prefaces a valedictory meditation in which she finds all to be for the best, and at last confronts the question of Guido's murder from a perspective which permits forgiveness: her parents were guilty and are punished, she, now her child is born, asks no more of life, and ends by denying that Guido was, in any real sense, the child's father. Her account of the elopement now ensures that this argument cannot be misunderstood, and allows her to confront, as her last gesture, the motive for her opening the door:

> It was the name of him I sprang to meet
> When the knock came, the summons and the end.
> 'My great heart, my strong hand are back again!'
> I would have sprung to these, beckoning across

> Murder and hell gigantic and distinct
> O' the threshold, posted to exclude me heaven:
> He is ordained to call and I to come!
>
> 1808-14

This is the first time she has mentioned Guido's impersonation of
Caponsacchi, and the accumulation of her monologue has prepared for
the appearance of this fact as an element, if not the proof of her innocence,
and, more than that, as her recognition of and response to Caponsacchi's
sanctity (the imagined 'call' of Caponsacchi invokes the parallel with
Christ's summoning of his disciples, as for her Caponsacchi *is* Christ, or
his representative). The logic of her apparently rambling discourse stands
revealed, achieves its purpose, and finally allows her to die.

It is only necessary try to imagine the effect of this presentation of
events in a solo monologue, unsupported by previous accounts, to realise
its difficulty as narrative. It is utterly radical. Pompilia enters the story
from its end, moves amongst its events with virtually no chronological
propriety, and omits everything which does not relate to her purpose
(including, almost, any mention of her husband). It would be impossible
to follow this presentation without a detailed prior knowledge of the
events. The development of her picture of the story takes the form of a
steadily thickening incrustation of interpretative detail and explanation
around a single, apparently minor event. This process, with its ellipses,
flash-backs, allusions and contempt for narrative, corresponds almost
exactly to Browning's own procedure in *Sordello*; it is repeated in all the
subsequent monologues; but the hinterland of exposition, continued as
an elaborate cross-reference and interpretative interdependence between
all the monologues of parts ii, iii, and iv, allows the reader to thread them
together, collate them, and emerge with a clear vision. But that vision was
not 'given' by the poem. It was assembled by the reader. In that sense, *The
Ring and the Book* indeed climaxes Browning's development, by
allowing him to combine his own priority of reader-creativity with the
reader's demand for explanation. In his middle period he had, as I have
shown, moved to meet his readers on or near the ground defined by them
as necessary to their approval; in response they, as he recognised in his
Preface to the *Selections* of 1872, moved to meet *him*:

> The readers I am at last privileged to expect, meet me fully half-way;
> and if, from their fitting standpoint, they must still 'censure me in their
> wisdom,' they have previously 'awakened their senses that they may
> better judge.'
>
> Preface to *Selections*, 1872

Notes

CHAPTER 1: THE PROBLEM OF POWER

1. *Essay on Shelley* (1852); in *Poems*, eds Pettigrew and Collins (Harmondsworth, Middx, 1981) [hereafter *Penguin*] i 1008.

2. On 16 Sept. 1845 E.B.B. wrote to Browning that Mr Moulton-Barrett 'never does tolerate in his family (sons or daughters) the development of one class of feelings' (*The Letters of Robert Browning and Elizabeth Barrett Barrett*, ed. E. Kintner [Harvard, 1969] [hereafter *LK*] 196). Browning's abhorrence of this attitude was expressed on 25 Sept. (*LK* 394). The passage I quote comes from a letter in which E.B.B. described the 'dreadful scenes' which followed her sister Arabel's attempt to lighten the tyranny (15 Jan. 1846: *LK* 394). A corroboration of Browning's political/religious reading of Mr Moulton-Barrett's conduct, though possibly inspired by him and therefore not independent evidence, comes in a letter in which Browning's friend Joseph Arnould described E.B.B.'s father as 'one of those tyrannical, arbitrary, puritanical rascals who go sleekly about the world, canting Calvinism abroad, and acting despotism at home' (to Alfred Domett, *Robert Browning and Alfred Domett*, ed. F. G. Kenyon [1907] [hereafter *RB & AD*] 133).

3. *The General Biographical Dictionary*, ed. A. Chalmers (1812–17).

4. *Biographie Universelle* (Paris, 1811–22).

5. See e.g. F. A. Pottle, *Shelley and Browning: a Myth and some Facts* (Chicago, 1923), and the edition of *Paracelsus* in vol i of *The Poetical Works of Robert Browning*, eds I. R. J. Jack and M. Smith (Oxford, 1983: hereafter *Oxford*).

6. Alexander Singleton coupled the two writers as 'pre-eminently human in the direction of their thought': 'Both act upon Pope's dictum that "the proper study of mankind is man"', with both and nature, outward, organic nature though acutely observed and sympathetically described, is never more than a background or foundation for the display in relief and testing of human character' :(Alexander Singleton, 'Goethe and Browning', *Publications of the English Goethe Society* [1912] 155). The precise degree of Browning's acquaintance with Goethe has not been studied: in particular, the extent of his knowledge of the German language remains controversial. In a letter of 1842 he asked his friend Alfred Domett, 'Do you prosecute German-study? I read pretty well now.' (To Alfred Domett, 13. Dec. 1842; *RB & AD* 49). This implies that when he wrote *Paracelsus* (1835) his competence was limited. However, *Faust* (part i) *Werter* and other works were available in translation: in a letter (to R. H. Horne, Autumn 1843; *NL* 32) Browning mentions two translations of *Faust* part i published in 1834 and 1835, and it seems probable that his reading of these stimulated him into both the writing of *Paracelsus* and the learning of German. It would equally seem reasonable to assume that he had considerable direct or indirect acquaintance with Goethe's work even before he knew the language well. Browning's interest in Goethe and in German poetry evidently continued: Eveline Forbes ('A Visit to

Balliol, 1879', *Nineteenth Century* xc [1921] 862-3) recalls a conversation in which 'He spoke of the German poets, of Goethe chiefly'; a late lyric (the conclusion of *Parleying with Gerard de Lairesse*) derives in part from Goethe's *Anakreons Grab*. See J. M. Carré, *Goethe en Angleterre* (Paris, 1921), E. Oswald, *Goethe in England and America* (1909) and (for a more general study), W. Stockley, *German Literature as Known in England 1750-1830* (1929).

7. I should add that the historical Paracelsus also had this idea, arguing that 'all things were made of nothing, by a word only, save man alone. . . . God took the body out of which He built up man from those things which he created from nothingness into something. That mass was the extract of all creatures in heaven and earth' (*Hermetic Astronomy*, in *The Hermetic and Alchemical Writings of Paracelsus*, ed. A. E. Waite [1894]: ii 289). The origin of this idea is Kabbalistic.

8. These are collected in the *Miscellanies*: see esp. those 'On History' and 'On Biography'.

9. To Alfred Domett 13 Dec. 1842: *RB & AD* 49.

10. Goethe himself felt some unease about his position, remarking 'I do not know that I ever joined in any way against the people; but it is now settled once for all, that I am no friend to the people. I am indeed no friend to the revolutionary mob. . . . I hate every violent overthrow, because as much good is destroyed by it as is gained by it' (*Maxims and Reflections* i 241). For a good account of Goethe's political career see G. P. Gooch, 'The political background of Goethe's life', *Publications of the English Goethe Society* n.s. iii (1928) 1-30.

11. See Book vi, where Sordello argues that to oppress the people really does them no harm, since 'Whence rose their claim but still / From Ill, as fruit of Ill – what else could knit / You theirs but Sorrow? Any free from it / Were also free from you!' (250-3).

12. I am grateful to Dr John Beer for the following comment: 'I have found it profitable to look at the question of liberty at this time under the separate headings of independence and freedom. That is, it seems to me that a primary concern and perhaps *the* primary concern in the seventeenth century was with independence: that is, the right of the individual to think in separation from the community. In this respect, Milton seems to me a dominant presence, in addition to figures such as John Lilburne. By the end of the seventeenth century that particular battle was largely won, and attention was focused more on the question of the nature of freedom, which involved the issue whether freedom was to be found in certain kinds of action or as a mental condition. Those who took the second line (notably Blake) could immediately find themselves facing also the issue of independence, since their society's dismissal could be so absolute as to drive them into a condition very close to madness as they continued to assert the validity of their own vision. Browning seems to me to be very much in the later tradition of 'freedom' and to move rapidly into that of asserting that true freedom exists in the individual rather than in the result of political action; but he is clearly aware also of the problems of independence that this raises and is carefully guarded against the dangers of isolation within his own society' (private communication).

13. Rousseau arrived, by a different route, at this position. His concept of the 'General Will' likewise considered the individual as subordinate to a larger collectivity. This is asserted in many passages in *The Social Contract*, as a consequence of the premise that 'the general will is always in the right' (*Rousseau's Social Contract etc*, trans. G. D. H. Cole [n.d.] 27), as here: 'As nature gives each man absolute power over all his members, the social compact gives the body politic absolute power over all its members also; and it is this power which, under the direction of the general will, bears, as I have said, the name of Sovereignty' (*Cole* 26–7).

14. The poem was commissioned by Andrew Reid for a volume entitled *Why I am a Liberal*. The book was published in 1885; Browning's poem appears on p. 11. He never collected it, but it has frequently been republished: see DeVane, *Browning Handbook* (2nd edn, New York, 1955 [hereafter *DeVane*]) 567.

15. *On Liberty* (Harmondsworth, Middx, 1974) 121, 126.

16. Browning first attacked Byron publicly in *Prince Hohenstiel-Schwangau, Saviour of Society* (1871): see n.24 below; the attack was repeated in *Fifine at the Fair* (1872), see l. 1105f. Byron and Rousseau were coupled in another attack in *La Saisiaz* (1877).

17. *Essay on Shelley, Penguin* i 1009. It is worth adding that Browning concurrently became disillusioned with Shelley. In 1851 Browning met Thomas Hookham, who had known Shelley, and who showed Browning papers connected with Shelley's elopement with Mary Godwin. Thereafter, Browning frequently expressed to correspondents his opinion that Shelley's conduct towards his first wife, Harriet, had been 'wholly inexcusable'; his letter of 12 Oct. 1883 to Edward Dowden (*Letters*, ed T. L. Hood [1933] [hereafter *LH*] 223–4) explains the matter very fully. In 1885 Browning refused to become President of the Shelley Society.

18. 'why not have . . . gone there and "jawed", if but in John Lilburne's method, who, when pilloried, or carted rather, "did justify himself to all men", whereon they gagged him and tied his hands lest he should gesticulate and explain something by that; "yet did he protest against them by a stamping with his feet", to the no small comfort of his stout heart, I warrant' (to Alfred Domett, 23 November 1845, *RB & AD* 118–19).

19. The historical Paracelsus held views very close to those of Browning's character, claiming, 'Now, man is not only flesh and blood, but there is within him the intellect which does not, like the complexion, come from the elements, but from the stars. And the condition of the stars is this, that all the wisdom, intelligence, industry of the animal, and all the arts peculiar to man are contained within them. From the stars man has these same things, and that is called the light of Nature' (*Hermetic Astronomy*, Waite ii 290). This concept is Gnostic. See H. Jones, *The Gnostic Religion* (1963). The central tenet of Gnosticism was that God made himself known to the believer through mystical knowledge rather than faith or works. This led to a dualistic cosmology in which the world and man's flesh were regarded as irredeemably corrupt, and historically links Gnosticism to Platonism before and Manicheanism after it. Browning's

researches into Cornelius Agrippa, Paracelsus, Boehme, and other occult thinkers gave him contact with belated variants of Gnosticism, and he was familiar with the apocryphal New Testament, much of which is Gnostic (in quoting, in *Sordello* iii 990–1021, from the *Acts of St John* he was referred to 'one of the most famous gnostic texts' [*The Gnostic Gospels*, E. Pagels [1979]73]). It is interesting to note that the original of Goethe's Faust-legend was the Gnostic Simon Magus, who also influenced Paracelsus.

20. The correspondence between Browning and his friend Amedée de Ripert-Monclar has recently been published for the first time, in vol. iii of *The Brownings' Correspondence*, eds P. Kelley and R. Hudson (Winfield, Kansas, 1985: hereafter *Correspondence*). Included (pp. 416–24) is a series of notes which Browning wrote on an abstract of *Paracelsus* sent to him by Monclar [hereafter *Monclar*].

21. Godwin, *Enquiry Concerning Political Justice*, ed. I. Kramnick (Harmondsworth, Middx, 1976) p. 82. Shelley, *Declaration of Rights*, 1812 (*Shelley's Prose*, ed. D. L. Clark, [Albuquerque, 1954]) p. 72.

22. See note 11.

23. For a different interpretation of this episode, see d. m. de silva, 'Browning's *King Victor and King Charles*,' *Browning Society Notes* [hereafter *BSN*] xi (Apr. 1981) 8–21.

24. See *Biographia Literaria* ch. xiii.

25. *Prince Hohenstiel-Schwangau* 517f. parodies and attacks various passages in *Childe Harold*, notably ii 217–34, iii 109–117, 590–8, 707–15, 896–905, iv 1603–1620.

26. Browning's note, written on a copy containing notes and a short notice of the poem by J. S. Mill (in the Victoria and Albert Museum, London), claims that *Pauline* was the first of a series in which he would 'assume & realise I know not how many different characters', and that 'the present abortion' (i.e. *Pauline*) was 'the first work of the *Poet* of the batch'.

27. 'He was, as I have said, reluctant to publish'. Browning goes on to quote various commentators who claimed that Paracelsus's published works were, in effect, either extorted from him or spurious.

28. *Correspondence* iii 417.

29. The poem appears to be a spoken apostrophe to Pauline, who is dramatically represented as present and listening, but is really 'the fragmentary text of the young man's written confession to Pauline, which she has read and, as she explains in a footnote to l. 811, reluctantly allows to be published' (*Poems*, eds J. Woolford and D. R. Karlin i (Longman, 1987/8): line ref. to 1st edn text.

CHAPTER 2: THE PROBLEM OF AUDIENCE

1. *Essay on Shelley*, Penguin i 1001.

2. *Christian Remembrancer* xxxi (1856) 267: *Richard Simpson as Critic*, ed. D. Carroll (1977) 77.

3. Note for instance Leslie Stephen's lofty comment that 'if literary fame could safely be measured by popularity with the half-educated, Dickens

Notes

must claim that highest position among English novelists' (*DNB* entry on Dickens, 1888). A. O. J. Cockshut questions 'the textbook account' of Trollope's reputation, that he was read and admired in his lifetime and 'then . . . execrated and afterwards forgotten', but his attempt to show that Trollope's unpopularity began in the 1860s uses a rather carefully-selected group of reviews (*Antony Trollope* [1955] 133f.). David Skilton, in *Antony Trollope and his Contemporaries* (Harlow 1972) agrees that 'Trollope's reputation declined slowly but significantly from the late 'sixties onwards' (30), but it was not until 1880 that the objections took their worst turn: 'Mr Trollope is not an artist according to the modern school of high art' (33).

4. See W. S. Peterson and F. L. Stanley, 'The J. S. Mill marginalia in Robert Browning's *Pauline*: a history and a transcription': *Papers of the Bibliographical Society of America* lxvi (1972) 135–70. In his note on the J. S. Mill copy Browning ascribed *Pauline* to 'a foolish plan which occupied me mightily for a time, and which had for its object the enabling me to assume & realise I know not how many different characters[.] . . . The present abortion was the first work of the *Poet* of the batch, who would have been more legitimately *myself* than most of the others[.]' (*Oxford* i 4). Browning quotes Mill's opinion twice in his letters to E.B.B., each time with the implication that that opinion could legitimately refer to *him*, rather than a fictitious character (*LK* 28, 75), so it is hard to reach a clear conclusion.

5. Forster was working on a biography of Strafford at the time, and Browning claimed that he himself completed it during Forster's illness. Interestingly, Browning's reading of Strafford's character is almost exactly the reverse of Forster's.

6. The sources of Browning's knowledge of the theory of Romantic irony remain obscure. Schlegel's *Athenaeum-Fragments* were, as far as I know, untranslated during this period, so Browning would have had to read them in German (see note 6 to chapter one on this). Secondary sources are to be found in A. W. Schlegel and Coleridge (see note 7 below), but Browning's thought is more radical than theirs, and closer to Friedrich Schlegel's. It is probable that he read an article entitled *The Modern German School of Irony* (*Blackwood's* xxxviii [Sept. 1835] 376–87, which, though condescending, contains some significant remarks and quotations: 'In one of his [Jean Paul Richter's] philosophical works, the *Vorschule der Aesthetik* . . . he describes humour as the adaptation of the finite to the infinite, of the understanding to the ideal' (379). And, quoting Jacobi: 'We aspire to Heaven, and strive to attain it here on earth. . . . therefore in the same degree that the ART of the Ancients was the securing of the extant, the attained, or delight in the divinity, the satisfaction of enjoyment, in the same degree is our ART, a yearning sigh for the unattainable hereafter, or an ironical transformation of the unsatisfied soul. . . . When Christ took Heaven from the earth, presenting the latter as a mere point of passage, and with this doctrine inspired a sense of the nothingness of all earthly things, he, at the same time, ingrafted on our soul raillery of their casual, their transitory nature' (377–8). It is at least possible that Browning read further in the works here referred to, though the essential doctrine was

already clear. Browning might additionally have picked up this idea from Coleridge (who admittedly probably got it from Schlegel), who writes in his 1818 lectures 'Yet still the consciousness of the poet's [i.e. poetic dramatist's] mind must be diffused over that of his reader or spectator: but he himself, according to his genius, elevates us' (*Coleridge's Essays and Lectures on Shakespeare*, n.d. p. 34). How far Coleridge recognised the principle of Socratic Irony is uncertain. In these lectures, he oscillates rather uneasily between insisting upon the reader's 'willing suspension of disbelief' (reprobating Johnson for having apparently denied this), and admitting that a consciousness of illusion is constant. He tries to resolve the conflict by claiming that '[w]e simply do not judge the imagery to be unreal; there is a negative reality, and no more' (p. 48); later, he puts it that 'These and all other stage-representations, are to produce a sort of temporary half-faith, which the reader encourages in himself and supports by a voluntary contribution on his own part, because he knows that it is at all times in his power to see the thing as it really is . . . The true stage-illusion in this and in all things consists – not in the mind's judging it to be a forest, but in his remission of the judgement that it is a forest' (p. 218). On the other hand, *Biographia Literaria* is now being read very much as an exercise in Socratic Irony: see K. L. Wheeler, *Sources, Processes and Methods in Biographia Literaria* (Cambridge, 1980).

CHAPTER 3: THE PROBLEM OF FORM

1. 'He asserts the poet's rank and right, / basing these on their proper ground, / recognising true dignity in service, / whether successively that of epoist, / dramatist, or, so to call him, analyst / who turns in due course synthesist'.
2. Coleridge, *Biographia Literaria*, eds J. Engell and W. J. Bate (Princeton, 1983) ii 27. Keats *Letters*, ed. H. E. Rollins (Cambridge, Mass., 1958) i 387.
3. B. W. Fuson, *Browning and his English Predecessors in the Dramatic Monolog* [sic] (Iowa 1948). Ina Beth Sessions, *A Study of the Dramatic Monologue* (San Antonio, Texas, 1933).
4. M. W. Macallum, 'The Dramatic Monologue in the Victorian Period', *Proceedings of the British Academy* ix (1924–25) pp. 265–83.
5. *Langbaum* 189.
6. These remarks are to be found in the series of Ms. notes which E.B.B. wrote, at Browning's request, on the poems which were published as *Dramatic Romances and Lyrics*. They will be published in *Browning* (Longman's Annotated English Poets), eds J. Woolford and D. R. Karlin (1987/88).
7. *Devane* 363.
8. B. R. Jerman, *Browning's Witless Duke, PMLA* lxxii (1957) pp. 488–93; L. Perrine, *Browning's Shrewd Duke PMLA* lxxiv (1959) pp. 157–9.
9. J. K. Stephen *The Last Ride Together (from her point of view)*. The point of the parody is that 'Mr B.' is composing his poem during the ride, and will not speak: 'He looked as he does when he's writing verse . . . I spoke of the

weather to Mr B., / But he neither listened nor spoke to me. . . . I wonder what he was thinking about. / As I don't read verse I shan't find out' (see *Parodies: an anthology* ed. D. Macdonald [1960] 129–31).

10. See e.g. *Fra Lippo Lippi*, *Mr Sludge 'the Medium'*, *Fifine at the Fair*, *Clive*.

CHAPTER 4: THE STRUCTURED COLLECTION

1. To John Forster, 12 Apr. 1853: *NL* 61.
2. E.B.B. wrote to Fanny Haworth in 1860: 'Robert deserves no reproaches, for he has been writing a good deal this winter – working at a long poem which I have not seen a line of, and producing short lyrics which I *have* seen, and may declare worthy of him' (18 May 1860: *Kenyon* ii 388). DeVane argues, convincingly, that most of the poems of *Dramatis Personae* were written after E.B.B.'s death in 1861 (*DeVane* 281).
3. To Sarianna Browning, 'end of March 1861', *Kenyon* ii 434–6.
4. 'Mr Browning seems to us to succeed best in his character-poems – what may with some latitude of meaning be called dramatic sketches – conversation-pieces, fictitious epistles, and the like. His loose execution, though not an improvement even here, does not jar so up on the sense of fitness as in his lyric poems' (*Spectator* 1434 [22 Dec. 1855] 1347).
5. Mill's essays on aesthetics were all written in the 1830s. The most important are *What is Poetry?* and *The Two Kinds of Poetry*, published in W. J. Fox's *Monthly Repository* in 1833, *Tennyson's Poems*, published in the *London Review* in 1834 and *Writings of Alfred de Vigny*, published in the *London and Westminster Review* in 1838. Page references are to *Mill's Essays on Literature and Society*, ed. J. B. Schneewind (New York, 1965).
6. William Stigand, *Edinburgh Review* cxxx (Oct. 1864) 537–65: 554, *CH* 231.
7. In *Biographia Literaria* Coleridge at one point remarks that images 'become proofs of original genius only as far as they are modified by a predominant passion' (ed. Symons [1906] 169). Mill's emphasis on unbroken unity in a poem evidently derives from Coleridge's similar campaign, and at this point Coleridge appears in part to authorise Mill's concept of mood; but generally it is 'Imagination' which he puts in charge of aesthetic unity.
8. *Literary Essays* (1888) 196, 240–1.
9. Dallas was not unaware of the oddity of his position, and added, 'It may seem strange at first sight that the lyric, wherein the poet's individuality is most apparent, should be the offspring of the law of unconsciousness; and that the drama, wherein it is least evident, should come of that law which is the most conscious. A second thought will convince the reader that we are most ourselves when we forget ourselves, and that in becoming self-conscious we become what we are not' (*Poetics* 84).
10. 'Wordsworth, Tennyson and Browning, or, Pure, Ornate and Grotesque Art in English Poetry' (*Prose Works*, ed. Stevas i 321–66: i 329).
11. *Biographia* 165. Shelley's attitude is similar to Mill's, though his perspective is Platonic rather than neurological: 'There is this difference between a story and a poem, that a story is a catalogue of detached facts, which have no other connection than time, place, circumstance, cause

and effect; the other is the creation of actions according to the unchangeable forms of human nature'.

12. Poe, 'The Poetic Principle', *Complete Works* (repr. New York 1965) xiv 266. W. Bagehot, 'Wordsworth, Tennyson and Browning, or, Pure, Ornate and Grotesque Art in English Poetry' (*Prose Works*, ed. Stevas ii 321–66.

13. Margaret Oliphant in *Blackwood's Magazine* lxxix (Feb. 1856) 135. Evidently the complaint was widespread, for H. B. Forman remarked in a review of *The Ring and the Book* that 'the shortness of the poems by which Browning is best known serves as a standpoint for detractors' (*London Quarterly Review* xxxii (1869) 325–57, 337; *CH* 336.

14. C. P. Chrétien, *Christian Remembrancer* xvii (1849) 381–401, 381: repr. *Victorian Scrutinies*, ed. I. Armstrong (1972) 200–22; 201. Charles Kingsley made the same point: 'It has often been asked why Mr Tennyson's great and varied powers have never been concentrated on one immortal work. The epic, the lyric, the idyllic faculties, perhaps the dramatic also, seemed to be all there, and yet all sundered, scattered about in small fragmentary poems'. (*Fraser's* xlii [1850] 245–55, 254: *Tennyson: the Critical Heritage*, ed. J. Jump [1967] 184).

15. *British Quarterly Review* xxii (1855) 467–98: 480.

16. 'Never since the beginning of Time was there, that we hear or read of, so intensely self-conscious a Society. Our whole relations to the Universe and to our fellow-man have become an Inquiry, a Doubt; nothing will go on of its own accord, and do its function quietly; but all things must be probed into, the whole working of man's world be anatomically studied. Alas, anatomically studied, that it may be medically aided! Till at length indeed, we have come to such a pass, that except in this same *medicine*, with its artifices and appliances, few can so much as imagine any strength or hope to remain for us. The whole Life of Society must now be carried on by drugs: doctor after doctor appears with his nostrum, of Cooperative Societies, Universal Suffrage, Cottage-and-Cow systems, Repression of Population, Vote by Ballot. To such height has the dyspepsia of Society reached; as indeed the constant grinding internal pain, or from time to time the mad spasmodic throes, of all Society do otherwise too mournfully indicate' ('Centenary' ed. *Misc.* iii 19–20).

17. Dallas *Poetics* (1833) 139.

18. G. Massey, *Edinburgh News and Literary Chronicle* (28 July 1855) 7.

19. See Chapter 7 below.

20. 'The habit too of writing such a multitude of small Poems was in this instance hurtful to him . . . I rejoice therefore with a deep & true Joy, that he has at length yielded to my urgent & repeated – almost unremitting – requests & remonstrances – & will go on with the Recluse exclusively. – A Great Work, in which he will sail; on an open Ocean, & a steady wind; unfretted by short tacks, reefing, & hawling & disentangling the ropes – great work necessarily comprehending his attention & Feelings within the circle of great objects & elevated Conceptions' (To Thomas Poole 14 October 1803; *Letters* ed. Griggs [Oxford, 1956] 1013. See also 1060).

21. Preface to *The Excursion* (1814).

22. *Works* ed. D. Masson (Edinburgh 1889) xi 313.

23. Goethe seems also to have anticipated the structured collection principle. Helen Mustard (*The Lyric Cycle in German Literature* [New York 1946]) notes that 'Goethe's arrangement of his poems in later collections from 1789 on' is designed 'to create a larger whole which would give the individual poem an added significance and a truer proportion in its position as a member of a higher unity' (62).

24. In a letter to the publisher Cottle, Coleridge asserted that he and Wordsworth 'regard the volumes offered to you as to a certain degree *one work*, in *kind tho' not in degree*, as an Ode is one work; and that our different poems are as stanzas, good, relatively rather than absolutely' (*Letters*, ed. Griggs 412).

25. *Saturday Review* ii (1856) 705; *Westminster Review* lxvii (1857) 310.

26. 'Heine's *Book of Songs*, like Tennyson's *In Memoriam*, draws its inspiration from a single theme' (*Saturday Review* ii [1856] 523).

27. George Eliot, *Westminster Review* n.s. ix (1856) 1–33; Milnes, *Edinburgh Review* civ (1856) 194; Fane, *Saturday Review* i (1855) 13–14.

28. Sol Liptzin, *The English Legend of Heinrich Heine* (N. Y. 1954) 65.

29. Browning was of course unable to prevent biographies of E.B.B. from being written, but when approached for his assistance invariably said something like, 'I am compelled to refuse any assistance whatever to the writer of the biography which your publisher projects' (to John H. Ingram, 21 Mar. 1880: *LH* 189: see also 76, 210–11).

CHAPTER 7: THE UNITY OF *THE RING AND THE BOOK*

1. George Santayana, 'The Poetry of Barbarism' in *Interpretations of Poetry and Religion* (New York 1900) 188–216; Henry James, 'The Novel in *The Ring and the Book*', *Transactions of the Royal Society of Literature*, 2nd series xxxi (1912) 269–98; also *Notes on Novelists* (1914) 306–26; Langbaum ch. 3: ' "The Ring and the Book": a Relativist Poem'. See also Chesterton's brilliant commentary in ch. 7 of his *Robert Browning* (1903) 160–76.

2. In *Research Studies of the State College of Washington* xi (1943) 193–233.

3. See P. Honan and W. R. Irvine, *the Book, the Ring and the Poet* (1974) 409.

4. The information in this paragraph takes one side of a controversy, caused by the claim of Rudolf Lehmann to have been told by Browning that the scheme of *The Ring and the Book* came to Browning during his first reading of the *Old Yellow Book*. See *DeVane* 322–3 for details. DeVane's acceptance of the Rossetti chronology relies on W. O. Raymond's 'New Light on the Genesis of *The Ring and the Book*' in his *The Infinite Moment*, 2nd edn (Toronto, 1965) 75–104.

5. 11 Mar. 1869: *New Letters of Carlyle*, ed. A. Carlyle (1904) ii 254.

6. 'By the way, my wife would have subscribed to every one of your bad opinions of the book; she never took the least interest in the story, so much as to wish to inspect the papers.' To Julia Wedgwood, 21 Jan. 1869: *LJW* 168.

7. *The Poetry of Experience* (repr. 1972) p. 109.

8. This passage would seem to owe something to one in Fox's review of

Pauline (see Chapter 2): 'The soul has its seasons, which may be sung with all their contrasted, yet connected phenomena, and with as many an episode to be naturally and gracefully interwoven, as the solar year' (op. cit., p. 252).

9. *VP* vi (1968) 253.
10. E. S. Shaffer, *Kubla Khan and the Fall of Jerusalem: the Mythological School in Biblical Criticism and Secular Literature, 1770–1880* (Cambridge, 1975) ch. 5, 'Browning's St John: the Casuistry of the Higher Criticism'.
11. 'The notion that truths external to the mind may be known by intuition or consciousness, independent of observation and experience is, I am persuaded, in these times, the greatest intellectual support of false doctrine and bad institutions. By the aid of this theory, every inveterate belief and every intense feeling, of which the origin is not remembered, is enabled to dispense with the obligation of justifying itself by reason, and is erected into its own, all-sufficient voucher and justification. There never was such an instrument devised for consecrating all deep-seated prejudices' (*Autobiography* [Columbia 1944] 58).
12. Preface to *The Cenci* (1819); *The Complete Works of Percy Bysshe Shelley*, ed. T. Hutchinson (1927) 274.
13. This is something of a contentious claim. DeVane made it in 1935, following earlier commentators; he notes in the 1955 edition of the *Handbook* (347–8) that various objections to his assertion had appeared in the interim, but maintains that it was nevertheless 'fundamentally correct'. I agree with him. The best study of the early reviews of the poem is in fact the work of one of the objectors, B. R. McElderry in two articles, 'Browning and the Victorian Public in 1868–9' and 'Victorian Evaluation of *The Ring and the Book*' in *Research Studies of the State College of Washington* v no. 4 (1937) 193–203; vii no. 2 (1939) 75–89. A more recent study, E. A. Khattab's *The Critical Reception of Browning's The Ring and the Book* (Salzburg, 1977) is very full but adds little to McElderry's conclusions.
14. *Cornhill* xix (1869) 253.
15. *Saturday Review* xxvi (1868) 832–4; *CH* 298.
16. *Tinsley's Magazine* iii (1869) 665–74, 667; *CH* 303.
17. Oral comment recorded in *Autobiography of Moncure D. Conway* (London, n.d.) ii 22.
18. Mortimer Collins *The British Quarterly Review* xlix (1869) 248–9; *CH* 307.
19. *Macmillan's* xix (1869) 544–52: 546. Mozley mentions *Childe Harold, Don Juan, The Excursion, and The Revolt of Islam* among the poems which, unlike *The Ring and the Book*, 'are single poems in nothing but the name; which are really collections of shorter poems'. I should add that McElderry argues, with statistical correctness, that reviewers were more inclined to reprehend than to approve the poem's bulk. All were, however, impressed.
20. H. B. Forman *London Quarterly Review* xxxii (1869) 325–57, 357; Walter Bagehot *Tinsley's Magazine* iii (1869) 665–74, 667; *CH* 303.
21. *North American Review* cix (1869) 279–83; 282, 283.

22.   *Edinburgh Review* cxxx (1869) 164–86; 172. R. W. Buchanan *Athenaeum* (26 Dec. 1868) 875–6; 875. *Macmillan's* xix (1869) 258–62; 258.
23.   Interestingly, Browning differentiates the two lawyers: all Arcangelis' classical citations are from Virgil, all but one of Bottinius' from Homer. In comparing Guido to Vulcan and Pompilia and Caponsacchi to Venus and Mars, Bottinius repudiates the story as too debased to be canonically Homeric, illustrating the general tendency to draw contrasts between epic and modern material.
24.   *North British Review* li (1869) 117; *British Quarterly Review* xlix (1869) 457.
25.   *Avant-Propos à la Comédie Humaine* ed. M. Bouteron (Paris, 1951) 11.
26.   Volume i of *The Ring and the Book* (books i–iii) was published. 21 Nov. 1868; volume ii (books iv–vi) 26 Dec. 1868; volume iii (books vii–ix) 30 Jan. 1869; volume iv (books x–xii) 27 Feb. 1869.
27.   *Fortnightly Review* xi (1869) 125–6; *CH* 307. *Spectator* xli (1868) 1464–6; *CH* 288.

Bibliography

PRIMARY TEXTS

Browning

Works

No complete edition of Browning's works is in print. The Penguin edition and the forthcoming Longman *Annotated* edition (see below) omit most of the plays. The Ohio edition and the Oxford Authors' edition will be comprehensive, but are not likely to be completed for many years. Line references in this book are to the Centenary edition: since this, like the Penguin, the Ohio and the Oxford Authors' editions, uses the text of Browning's last supervised edition (but see below), its lineation corresponds to theirs, except in the case of the prose passages in two plays, *Pippa Passes* and *A Soul's Tragedy*; for convenience of reference, the Penguin line numbers are used for these passages. In cases where I use manuscript or first edition texts, Penguin line numbers are again given, though they do not necessarily correspond. Line numbers for the *Essay on Shelley* are also taken from Penguin; those for the *Essay on Chatterton* from the edition by Donald Smalley (see below). Browning's works for the period covered in this book (1833–69) were published as follows:

1833 *Pauline, a Fragment of a Confession*, published anonymously, London (Saunders & Otley).
1835 *Paracelsus*, (London, Effingham Wilson).
1837 *Strafford: a Tragedy*, (London, Longman).
1840 *Sordello*, (London: Edward Moxon).
1841 – *Bells and Pomegranates*, (London, Edward Moxon). The eight pamphlets comprise the following works:

1. *Pippa Passes* (Apr. 1841).
2. *King Victor and King Charles* (Mar. 1842).
3. *Dramatic Lyrics* (Nov. 1842).
4. *The Return of the Druses* (Jan. 1843).
5. *A Blot in the 'Scutcheon* (Feb. 1843).
6. *Colombe's Birthday* (Mar. 1844).
7. *Dramatic Romances and Lyrics* (Nov. 1845).
8. *Luria* and *A Soul's Tragedy* (Apr. 1846).

1842 Essay on Chatterton and Tasso *Foreign Quarterly Review* xxix (July 1842) 465–83. Published anonymously: reprinted *Browning's Essay on Chatterton*, ed. D. Smalley (Cambridge, Mass., 1948).
1849 *Poems*, London, Chapman & Hall (a collected edition of his works published in volume form to date, except *Pauline*, *Sordello*, and some shorter poems).
1850 *Christmas Eve and Easter Day* (London, Chapman & Hall).

1852 Introductory Essay in *Letters of Percy Bysshe Shelley*, (London, Moxon).
1855 *Men and Women*, (London, Chapman & Hall).
1863 *Poetical Works*, (London, Chapman & Hall) (the second edition [see 1849], including all works previously published in volume form except *Pauline*).
1864 *Dramatis Personae*, (London, Chapman & Hall).
1868 *Poetical Works*, (London, Smith Elder), (including all works published in volume form; the first appearance of *Pauline* since 1833).
1868–69 *The Ring and the Book*, (London, Smith Elder).
1872 *Selections*, (London, Smith Elder).

I exclude from the above table the (few) fugitive poems published in periodicals which Browning did not subsequently collect, reprints of his published works, and selections from his works (apart from the 1872 set). It is worth mentioning, however, that the 1865 reprint of the 1863 *Poetical Works* was revised, and that some volumes of selections involved textual change. For this period of his career, *Paracelsus* and *Dramatis Personae* are the only major works for which a (late) manuscript survived: that of *Paracelsus* is reprinted in *Oxford* i.

Modern editions to which I make reference are:
The 'Centenary' edition of the Complete Works, ed. F. G. Kenyon (1913). Based on the final authorially supervised edition of 1888–9, with added line numbers.
Poems, eds J. Pettigrew and T. J. Collins (Harmondsworth, Middx, 1981). This edition omits the plays, except *Pippa Passes*; it includes nearly all Browning's unpublished works, some of which had previously appeared in *New Poems of Robert and Elizabeth Barrett Browning*, ed. F. G. Kenyon (1914). Its text incorporates alterations recorded by Browning for inclusion in 1888–89, but not implemented there.
The Poetical Works of Robert Browning, eds I. R. J. Jack *et al*. (Oxford, 1983–   ). This edition, two volumes of which, covering the years 1833–40, have so far appeared, will be complete, and includes a comprehensive collation of textual variants between editions.
Robert Browning in Longman *Annotated English Poets*, eds J. Woolford and D. R. Karlin. This edition includes those plays which were not written for the stage, and therefore includes *Pippa Passes, Luria* and *A Soul's Tragedy*. Its first volume, to be published 1987–88, will include all works to 1846, in their first edition form.

Letters
No complete edition of Browning's letters exists. *The Brownings' Correspondence*, eds P. Kelley and R. Hudson (Winfield, Kansas, 1984–   ), will be complete; it includes reviews of the Brownings' works and supplementary material. Three volumes, covering the years up to 1837, have so far appeared. Below I cite only a selection from the many volumes of letters which have appeared, comprising those actually cited in this book, and others which I have extensively consulted:

The Letters of Robert Browning and Elizabeth Barrett Barrett, ed. E. Kintner (Harvard, 1969).
Letters, ed. T. L. Hood (1933).
New Letters, eds W. C. DeVane and K. L. Knickerbocker (Yale, 1950).
Robert Browning and Alfred Domett, ed. F. G. Kenyon (1907).
Robert Browning and Julia Wedgwood, ed. R. Curle (New York, 1936).

218   *Bibliography*

Dearest Isa, ed. N. MacAleer (Texas, 1951).
D. DeLaura, 'Ruskin and the Brownings: twenty-five unpublished letters', *Bulletin of the John Rylands Library* lxiv (1972) 314–46.
Browning's Trumpeter, ed. W. S. Peterson (Washington, D. C. 1979).
The Letters of Elizabeth Barrett Browning, ed. F. G. Kenyon (1898).

Biographies
Life and Letters, A. Orr (1891).
Robert Browning, G. K. Chesterton (1903).
Robert Browning: a Portrait, B. Miller (1952).
The Book, the Ring and the Poet, P. Honan and W. R. Irvine (1974).
Browning's Youth, J. Maynard (Harvard, 1977).
The Courtship of Robert Browning and Elizabeth Barrett, D. R. Karlin (Oxford, 1985).

Bibliographies and Works of Reference
Handbook, Mrs A. Orr (1885).
Browning Cyclopaedia, E. Berdoe (1892).
    Guide-Book to the Poetic and Dramatic Works of Robert Browning, G. W. Cooke (Boston 1891).
Concordance, L. Broughton and B. F. Stelter (New York, 1926).
A Browning Bibliography, eds L. N. Broughton, C. S. Northrop, R. Pearsall (Ithaca, New York, 1953).
A Browning Handbook, W. C. DeVane, 2nd edn (New York, 1955).
Vol vi (Browning, Ruskin, Swinburne, ed. J. Woolford) in *Sale Catalogues of the Libraries of Eminent Persons* (gen. edn A. N. L. Munby) 1972.
Robert Browning and Elizabeth Barrett Browning: an Annotated Bibliography 1951–70, ed. W. S. Peterson (New York, 1974).
Browning: the Critical Heritage, eds Boyd Litzinger and Donald Smalley (1970).

The annual volumes of *Browning Institute Studies* contain bibliographies for the years following the Peterson bibliography.

Other Writers

Matthew Arnold, *Poems*, ed. K. Allott (1965).
The Complete Prose Works of Matthew Arnold, ed. R. H. Super, 11 vols (Ann Arbor, 1960–77).
Blake, *Songs of Innocence and Experience* (1789, 1794).
Elizabeth Barrett Browning, *Sonnets from the Portugese* (1850).
Aurora Leigh (1856).
Selections (ed. Browning) 1865.
Poems before Congress (1860).
Byron, *Hours of Idleness* (1807).
Carlyle, *Complete Works* ('Centenary' edn) 1896.
Coleridge, *Sybilline Leaves* (1817).
Biographia Literaria, eds J. Engell and W. J. Bate (Princeton, 1983).
Coleridge's Essays and Lectures on Shakespeare (n.d.).
Notebooks, ed. K. Coburn (1957).
Letters, ed. Griggs (Oxford, 1956).
E. S. Dallas, *Poetics* (1853).

The Gay Science (1865).
Dickens, *Letters*, ed. W. Dexter (1938).
Speeches, ed. R. H. Shepherd (1884).
Dryden, 'A Discourse Concerning Satire', *Of Dramatic Poetry and other Essays*, ed. G. Watson (1962).
Ebenezer Elliot, *Corn-Law Rhymes* (1831).
Godwin, *Enquiry Concerning Political Justice*, ed. I. Kramnick (Harmondsworth, Middx, 1976).
Goethe, *Goethe's Opinions*, ed. O. Wenckstern (1853).
Conversations with Eckermann, trans. J. Oxenford (1850).
Torquato Tasso, trans. Des Voeux (1827).
Müller's Characteristics of Goethe, trans S. Austin (1833).
H. Heine, *Buch der Lieder* (1828).
R. H. Horne, *A New Spirit of the Age* (1844; 1907).
Victor Hugo *Les Contemplations* (1856).
La Légende des Siècles (Paris, 1859; 1962).
Samuel Johnson, *Review of a Free Enquiry into the Nature and Origin of Evil* (1757) in *Johnson's Works* vi (Oxford, 1825) 47-76.
Keats *Letters*, ed. H. E. Rollins (Cambridge, Mass., 1958).
W. S. Landor, *Heroic Idyls* (1863).
R. Lytton, *The Wanderer* (1859).
G. Massey, *Craigcrook Castle* (1856).
W. Meredith, *Modern Love* (1862).
J. S. Mill, *Works*, ed. J. M. Robson (Toronto, 1977).
Autobiography (Columbia, 1944).
On Liberty (Harmondsworth, Middx., 1979).
Mill's Essays on Literature and Society, ed. J. B. Schneewind (New York 1965).
Paracelsus, *The Hermetic and Alchemical Writings of Paracelsus*, ed. A. E. Waite (1894).
Coventry Patmore, *The Angel in the House* (1854-62).
Pope, *Poetical Works*, ed. H. Davis (1966).
D. G. Rossetti, *The House of Life* (1869).
Rousseau, *Rousseau's Social Contract etc*, trans. G. D. H. Cole (n.d.).
Ruskin, *The Works of John Ruskin*, eds Cook and Wedderburn, 39 vols (1903-12).
A. W. Schlegel, *Lectures on Dramatic Poetry*, trans. J. Black (1815).
F. Schlegel, *Friedrich Schlegel: Dialogue on Poetry and Literary Aphorisms*, trans. E. Behler and R. Struc (Pennsylvania, 1968).
Shelley, *The Complete Works of Percy Bysshe Shelley*, ed. T. Hutchinson (1927).
Shelley's Prose, ed. D. L. Clark (Albuquerque, 1954).
Swinburne, *Songs before Sunrise* (1871).
H. Taylor, Preface to *Philip van Arteveldte* (1834).
Tennyson, *In Memoriam* (1849), *Maud* (1855) in *Poems*, ed. C. Ricks (Harlow, 1969).
Tennyson: the Critical Heritage, ed. J. Jump (1967).
Thackeray, 'A Box of Novels' in *Barry Lyndon* etc (Oxford, n.d.).
Trollope, *Autobiography* (Leipzig, 1883).
Whitman, *Leaves of Grass* (1855).
Wordsworth *Poems*, ed. J. O. Hayden (Harmondsworth, Middx, 1977).
Gerrard Winstanley *The Works of Gerrard Winstanley*, ed. G. H. Sabine (Cornell, 1941).

SECONDARY TEXTS

I include only texts actually cited in this book. Where possible, page references
relate to editions currently in print, and easily available. Contemporary reviews
are listed under the names of the journals, with the author, where known, cited in
brackets, except in cases where the author was known to Browning.

W. Allingham, *Diary*, eds H. Allingham and D. Radford (1907).
Athenaeum 657 (30 May 1840) 431–2.
Athenaeum 1464 (17 Nov. 1855) 1327–8.
Athenaeum 2148 (26 Dec. 1868) 875–6 (R. W. Buchanan).
Atlantic Monthly xxiii (1869) 256–9.
G. E. Aylmer (ed.), *The Levellers in the English Revolution* (1975).
W. Bagehot, 'Wordsworth, Tennyson and Browning, or, Pure, Ornate and
  Grotesque Art in English Poetry' (*Prose Works*, ed. Stevas ii 321–66).
Biographie Universelle (Paris, 1811–22).
Blackwood's Magazine xxxviii (Sept. 1835) 376–87 (*The Modern German School of
  Irony*; Mrs W. Busk).
Blackwood's lxxix (Feb. 1856) 135–7 (Margaret Oliphant).
British Quarterly Review xxiii (Jan. 1856) 151–80.
British Quarterly Review xxii (1855) 467–98.
British Quarterly Review xlix (1869) 248–9 (Mortimer Collins).
J. Bryant *War of Troy* (1799).
Carlyle, *Letters to Mill, Sterling and Browning*.
New Letters of Carlyle, ed. A. Carlyle (1904).
'Joanna Baillie', *New Edinburgh Review* i (Oct. 1821).
Balzac *Avant-Propos à la Comédie Humaine*, ed. M. Bouteron (Paris, 1951).
J. M. Carré, *Goethe en Angleterre* (Paris, 1921).
D. Carroll (ed.), *Richard Simpson as Critic* (1977).
A. Chalmers (ed.), *The General Biographical Dictionary* (1812–17).
Christian Remembrancer xvii (1849) 381–40 (C. P. Chrétien) repr. *Victorian
  Scrutinies*, ed. I. Armstrong (1972) 200–22.
Christian Remembrancer xxxi (1856) 267.
M. D. Conway, *Autobiography of Moncure D. Conway* (London, n.d.)
Cornhill xix (1869) 249–56 (F. Greenwood).
T. De Quincey *Works*, ed. D. Masson (Edinburgh, 1889).
d. m. de silva, 'Browning's *King Victor and King Charles*,' *Browning Society Notes*
  xi (Apr. 1981) 8–21.
Domett, *Diary*, ed. E. A. Horsman (Oxford, 1953).
Edinburgh News and Literary Chronicle (28 July 1855) (G. Massey).
Edinburgh Review civ (1856) 192–209 (Monckton Milnes).
Edinburgh Review cxx (Oct. 1864) 537–65 (William Stigand).
Edinburgh Review cxxx (1869) 164–86 (Julian Fane).
Eveline Forbes 'A Visit to Balliol College', *Nineteenth Century* xv (1921) 862–3.
Fortnightly Review xi (1869) 331–43.
W. J. Fox, review of *Pauline*, *Monthly Repository* n.s. vii (1833) 252–62.
Fraser's Magazine xlii (1850) 245–55 (C. Kingsley).
Fraser's liii (Jan. 1856) 105–16 (G. Brimley).
J. A. Froude *Short Studies on Great Subjects* (1867–83).

B. W. Fuson, *Browning and his English Predecessors in the Dramatic Monolog* [sic] (Iowa, 1948).
R. Garnett, *Life of Carlyle* (1887).
Guardian xi (Jan. 1856) 34–5.
G. P. Gooch, 'The Political Background of Goethe's life', *Publications of the English Goethe Society* n.s. iii (1928) 1–30.
R. H. Hutton, *Literary Essays* (1888).
Henry James, 'The Novel in *The Ring and the Book*', *Transactions of the Royal Society of Literature* 2nd ser. xxxi (1912) 269–98
Notes on Novelists (1914).
B. R. Jerman, *Browning's Witless Duke*, *PMLA* lxxii (1957) 488–93.
H. Jones, *The Gnostic Religion* (1963).
E. A. Khattab *The Critical Reception of Browning's The Ring and the Book* (Salzburg, 1977).
R. Langbaum *The Poetry of Experience* (repr. 1972).
G. H. Lewes 'The Principles of Success in Literature', *Fortnightly Review* i (May–Aug. 1865).
S. Liptzin, *The English Legend of Heinrich Heine* (New York, 1954).
London Quarterly Review xxxii (1869) 325–57 (H. B. Forman).
R. Lytton *Letters*, ed. Lady Betty Balfour (1906).
M. W. Macallum, 'The Dramatic Monologue in the Victorian Period', *Proceedings of the British Academy* ix (1924–5) 265–83.
B. R. McElderry, 'Browning and the Victorian Public in 1868–9', *Research Studies of the State College of Washington* v no. 4 (1937) 193–203.
'Victorian Evaluation of *The Ring and the Book*' ibid., vii no. 2 (1939) 75–89.
Macmillan's xix (1869) 544–52.
J. Martineau, 'John Stuart Mill', *National Review* ix (1859) 474–508.
Metropolitan Magazine (literary suppl.) xxvii (Feb. 1840) 108–9.
Helen Mustard *The Lyric Cycle in German Literature* (New York, 1946).
North American Review cix (1869) 279–83.
North British Review li (1869) 97–126 (R. Simpson).
E. Oswald, *Goethe in England and America* (1909).
M. Peckham 'Historiography and *The Ring and the Book*' *VP* vi (1968) 243–57.
L. Perrine, *Browning's Shrewd Duke* *PMLA* lxxiv (1959) 157–9.
W. S. Peterson and F. L. Stanley, 'The J. S. Mill marginalia in Robert Browning's *Pauline*: a history and a transcription': *Papers of the Bibliograhical Society of America* lxvi (1972) 135–70.
E. A. Poe, 'The Poetic Principle', *Works*, ed. J. A. Harrison (repr. New York, 1965).
F. A. Pottle, *Shelley and Browning: a Myth and some Facts* (Chicago, 1923).
The Rambler, n.s. v (1856) 54–71 (R. Simpson).
W. O. Raymond *The Infinite Moment*, 2nd edn (Toronto, 1965).
Ernest Renan *La Vie de Jésus* (1863).
Rossetti Papers (1903).
George Santayana, 'The Poetry of Barbarism' in *Interpretations of Poetry and Religion* (New York, 1900) 188–216.
Saturday Review i (5 Nov. 1855) 13–14 (J. Fane).
Saturday Review ii (1856) 523.
Saturday Review xxvi (1868) 832–4.

Ina Beth Sessions *A Study of the Dramatic Monologue* (San Antonio, Texas 1933).

E. S. Shaffer, *Kubla Khan and the Fall of Jerusalem: the Mythological School in Biblical Criticism and Secular Literature, 1770–1880* (Cambridge, 1975).

Alexander Singleton, 'Goethe and Browning', *Publications of the English Goethe Society*, 1912.

David Skilton *Antony Trollope and his Contemporaries* (Harlow, 1972).

Spectator xxviii (22 Dec. 1855) 1346–7.

Spectator xli (1868) 1464–6.

W. Stockley, *German Literature as Known in England 1750–1830* (1929).

Beryl Stone, *Browning and Incarnation* (unpublished MA thesis), quoted W. Whitla, op. cit., below.

David Strauss *Das Leben Jesu*, trans. George Eliot (1846).

Tinsley's Magazine iii (1869) 665–74 (W. Bagehot).

Victoria Magazine ii [1864] 298–316 (M. D. Conway).

Westminster Review lxv (n.s. ix) (1856) 1–33 (George Eliot).

Westminster Review xci (n.s. xxxv) (1 Jan. 1869) 298–300 (J. R. Wise).

K. L. Wheeler, *Sources, Processes and Methods in Biographia Literaria* (Cambridge, 1980).

W. Whitla *The Central Truth: the Incarnation in Browning's Poetry* (Toronto, 1963).

G. Wilkins, *The Growth of the Homeric Poems* (1855).

J. Woolford, *Periodicals and the Practice of Literary Criticism 1855–1864* in *The Victorian Periodical Press*, eds J. Shattock and M. Wolff (Leicester, 1982).

Index